Captives of Conquest

THE EARLY MODERN AMERICAS

Peter C. Mancall, Series Editor

Volumes in the series explore neglected aspects of early
modern history in the western hemisphere. Interdisciplinary
in character, and with a special emphasis on the Atlantic World
from 1450 to 1850, the series is published in partnership with the
USC-Huntington Early Modern Studies Institute.

Captives of Conquest

Slavery in the Early Modern Spanish Caribbean

Erin Woodruff Stone

PENN

UNIVERSITY OF PENNSYLVANIA PRESS

PHILADELPHIA

Published by
University of Pennsylvania Press
Philadelphia, Pennsylvania 19104-4112
www.upenn.edu/pennpress

Printed in the United States of America on acid-free paper
10 9 8 7 6 5 4 3 2 1

A Cataloging-in-Publication record is available from the Library of Congress
ISBN 978-0-8122-5310-8

CONTENTS

From a "Structure of Conjuncture" to a "Shatter Zone"

Taking advantage of the early morning calm, Miguel de Ibarra and Juan de Urrutia hurried their cargo to the awaiting "pataje." They pushed the chained men and women, all of whom had the letter R for "rescate" or G for "guerra" branded on the left side of their faces, onto the crowded ship. The brands sealed their fate, declaring them as legally acquired slaves. By the time they were all loaded, there was only room to stand on the small vessel. Fear rippled through the group. Many of the captives were from the interior and had no idea where they were going. Some might have never seen the ocean before today. Most did not understand the Spanish spoken by their captors.

On the other hand, some could have heard tales of what their future life as slaves would hold. Stories of the Spanish and their practices spread quickly after their arrival, often preceding them. Whether out of fear of the unknown or to avoid toiling on plantations, some captives were able to slip from their chains to throw themselves overboard. They chose drowning over removal and enslavement in the Spanish colonial regime. Their suicides were remembered by many, even causing some colonists to question the practice of enslavement.

And this pataje was only one of many loaded with captives. Of the thousands of slaves removed from the region in 1528, hundreds perished in the coming months. Whether they took their own lives, died of thirst or hunger during transport, or perished within a few months of laboring in a foreign land, most of the branded men and women did not live past 1529. Nevertheless, Urrutia, Ibarra, and dozens of other merchants did not let these statistics deter them. Instead they looked forward to selling their surviving "piezas" (pieces) in the central plazas of Santo Domingo and Havana. There, merchants, officials, judges, landholders, Crown representatives, and even priests and friars all vied to purchase the strongest and most skilled slaves. Those adept at diving commanded the highest prices, as they were destined for Venezuela's prosperous pearl beds. Most colonists did not inquire as to how the slaves were obtained, or whether the brand on someone's face was indeed legal. For the majority, the need for laborers overcame moral and legal concerns. Secure in the value of their captive cargo, Ibarra and Urrutia sailed into the blue horizon for the Greater Antilles.

*   *   *

Most have probably read about similar scenes that took place on the West African coast at the start of the infamous Middle Passage. While the episode described above does invoke the experiences of thousands of enslaved Africans beginning the terrifying journey across the Atlantic, the ships of Ibarra and Urrutia prepared to sail from the opposite side of the ocean. They left the port of Santisteban, located on the Gulf of Mexico in the province of Pánuco. Nor were the ships loaded with enslaved Africans, but with indigenous slaves. The pervasive and at times lucrative trade in Indians was the other face of slavery in the early Spanish Empire—a slavery overlooked until recently.

The trade in Indian slaves, beginning in 1493, grew to encompass all the Caribbean islands, along with much of North and South America. As the trade evolved, it influenced the creation of the Spanish Empire. Indigenous populations did not simply collapse from disease or warfare; a significant number were first removed through the business of Indian slavery, a business that helped to construct economic, legal, and religious colonial policies in the nascent Spanish Empire. But how and why did the trade grow to become an integral part of the Spanish colonial experience?

To begin, the enslavement of and trade in Indians was central to the processes of conquest. Specifically, the search for new sources of Indian slaves propelled much early Spanish exploration, from the discovery of Mexico to *entradas* into the interior of South America. Slaving operations were inextricably linked to the military, economic, and spiritual conquests of the Americas. After initial contact, Indian slavery remained central to growing colonial enterprises, from the pearl fisheries of Venezuela to sugar cultivation in the Greater Antilles. The indigenous slave trade connected the colonists, colonies, and indigenous populations throughout the early Spanish Empire.

Even as the number of African slaves grew in the Americas, enslaved Indians did not disappear. African and Indian slaves worked side by side, the methods and practices of both types of slavery influencing one another throughout the centuries. Together the two forms of slavery helped to create the greater Spanish Caribbean, a space and economy founded on the bondage and coerced labor of both indigenous and African peoples.[1] From Christopher Columbus in the 1490s to German conquistadors of the 1530s and beyond, European explorers, raiders, and colonizers enslaved thousands of Indians.[2] Some were shipped as commodities to various islands, or as far away as Spain, to be sold for immediate profit. Others became military auxiliaries, guides, miners, pearl divers, servants, or, in the case of women, unwilling sexual partners. In all these roles and experiences, Indian slaves helped mold the greater Spanish Caribbean.

The greater Spanish Caribbean or circum-Caribbean was the center of the burgeoning Spanish Empire. It stretched outward from Spain's first colonies (Española, Puerto Rico, and Cuba) to both the north and south, encompassing the Bahamas, Florida (which, per Spanish definitions, reached as far north as the Chesapeake Bay), the Lesser Antilles, and the northern coast of South America. By the third decade of Spanish imperial activity, the region reached deep into both Central America and today's southeastern United States. The entire circum-Caribbean was governed by the *Audiencia* (court) of Santo Domingo until 1535.[3] The colonies and territories were all connected through economic, legal, and social networks. It was within this system that the business of Indian slavery developed and operated, with the indigenous slave trade lying at the heart of many of these connections.

My project views the earliest Indian slave trade through this wide geographic lens. Through this larger window, I see how the early slave trade moved Indians in many different directions. While some slaves were taken from one location and sold in another, many others were displaced numerous times. For example, Indians taken from present-day Mexico to Cuba and Española later served as slaves during expeditions to Florida. A few traveled through the entire Atlantic World, visiting Europe and the Canary Islands.[4] For most of these Indians, Española served as a nexus, where slaves first disembarked and from where they were taken to disparate locations. Thus, *Captives of Conquest* begins in Española but quickly looks outward. The multidirectional movement of slaves underscores that the removal of Indians was a key component to the early colonial project.

I am able to paint this picture of early indigenous slavery with broader strokes because of the work of many previous historians. Indeed, this book is not the first to address early indigenous slavery in the Spanish Empire. However, previous works were limited by a focus on indigenous slavery within national boundaries or industries.[5] Recent scholarship, especially ethnohistorical works, has begun to unravel the magnitude and impact of Indian slavery in the Americas. Though groundbreaking, the majority of these studies begin in the seventeenth century, more than one hundred years after the origins of the Indian slave trade, and concentrate on Dutch, French, or English colonies and slaveries.[6] Additionally, most works focus on territories that became the continental United States.[7] Andrés Reséndez's *The Other Slavery: The Uncovered Story of Indian Enslavement in America* serves as the benchmark example of this type of scholarship.[8] While Reséndez does begin his work with a brief study of the earliest years of the Caribbean indigenous slave trade, he mainly focuses on northern Mexico and the U.S. Southwest. *Captives of Conquest* focuses solely on the formation and earliest years of the Indian slave trade in the circum-Caribbean, serving as a key precursor to indigenous slavery in the seventeenth and eighteenth centuries.

The Greater Antilles in the Sixteenth-Century Circum-Caribbean Slave Trade

Despite Española's significance as the first European settlement in the New World, previous scholarship minimized the importance of the Caribbean, characterizing it as merely a "staging ground" or "antechamber" for the more important conquests of Mexico and Peru.[9] On the contrary, the Caribbean was of vital importance to the formation of the Spanish Empire, and it continued to be so well after the discoveries of the Mexica or Inca Empires. The region was also central to the business of conquest and by extension indigenous slavery.[10] This project highlights the role that Española, and later Puerto Rico and Cuba, had on the formation of colonial institutions throughout Spanish America. Economic, religious, political, legal, and social policies cultivated in Española provided the model for future conquest and colonization in the entire Spanish Empire.

Indigenous slavery was one of the most significant practices that developed through the process of "pacifying" and populating Española. The conquest of the Caribbean and the rise of the indigenous slave trade were inextricably linked. It was the act of conquering the Americas that created the indigenous slave trade. In turn this trade pushed further Spanish expansion and exploration as colonists searched for new sources of captives. Both in the Caribbean and beyond, the reliance on indigenous slaves led to the rapid decline of indigenous populations, eventually leading to large-scale African slavery.[11] In fact, some of the loudest defenders of Americas' indigenous peoples, like Bartolomé de las Casas, advocated a rapid expansion of the African slave trade to ameliorate the suffering of indigenous peoples of the Americas, particularly the Taíno.[12] The growth of the Atlantic African slave trade in the mid-sixteenth century was directly linked to the challenges presented by several decades of a brutal and pervasive indigenous slave trade.

The Evolution of the Legal Indigenous Slave Trade

The circum-Caribbean indigenous slave trade took many forms, with conquest and colonization pushing its transformation. From 1493 to 1542 and beyond, the Indian slave trade evolved, depending on which Indians could legally be enslaved and for what reasons. Resistant Taínos of Española served as the earliest victims of the slave trade. Most Taíno captives were sent to Spain to serve as galley slaves, urban servants, or workers on the sugar plantations of the Canary Islands. The Spanish justified their enslavement through the doctrine of "just war."[13] Then in 1503 Queen Isabela made it legal to enslave "Carib" Indians, designating the coastlines of Colombia and Panama as territories where "Caribs," meaning cannibals, lived. In 1508 King Ferdinand legalized the enslavement of all Indians living in "useless" islands, which essentially meant those areas that lacked gold. In the wake of indigenous rebellion on Puerto Rico, in which Indians from the Lesser Antilles were also implicated, the Crown greatly expanded the definition of "Carib" lands to include most of the Lesser Antilles. Finally, in 1518, the Jeronymite government legalized the enslavement of "Caribs" living on the coast of South America. In addition to those taken through "just war" or declared as "Caribs," the Spanish had one more way to obtain indigenous slaves legally: *rescate*. While "rescate" literally means ransom and did in certain situations mean the ransoming of a Christian captive, in the Americas it usually meant bartering for previously enslaved Indians. According to Spanish law it was legal, until 1542, to purchase or barter for Indians already held in bondage. In other words, the Spanish (as well as the French and Portuguese in Africa) used the preexistence of slavery in the Americas to justify the continued enslavement of indigenous peoples. Over time the practice of rescate became more violent, signifying trade for slaves under pressure, force, or violence.[14] Map 1 shows the evolution of the "legal" trade. Alongside the legal trade existed an endemic illegal, and undocumented, indigenous slave trade. The contraband trade in indigenous slaves flourished due to

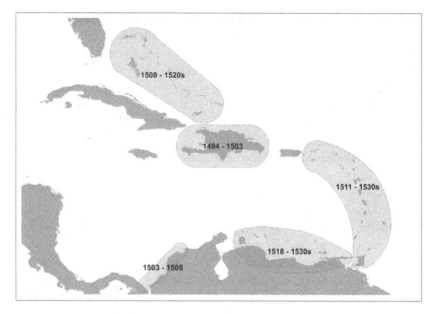

Map 1. Sources of Indian slaves for the Spanish Empire, 1494–1530s. Map created by Richard Stone.

the contradictory nature of Spanish laws, the distance of American territories from Spain, and the general ambivalence of Spanish officials toward the plight and legal status of indigenous peoples.[15] And while the legal slave trade operated in a fairly limited space, the illegal trade ranged far and wide, encompassing territories from Mexico to Brazil and to North America as far north as the Chesapeake.

It is equally important to note that the Indians of the Caribbean played a central role in forming the *early* Indian slave trade. Taíno politics, connections, and knowledge in many ways dictated who was enslaved in the first two decades after contact. For example, the enslavement of the "Carib" peoples by Columbus can be traced to their antagonistic relationship with the Taínos. Here, the Taínos were able to direct some early policies of conquest and colonization; however, this did not last. Due to population loss and an influx of both Spaniards and foreign Indians, indigenous leaders lost any control of the slave trade and the larger colonial project that they initially possessed. As native leaders' statuses diminished, Spanish colonists acted with more impunity, leading to large increases in the Indian slave trade from the 1520s to 1542. During this period the Caribbean became a "shatter zone" ripped apart by violence, warfare, disease, and slavery.[16] Indigenous peoples within this zone of destruction lost their independence, their power, and, in many cases, their lives.

More Than a Numbers Game

It is difficult to estimate the exact number of Indian slaves shipped across the Caribbean or Atlantic from 1493 to 1542. During my research I was able to find concrete records of approximately seventy thousand enslaved Indians, including some Taínos from Española sent to Spain, displaced Lucayan Indians moved to Española, and thousands of Indians labeled as "Caribs" removed from South America. However, this is a very conservative estimate. In 1515 one group of slavers captured and sold fifty-five Indian slaves from the Pearl Islands in Santo Domingo. In the same year twelve other slaving expeditions sailed from Española to Trinidad, the Pearl Islands, and Panama. Documents detailing how many slaves each of these expeditions captured have yet to surface. However, if we estimate that each one took between fifty and one hundred slaves, then in 1515 up to 1,200 more Indian slaves likely disembarked in Santo Domingo alongside the one recorded ship. In later years island officials reported the arrival of as many as fifteen thousand Indian slaves annually.[17] While this number seems high, at least five thousand (with some witnesses estimating twelve thousand) Indian slaves came from a single port in Mexico in 1528. And by the 1530s the number of Crown-issued slaving licenses numbered in the hundreds. If most of these led to slaving expeditions, the actual number of enslaved Indians would have been in the hundreds of thousands. Illegal slaving expeditions only added to the number of displaced and captive Indians. This high number corroborates the incessant letters from colonists and religious officials to the Crown complaining about the negative impacts of the Indian slave trade on Honduras, Venezuela, and Colombia: the areas most affected by slave raids in the 1520s and 1530s. Given all of this, I estimate that the actual number of Indians enslaved from 1493 to 1542 in the circum-Caribbean was between 250,000 and 500,000. If we count those taken captive temporarily to serve as porters in exploratory ventures, most of whom did not survive, the numbers are even higher.[18]

The mechanisms of the Indian slave trade help to explain the lack of clear, detailed records. Indigenous slaves did not have to travel across the Atlantic in large vessels, passing through the hands of multiple merchants. Instead a few dozen slaves were caught by a couple of raiders and then transported in small *naos* or *caravels* from island to island. These smaller ships often escaped formal records. Indian slaves also were usually not taxed and thus were not "worthy" of royal recognition. Indian slaves were never insured like their African counterparts. Other than a few very detailed court cases (generated by especially egregious actions), most Spanish sources that mention Indian slaves are vague, short, and inconsistent. The majority fail even to include where or how slaves were captured, let alone their gender or ethnicity. The dearth of detailed records makes tracking and quantifying the indigenous slave trade even more difficult than it is for the African Atlantic trade.[19]

While calculating the number of enslaved Indians during the first half of the sixteenth century is nearly impossible, tracing the evolution of the trade reveals a great deal about the transformation of colonial economies. The selling of Indian slaves in Iberia was Columbus's first plan to exploit the Americas. When the Spaniards discovered gold and later pearls, Indian slaves became laborers and miners. Later, when both gold and pearls became scarce in the Caribbean, Indian slaves were transformed back into commodities or were sent to labor on sugar plantations. The search for Indian slaves led to the "discovery" of new lands and the expansion of the Spanish Empire. Indigenous populations, both enslaved and free, across the circum-Caribbean actively impacted the process of European colonization. Indigenous slaves served as laborers, profit, and settlers. They were at the center of the enterprise of conquest and colonization and were active, though not always voluntary, players in it.

Beyond economics, religious and secular debates about Indian slavery changed colonial legislation from the Laws of Burgos in 1512 to the New Laws of 1542 and beyond. While the discussions did create reforms, they also contributed to the creation of the Black Legend, a myth perpetuated by other European powers painting Spanish conquistadors as villains in order to discredit Spanish claims in the Americas. The attempts at reform also impacted the creation of colonial laws and policies that changed dozens of times over the first decades of colonization. By examining the evolution of laws governing the Indian slave trade, we see the gradual, and difficult, imposition of the power of the Crown over its distant colonies. While the colonies began as largely private ventures, with Crown supervision and funding, by the mid-sixteenth century royal officials imposed Crown law and policies much more effectively, including over Indian slavery.

At its highest point (1518–1542), the circum-Caribbean indigenous slave trade scattered diverse ethnic groups and cultures across the Americas. Indigenous slaves from Mexico, Colombia, Florida, Venezuela, and Brazil all found themselves transported to Española, Cuba, Puerto Rico, and the Pearl

Islands. The experience of movement and displacement was at the heart of the Indian slave trade. While illustrating how the trade operated, *Captives of Conquest* simultaneously attempts to reveal the indigenous experience of captivity and removal across the Caribbean. The indigenous slave trade displaced thousands of Indians across the Americas, causing untold pain, suffering, and disorientation. Many Indian slaves lost their lives before even arriving at their new homes. But there is also evidence of survival, incorporation, and knowledge sharing in the process, especially when we consider precolonial relationships between and across islands. Indigenous groups contributed greatly to this system, both voluntarily and through force. They resisted Spanish incursions, at times forcing the Spanish to alter their practices and policies of colonization. At this very early stage of colonization, Indians, even some enslaved, were still able to influence and inhibit the Spanish conquest of their lands. My work examines these instances to uncover the indigenous perspective on and contributions to both the Indian slave trade and, more generally, the early contact period.

Methodology and Sources

Captives of Conquest is a work of ethnohistory that combines the use of Spanish documents with the application of archaeology (when available) to access the indigenous perspectives of the circum-Caribbean.[20] Archaeology can help to determine pre-contact cultural patterns and provide clues to pre-Hispanic relations among ethnic groups in the Caribbean. Key pieces of archaeological evidence that I consult include ceramics, *cemis*, paleoglyphs, and burial sites, all of which help me to explore the process of cultural persistence and adaptation.[21] Unfortunately, the majority of archaeological sources shed light only on pre-contact indigenous lives, with few vestiges of indigenous life after the arrival of Europeans. The dearth of post-contact artifacts likely serves as evidence of the upheaval and suffering experienced by Taínos after the onset of Spanish colonization.

On the other hand, there are thousands of Spanish documents detailing the conquest and the early project of colonization in the Caribbean. These documents include court cases, testaments, lawsuits, royal proclamations, petitions, and everyday correspondence. Within these largely institutional sources lie references to and hints about the often-obscured Indian slave trade. As mentioned previously, few documents focused on the indigenous slave trade alone. Instead, references to the trade were hidden in long reports on the general status of a colony or appear in a short royal provision. A small number of court cases provide us with more detailed accounts of the trade, focusing on a single episode or trader who pushed the limits of colonial policy. The diffuse nature of the documents is perhaps what has prevented many scholars from investigating the early indigenous slave trade.

In addition to mining Spanish archives, I utilized more commonly referenced early chronicles, including the writings of Fray Bartolomé de las Casas, the royal historian Gonzalo Fernández de Oviedo, the Jeroynimite friar Ramón Pané, the Italian historian Pedro Mártir de Anglería, and Christopher Columbus. While these sources are full of detail, they must be approached with caution as they were written for specific purposes. Thus Las Casas's descriptions of Spanish violence in his fight for reform were probable exaggerations. They were also often written years after the authors lived in the Americas and in some cases, like Mártir, were written by men who never ventured across the Atlantic. To overcome some of the biases and inconsistencies of the early Caribbean chronicles, I approached them from an anthropological perspective, reading between the lines in search of salient details supported by other sources.

Here I follow in the footsteps of Neil Whitehead in his analysis of Sir Walter Raleigh's *Discoverie of Guiana* text, which historians labeled as an exaggeration and unreliable due to its mythical descriptions. Whitehead reveals what we can still discover in travel accounts or chronicles through careful reading and simultaneous consideration of anthropological and archaeological findings. He isolates numerous details (for example, Raleigh's description of natives with heads in their chests instead of on their necks) that point to real indigenous traditions and provide an avenue to indigenous cosmology.[22] For Whitehead the reading of historical texts through anthropological (and at times literary) methods provides a "refraction," not a reflection, of an indigenous culture. Nevertheless, this refraction brings us closer to a native perspective than traditional historical readings of early chronicles.

The refractory nature of early sources, in that they can show only glimpses of indigenous cultures and practices through the lens of European cultural schemas, is a result of what anthropologist Marshall Sahlins calls the "structure of the conjuncture."[23] The structure of the conjuncture takes place when two distinct cultural systems collide to produce a moment in which multiple cultural schemas (cosmologies or, more generally, ways of thinking) are present and interpreted in distinct ways. My work borrows from Sahlins's theory and approaches the conquest of Española, and the consequent rise of the Indian slave trade, as a structure of the conjuncture. It is from this newly negotiated set of structures, and certain actors' ability to manipulate them, that some Indians gained agency.[24] It is also within this set of structures that the initial rules and practices of the indigenous slave trade were created: for example, the trope of the "Carib" that drove much of the trade. The level of an actor's agency was limited by their place in the social hierarchy; therefore indigenous leaders were able to harness agency with more ease than an African slave who did not possess the equivalent social reach to engage in open contestation of the social hierarchy.[25] But the structure of the conjuncture was temporary, replaced by the "shatter zone" and Spanish dominance of the greater Caribbean by the middle of the sixteenth century.

* * *

To properly gauge the effect of the Indian slave trade on both the nascent Spanish Empire and the pre-contact inhabitants of the Caribbean, the timeline of this project begins in 1491, before the arrival of Europeans in the region. Mapping the ethnic, mercantile, and cultural connections among indigenous peoples in the pre-contact Caribbean reveals the interconnectedness of the region. Next, I briefly turn to the opposite side of the Atlantic, examining the world that created Columbus, in particular the recent colonization efforts in the Canary Islands that influenced European perceptions of and actions in the Americas. Following investigations into the cultures of the Caribbean and Iberia in isolation, *Captives of Conquest* then moves to the collision of cultures, which began with Columbus's first encounters with the peoples of the Bahamas, Cuba, and Española. Here is the foundation of the circum-Caribbean indigenous slave trade. From 1492, I move forward, tracing the policies and ideologies that pushed the growth and expansion of the Indian slave trade, including the creation of the Carib trope and the implementation of "just war" when faced with indigenous resistance across the islands.

By the third decade of colonization, the circum-Caribbean Indian slave trade was fully operational, driving many early colonial enterprises, resulting in calls for reform from religious groups. While the Dominicans, Franciscans, and Jeronymites all worked to limit or even end the indigenous slave trade, their efforts were thwarted by greed, the needs of military conquest, and even the interests of the indigenous populations in question. Here I illustrate both the connections and contradictions between the "spiritual conquest" and military conquest of the Americas. This was especially true during times of exploration and pacification of new territories. As the Spanish colonists moved away from Española, widening their lens to incorporate the larger circum-Caribbean to search for new sources of indigenous slaves, they also discovered new territories. This book follows the slavers and explorers on this enterprise, documenting how the Indian slave trade promoted and inspired further Spanish exploration. But indigenous captives were more than the goal of these voyages. Indian slaves played important roles, whether forced or willing, during these missions of conquest and exploration. As the Indian slave trade incorporated much of South, Central, and North America, it developed into an industry or business of its own. Later chapters examine the operation of the business of Indian slavery, including how the industry connected diverse colonies, colonists, and other economic enterprises. The business of capturing and selling slaves was central to the creation of the Spanish Empire. But it also had unintended consequences.

Captives of Conquest ends by examining some of the larger implications of the slave trade. Both for displaced indigenous captives and for the original inhabitants of the Greater Antilles, the Indian slave trade was a nightmare they likely could not have imagined in 1491. While captives were violently removed from their homelands, the Taínos who remained in their territories were equally impacted by the arrival of thousands of foreign slaves. In the early years of conquest many indigenous leaders were able to temper Spanish power by playing the role of intermediary between Indian laborers and Spanish *encomenderos*. With the influx of Indian slaves and, later, African slaves, this was no longer the case. Unrest and abuse of both enslaved and free Indians erupted in rebellions by the third decade of conquest. As Indians tried to take back their lands, they inspired new legislation meant both to quell discontent and to make the colonies profitable. These reforms included the push for more African slaves over indigenous.

Where most works of slavery in the Americas start, this one ends. Using a diversity of sources and approaches, *Captives of Conquest* illustrates the breadth, scope, and significance of the earliest Indian slave trade in the circum-Caribbean.

CHAPTER 1

_____

Migration, Exchange, and Conquest

Slavery in the Pre-Contact Atlantic

When Christopher Columbus and his fellow Europeans "discovered" the Caribbean, they did not enter an empty landscape.[1] Instead they stumbled on a highly populated and culturally sophisticated web of islands whose inhabitants were connected to one another through ties of kinship, political alliances, and trade networks. In many ways the Caribbean Sea acted as a highway tying various indigenous cultures and peoples to one another. Some maintained ties as far afield as the South American and Mesoamerican mainland. All of these connections helped to shape both the pattern of Spanish conquest and the development of the earliest indigenous slave trade. In particular, the Spanish used an imagined, or at the very least exaggerated, conflict between indigenous groups in the Antilles to justify the capture of thousands of enslaved Indians during the first decades of contact.

While there were cultural and linguistic differences between the populations of the Greater Antilles (those who would become Taínos) and the Lesser Antilles (those who would be known as the first "Caribs"), these two groups were not isolated from one another.[2] Nor were their relationships solely violent and antagonistic, as in the Spanish version. Archaeological evidence points to the growth of closer relationships between the two groups during the fifteenth century. The firm distinction between the Taínos and the "Caribs" was a Spanish construction designed to enslave Indians.[3]

Indigenous Cultures of the Greater Antilles

Diverse indigenous groups inhabited the Caribbean in the fifteenth century, including the Taíno, Ciguayos, Macorixs, and "Caribs." The Taíno, a

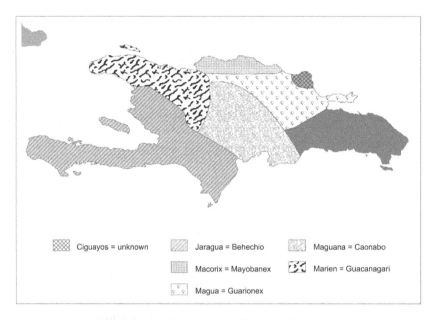

Map 2. Cacicazgos of Española. Map created by Richard Stone.

linguistically diverse ethnic group, inhabited most of the Greater Antilles, including Española, the Lucayos Islands, Jamaica, Puerto Rico, and most of Cuba.[4] After brief interactions with the Lucayan Indians of the Bahamas, the Spanish encountered the Taíno of Cuba and Española. Taíno means "noble" or "good," and it is a derivative of the adjective *nitaíno* in the Taíno language. It was used by the Spanish to differentiate the supposedly peaceful Indians of the Caribbean from the more savage or wild "Caribs."[5] The Taínos in Española, as well as the rest of the Greater Antilles, lived in kin-based villages called *cacicazgos* (chiefdoms).[6] At the time of the Spaniards' arrival there were five paramount cacicazgos led by five very powerful *caciques* (chiefs). Map 2 shows Española's cacicazgos circa 1492.

All of the caciques who are listed in the legend for Map 2 were paramount caciques governing several villages from which they collected tribute. Beneath these powerful individuals were the shamans, or *behiques*, who performed powerful rituals and served as doctors and diviners. The remaining Taínos were broadly grouped into two social classes: the nitaínos (nobility) and the *naborías* (tribute-paying commoners).[7] After their arrival in the Caribbean, the Spanish mistook the second group for a type of slave. Despite what the Spaniards assumed, or may have wished, the Taínos did *not* possess a distinct class of slaves. Nor did they view captives or enslaved individuals as property. While captives were taken in war and raids, both by the Taínos and their "Carib" neighbors to the South, they were rarely enslaved according to European definitions. Often captives were assimilated into the larger society, albeit usually as servants but at times into kinship networks.[8] This was especially true of female captives and children, the majority taken in raids.[9] This is not to say that Taíno societies were egalitarian, and captivity was inherently violent. For example, many boys or adult males captured in war by the "Caribs" of the Lesser Antilles were castrated or emasculated prior to entering servitude.[10] Some men might also have been executed and consumed in cannibalistic rituals.[11] That could explain the animosity felt by the Taíno families who had lost loved ones to "Carib" raids and why they might have used the Europeans to gain revenge on their neighbors.

Still, neither the Taíno tribute system nor the captivity experienced in the Greater and Lesser Antilles prepared the Indians of the Caribbean for the large-scale slave raiding and eventual chattel slavery initiated by the Spanish.[12] Instead, the exchange of slaves was often a part of diplomacy or alliance formation. Alliances between caciques and cacicazgos were solidified both through marriage and the exchange of gifts. Gifts came in the form of valuable items, slaves, and names. Additional names not only bestowed status on caciques, but also, more importantly, created reciprocal fictive kinship relationships between caciques. The more names that a cacique had, the more allies and power he possessed. For example, the Taíno cacique Behechio had over forty names when the Spanish arrived in Española and he expected to be addressed by each one.[13]

In addition to the exchange of captives and women, Taínos also traded religious symbols and figures, most notably cemíes and *guaízas*. Cemíes are painted stone, wood, cotton, or seashell figures that come in many shapes, including doglike, three-pointed, or even in the form of a human body.[14] These often include bones (usually skulls or teeth) from ancestors meant to increase the cemí's power.[15] See Figure 1 for an example of a cemí.

Cemíes were mainly portable objects (which belonged to one cacique or behique) but also came in the form of pictographs and petroglyphs painted or carved on cave walls or into boulders. Cemíes like these would have been accessible to the entire village and likely denoted sacred spaces.[16] Of great significance is that the Taínos viewed their cemíes as vital forces or spirits closely linked to one specific human (always a cacique or behique) who could "unveil its identity or personhood."[17] The cacique and the cemí were like partners, with the cacique's success perceived as emanating from the cemí's

Figure 1. A typical three-pointed cemí from Museo
de Altos de Chavón, Dominican Republic. Photo by
author.

power. As with caciques, different cemíes possessed different levels of power
along with their own kinship networks and genealogies.[18] While cemíes were
carefully guarded by their cacique during his lifetime—though especially
important alliances were cemented with the exchange of cemíes—upon his
death foreign caciques inherited at least some of the deceased cacique's most
powerful belongings, including cemíes. This exchange sought to create new
alliances, to bolster the rule of the new cacique inheriting the position, and to
strengthen already-existing alliances between kin groups related by marriage.

Beyond the exchanging or inheriting of cemíes was the more prevalent
practice of gifting guaízas. Guaízas are small face masks usually made of
stone or shells. For the Taíno the skull, and by extension the face, was the key
part of the human anatomy and where a cacique's power resided. Thus, by
giving carvings of faces to stranger caciques as part of an alliance ceremony,
caciques were exchanging representations of the most important portion of
the living soul. The giving of guaízas usually accompanied the exchanging
of names and/or wives as a sign of alliance both within and between islands.
Although guaízas were endowed with some power, they were not as significant as cemíes; thus it makes sense that the number of guaízas that circu-
lated the Caribbean was much larger than the number of cemíes. Columbus

received guaízas from the caciques Caonabó and Guacanagarí during his early negotiations with them.[19]

While cemíes and guaízas played crucial roles in both the lives and deaths of Taínos, especially caciques, sacred landscapes were also key to a cacique's power and how Taínos understood their realities. One can see this in the funerary rituals and burials of caciques and other higher-status Taínos. While naborías and lower-level nitaínos were buried in either village middens or just outside of settlements in places akin to cemeteries, caciques and their families were usually interred in caves. Most burial caves also house petroglyphs and pictographs showing signs that caves chosen for interment were already considered sacred by the Taínos.[20] Caves also served as places of refuge, particularly during hurricanes. Taínos, and later African slaves, continued this practice of hiding from the Spanish in the Cibao and Bahoruco mountain cave systems. Map 3 shows some of the known Taíno sacred spaces (largely caves) and landscapes.

Following the conquest, caciques were forced to move across the island, deserting their caves, ancestors, and less portable cemíes (like the petroglyphs). Because the caciques derived their spiritual and political authority from these elements, they likely felt this desertion emotionally, spiritually, and politically.[21] This was especially true for the more powerful caciques, leaders whose territories held some of the most important sacred elements. It is interesting to note that almost all the most significant spaces and caves were found in the cacicazgos of Magua, Maguana, and Higuey. All of these

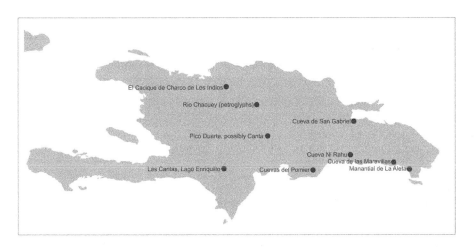

Map 3. Sacred spaces of Española. Map created by Richard Stone.

cacicazgos and their corresponding caciques (Guarionex, Caonabó, and Higuanamo) violently protested Spanish presence and infiltration of their lands. On the other hand, the cacique Guacanagarí of Marién, a less power-ful cacicazgo that held no identifiable sacred spaces, sought out an alliance with Columbus and even remained loyal to the Europeans when the rest of the island rose against them. Guacanagarí may have thought that an alliance with the Europeans would increase his own power and status on the island, something that the other more dominant caciques did not see as necessary or even appealing. These dominant caciques, with their sacred territories, suf-fered most from the upheaval of Spanish colonization, especially as surviving caciques were forced to desert their ancestral lands and faced an influx of foreign Indian slaves beholden not to Taíno rulers, but to the Spanish in the third decade of conquest.

A Closer Look at Indigenous Connections
Across the Caribbean

There was significant fluidity among indigenous groups in the pre-contact circum-Caribbean.[22] A great range of movement within the Caribbean was possible since the Taínos and others possessed a range of wooden canoes. Some could hold from fifty to one hundred men, while others were smaller, personal-sized canoes. The larger canoes could make long-distance voyages. Chroniclers such as Bartolomé de las Casas and Dr. Chanca marveled at the craftsmanship of the Taíno canoes.[23] Some of the largest and most artfully decorated canoes were found in Jamaica, where European explorers reported seeing canoes painted with brilliant colors.[24] Both the Taínos and Caribs possessed hundreds if not thousands of canoes. For example, Guacanagarí of Española greeted Columbus with no fewer than 120 canoes, all filled with men.[25] The Indians also possessed detailed knowledge of the Caribbean basin, something of great value to the conquistadors. The extent of this knowledge can be seen in the interrogation of two captive Lucayan Indians by the king of Portugal in 1493. During the interview, the Indians used beans to create a map of the Caribbean that included the Bahamas, Cuba, Española, Puerto Rico, and several islands of the Lesser Antilles.[26] During the colonial era, Indians used their canoes and knowledge of the region to escape the Spaniards, flee-ing to Florida, Cuba, or the Lesser Antilles. This frustrated the Spanish to the point that they began to burn any canoes they found.[27] It also inspired further exploration and the taking of "rebellious" Indians as slaves.

The mobility of indigenous populations across the Caribbean calls into question the long-accepted division between the "Caribs" of the Lesser Antilles and Taínos of the Greater Antilles. Though few details about the "Caribs" can be agreed upon, it is highly probable that the Indians who the Spanish first designated as Caribs were recent arrivals to the Lesser Antilles, populating the islands in the 1300s.[28] Shortly thereafter, the Caribs, especially those living in the northernmost Lesser Antilles or the Leeward Islands, began to have sustained contact with the Taínos of Puerto Rico and the rest of the Greater Antilles.[29] On the other hand, the residents of the more southern islands, the Windward Islands, remained within the sphere of mainland South American politics and culture.[30]

Burial sites across the Antilles reveal the connections between the two societies. For example, in the Windward Islands, pottery appears that signifies close interactions with the inhabitants of the Guianas and Amazonia throughout the pre-contact period.[31] It was with these peoples, the inhabitants of the Windward Islands and the mainland of South America, not the residents of the more northern Leeward Islands, that the Taíno described having hostilities, including slave raids. Even these conflicts seem to have been carried out within a single cultural landscape, with both sides conducting reciprocal raids. Neither side was engaged in conquering territories but had augmented small populations (hence the preference for taking women captive).[32]

Additionally, there is evidence of cultural sharing between the Greater and Lesser Antilles just before Spanish arrival. Specifically, a type of ornamentation was found on higher-status and religious artifacts in Grenada, Guadeloupe, St. Vincent, and Dominica that is almost identical to Taíno bowls of the Greater Antilles.[33] This type of pottery, often featuring bat and owl faces, shows a high degree of craftsmanship. Both bats and owls held significant meaning in Taíno cosmology.[34] The fact that similar decorations appear on ceramics in the Lesser Antilles points to Taíno influence on Carib culture.[35]

Connections and relationships between the Taínos of the Greater Antilles and the Caribs of the Lesser Antilles likely extended to voluntary marriage alliances.[36] It follows that the presence of Arawak-speaking women in the Lesser Antilles was possibly not the result of kidnapping during Carib raids, as the Spanish assumed. Instead, it suggests Taíno attempts at extending political and social alliances into the Lesser Antilles in the fifteenth century. Columbus first encountered the Caribs during his second voyage in 1493, when he spent six days on the island of Guadeloupe. During his stay he captured ten or twelve women from the island of Boriquen (Puerto Rico). He assumed the women were captives stolen or enslaved by the Caribs. While this is a possibility, it could also be that during recent diplomatic missions caciques of Boriquen gave the women to the Caribs to solidify new alliances. Either way, Columbus and the Spanish took the women from Guadeloupe and sent them to Spain, using their presence on the island to prove the barbarity of the Caribs while also depriving the women of their freedom.[37] The Spanish relied on the dichotomy between the Taínos and the Caribs, despite its deficiencies, to legitimize the circum-Caribbean indigenous slave trade in the early sixteenth century.

In addition to marital or kinship connections, trade also linked the Antilles. The Caribbean Sea tied various indigenous peoples to one another, as far south as South America.[38] At the time of Spanish occupation, both Taíno and Carib ceramics were present on the island of Trinidad.[39] It can thus be inferred that the Taíno of the Greater Antilles ventured as far south as Trinidad and the coast of South America to conduct trade in raw materials, finished pottery, and even pendants made from exotic materials like jade, turquoise, and quartz.[40] For example, two quartz pendants found in Jamaica were almost certainly made in South America because quartz, along with jade and turquoise, is not naturally found in the Antilles.[41] One of the best examples for trade in raw materials is the presence of stone tools made from flint or chert throughout the Lesser Antilles, even though chert is only naturally available in the Windward Islands or southernmost Antilles.[42] These pre-contact exchange networks also help explain the presence of *guanín* in Española in the fifteenth century. Guanín is a mixture of gold, copper, and silver. It does not occur naturally in the Caribbean, nor did the Taíno know how to refine or forge the metal. Therefore, guanín likely originated from Colombia, whose inhabitants possessed the technology necessary for the refinement of precious metals.[43] Contacts between the Greater Antilles and Colombia are further reinforced by the presence of guinea pig, or cuy, remains in ceremonial settings in Puerto Rico. The cuy was not native to the Antilles or northeastern South America, but to the Andes, and was considered a luxury food for the elite during important festivals or for use in long-distance trade. The fact that guinea-pig bones were located in ritual contexts in the Taíno settlement of Tibes, Puerto Rico, suggests that the animal was brought from northwestern South America as part of a prestigious exchange.[44]

Evidence also suggests the exchange of higher-prestige items between the Greater and Lesser Antilles, though not to South or Central America, revealing the deeper connections shared within the Antilles. High-prestige items included *duhos* (chiefly stools used during rituals and welcoming ceremonies), guaízas, and some cemíes.[45] The trade or gifting of these was more significant than acquiring subsistence items because they suggest political and social relationships, not just economic.[46] Cemíes and guaízas gifted at funerary rituals were especially noteworthy as they cemented alliances between the new cacique and more established caciques throughout the region. By accepting a cemí or other gift, including names or wives, foreign caciques (who could be from different islands or simply distinct chiefdoms) became indebted to and publicly demonstrated their support for the new cacique.[47] The importance of the exchange of cemíes helps to explain the lack of cemíes found in burial sites across Española and Puerto Rico, as cemíes remained in circulation to solidify military or political alliances.[48]

While archaeologists have found the majority of cemíes, duhos, and guaízas in Puerto Rico, Cuba, and Española, they also unearthed these items (especially guaízas) across the Antilles, underscoring the connectedness of the region.[49] For example, archaeologists discovered numbers of shell guaízas on the Leeward Islands of Anguilla, Antigua, and Monserrat, and on the Windward Islands of Guadeloupe, Desirade, and Marie-Galante.[50] These discoveries could serve as evidence that the northern Lesser Antilles were a part of the larger Taíno cultural sphere that spread eastward from the Greater Antilles in the Late Ceramic Age.[51] Though fewer in number, some shell guaízas have also been found as far south as the Grenadines Islands.[52] Additionally, archaeologists have found cemíes, though most were broken, in the Lesser Antilles closest to South America.[53] Just as ceremonial objects spread southward to the Lesser Antilles, so did styles and forms of petroglyphs. By the 1400s, petroglyphs in Grenada and St. Vincent began to resemble those found in the Greater Antilles, becoming larger and more elaborate. Some even resemble carved images of the three-pointed Taíno cemíes.[54] In addition, more petroglyphs were produced in the years leading up to European contact, indicating the sharing of cultural and political ideas. Many of the newer petroglyphs are located near the coast, making them highly visible to visitors. Thus, they may have denoted territorial, ethnic, or political markers, as many did in both Española and Puerto Rico.[55]

The close ties between the Greater and Lesser Antilles, possibly extending to both Central and South America, through marriage and trade, explain common practices within the greater Caribbean. These include the use of marriage to create alliances, the common practice of hereditary succession to chiefly status of uncle to nephew, and the sharing of myth cycles and sacred objects.[56] It seems increasingly likely that Caribs were Arawakan speakers, longtime residents of the Lesser Antilles, with connections to both the Greater Antilles and the South American mainland through trade and alliance networks.[57] These connections and alliances were crucial to the survival of the island populations, who relied on trade and exchange to garner both subsistence and prestige items.

Much evidence also points to pre-contact Taíno trade networks extending westward to Central America. A Taíno vomiting stick, used to purge oneself prior to the *cohoba* ritual, was found on the coast of Belize.[58] Moreover, in 1518 Bernal Díaz de Castillo found a Taíno woman from Jamaica living on the Maya island of Cozumel, where she was shipwrecked after blowing off course in a fishing expedition. Her presence suggests that the Taínos traveled regularly to waters near Central America.[59] Strong evidence also points to ties between Cuba (especially western Cuba) and Central America into the fifteenth century.[60] This connection may help shed light on why the Taíno of both Cuba and Española could communicate with the indigenous inhabitants of Mexico and Honduras.[61] It also might explain the similarities present between the ball court, or *batey*, of the Taíno and that of the Maya and Mexica (Aztec) of Central America.[62] Some postulate that the Mesoamerican ball game, or some version, arrived in the Greater Antilles around 600 BC. By the fifteenth century there were hundreds of bateys in Española and Puerto Rico as well as some on the Lucayos Islands. Sustained contact between Mesoamerican cultures may have also exposed islanders to a system of slavery closer to that of Europe. In Mesoamerica, slaves, *tlatlacotlin* in Nahuatl, were not simply gained by raiding, but were obtained through warfare, tribute payment, punishment, and debt. Once enslaved, if they were not killed or sacrificed as many thousands were annually, the slaves became the property of their masters. However, masters did not just elicit labor (usually household service, agricultural work, or weaving) from their slaves. Owners also had to care for their slaves, providing food, clothing, and shelter. Many compared the treatment of slaves to that of children. That could explain why some individuals sold themselves into slavery. Slaves were also permitted to earn money, marry a free person, and sue for their liberty.[63] Yet the descriptions of slave markets, complete with branding and chains around slaves' necks, paint a different picture.[64] This type of slavery spread across the Americas with the arrival of the Europeans, uniting the circum-Caribbean in a violent slave trade.

The pre-contact Caribbean basin was a highly permeable environment populated by diverse peoples with complex networks of kinship, alliance, and exchange, all connecting the various islands. Of course, the connections were not always peaceful, with warfare and raiding also occurring across the region. Both peaceful and contentious relationships greatly impacted how indigenous populations reacted to Spanish conquistadors as Indians shared knowledge of the Spanish, as some found sanctuary on nearby islands, and, most dramatically, as islands rose up together to contest Spanish presence. Preexisting connections also determined the ability of Española's chiefdoms to incorporate the influx of diverse indigenous slaves following the increase in slaving expeditions of the early 1500s. The initial victims of the Spanish slave trade originated from islands that already formed part of the Taíno cultural zone, for example, the Lucayos Islands or Carib Guadeloupe. However, assimilation was more difficult (though not impossible) for Indians captured in more disparate regions such as the interior of South America or the southeastern United States, populations that had different conceptions of slavery and power. In many ways indigenous pre-contact patterns, ideas, and networks molded the Spanish conquest and colonization of Española and the larger Caribbean. They also, especially in the first decades of contact, shaped the creation of the indigenous slave trade.

Iberian Exploration Expands into the Atlantic

Just as the Taínos, Caribs, and other indigenous groups of the greater Caribbean were expanding their horizons, the residents of Iberia, on the other side of the Atlantic, were embarking on new missions of exploration. In response to the Muslim capture of Constantinople in 1453, the successful Reconquista of the Iberian Peninsula culminating in 1492, and Portuguese journeys into the Atlantic throughout the fourteenth and fifteenth centuries, the Spanish began looking outside of the Mediterranean world. Exploration first took them to the Canary Islands off the coast of Africa.

Beginning in the first decades of the fourteenth century, various Genoese, Castilian, Norman, Florentine, and Portuguese merchants and traders visited and explored the Canary Islands, with goals ranging from trade to conversion and colonization.[65] The Spanish Crown sent Christian missionaries, first Franciscan friars, to the Canaries, who endeavored to preach to the indigenous peoples of the islands in their own languages while setting up exchange programs, schools, and churches.[66] In 1351 Pope Clement VI joined with the king of Aragon to send two captains to the Canaries in an ambitious plan to bring the inhabitants into the Christian fold. Up to thirty missionaries (from both Carmelite and Franciscan orders) accompanied two ships from Majorca. Along with the captains and missionaries there were up to twelve Canary Islanders who had been captured and brought to Europe on previous expeditions of exploration or pillaging. In Europe, the Canarians had received instruction in the Catholic faith and Catalan language. They were now to serve as intermediaries for the Spanish conquest and colonization of the islands, at least in theory. The pope commented about their zeal to return to their homelands, supposedly to help indoctrinate their fellow Canarians in Christianity.[67] While the islanders might have truly wanted to help the missionaries, it is just as likely that they simply sought to return to their native lands. These were the first native (captive) peoples brought to Iberia specifically to be trained in Catholicism and European languages before returning to their homelands as guides and translators to assist in conquest. The same practice was carried out in nearly every New World conquest, at times greatly assisting the Spanish, and at other times backfiring when native allies turned against them.[68]

Upon arriving in Gran Canaria, the friars set up a mission in Telde, the seat of one of the most important leaders of the island. There they built a small church and attempted to convert the Canarians. However, the local population was very distrustful of the friars, and not many were willing to adopt their faith. Much of the fear and caution displayed by the Canarians can be linked to the dozens of slave-raiding expeditions that assaulted the island throughout the fourteenth century, and which continued despite the presence of the missionaries.[69] But the church did not give up. While the exact fate of the first thirty friars is unclear, in 1366 the king of Aragon supported an expedition from Majorca meant to clear the islands of other European intruders, specifically slave traders and raiders. Despite this effort, along with the arrival of more missionaries and supplies in 1370 and 1386, the missions came to a dramatic end in 1393. By the 1390s Catalans, Cantabrians, and Andalusians were all assaulting the island, carrying off dozens of slaves on each visit. As slave raids increased, the island also experienced severe famine. Unable to support their people, and perhaps blaming the missionaries for the recent hardships, the islanders killed all the friars, two of whom they threw down a volcanic shaft.[70]

But the Spanish did not give up. With the Reconquista coming to a close at the end of the fifteenth century, the Spanish refocused on the archipelago, a territory that they hoped would link them to the gold mines of Ethiopia.[71] By 1478 they controlled the islands of Lanzarote, Fuerteventura, and Hierro, and they began to undertake the conquest of the larger and most densely populated island of Gran Canaria.[72] Soon thereafter, they began the difficult conquests of La Palma and the largest island, Tenerife, which was not pacified until 1496.[73] Faced with armed resistance in the Canaries, the Spanish responded with increased violence and enslavement of combatants, as they later would in the

Americas. Because these captives were pagans taken in what the Spanish considered legitimate or "just war," they could legally be enslaved.[74] Captives taken in "just war" who were "enemies of the faith" could be enslaved rather than killed, according to the Siete Partidas, a law code dating from the thirteenth century, influenced by Roman law.[75] Justifiable war included when one was under attack or fighting in defense of one's own sovereignty or an ally's safety. Usually Christians were exempt from bondage.[76] However, the inhabitants of the Canary Islands presented Spain with a quandary. Because the islanders had not previously been introduced to Christianity, they did not qualify as heretics or infidels like Muslims or pagans of Africa and Eastern Europe. To enslave them, Iberians had to complicate their definition of "just war," something they later used on the indigenous peoples of the Americas. Essentially, they divided the islanders into two groups: "rebellious," meaning those who refused Christian conversion, and "peaceful," or those who willingly accepted Christianity. All "rebellious" Canarians could be enslaved.[77]

But conversion to Christianity did not always mean safety from enslavement, particularly during the chaotic process of military conquest. While the small island of Gomera submitted to the Spanish in the 1440s, its residents continued to be enslaved and used during conquests of other islands, like Gran Canaria in 1478. Because of this abuse, the Gomerans revolted against the Spanish in 1488, killing the Spanish governor Peraza and providing the Spanish with the perfect excuse to wage "just war" on the island. In the process thousands of Gomerans were enslaved and transferred to the ports of southern Andalucía and the greater Mediterranean in 1488 and 1489. The arrival of so many Gomeran slaves caught the attention of Queen Isabela and King Ferdinand, who declared the Gomerans as free, Christian vassals despite the rebellion. According to the Crown's order, officials needed to locate all the recently enslaved Gomerans from across the Mediterranean and return them to their homes. The task took decades to complete, with the bulk of the Gomerans never gaining their freedom.[78]

Nor were the Gomerans an anomaly. Throughout the fifteenth century, until 1496 and the surrender of Tenerife, Spanish forces battled the Canarians of Gran Canaria and the Guanches of Tenerife, enslaving thousands in the process.[79] During the fourteenth and fifteenth centuries, the most lucrative product of the Canary Islands was its people. Other than the capture of slaves, Europeans also profited from the sale of sheep, goats, and wild pigs. But, by far, the best business was the slave trade.[80] In fact, the *quinto de esclavos* (the fifth collected on the sale of slaves) served as one of the larger incentives included in conquistadors' royal contracts of conquest.[81] After their capture the slaves were sold in the coastal markets of Iberia from Andalu-cía (the future heart of the American enterprise) to Catalonia. For example, in 1490 a *corregidor* in Palos purchased several Canarian slaves in the port city of Palos.[82] One might expect the presence of high numbers of enslaved Canary Islanders in Andalucía; however, some of the largest numbers were destined for the port city of Valencia.[83] One German traveler, Jerónimo Mun-zer, described the sale of eighty-six enslaved Guanches in Valencia in Octo-ber 1494 (at the high point of the military conquest of Tenerife).[84]

A steady stream of enslaved Canary Islanders arrived in Iberian ports throughout the 1480s and 1490s, with spikes in the numbers of slaves after a pitched battle. In the spring of 1496 the official conquistador of Tenerife, Alonso de Lugo, journeyed to Andalucía and later Valencia to sell many Guanche slaves. He used the profit to recover his costs from the conquest of the island, including to pay his debtors.[85] Nor did slaving stop after the end of formal conflict in December 1495. Instead, the Spanish used the presence of small pockets of resistant Guanches to continue waging "just war" and/or pacifying the island. In many cases the pockets of "rebellious" islanders were simply those who lived far from Spanish settlements, many having purpose-fully fled the coast during the process of conquest. The greater part of these populations were labeled as "rebellious," or *alzados*, and enslaved, their only crime being geographical distance from the Spanish.[86] All Guanches defeated during this period of *limpieza* (cleaning up) were taken as slaves and deliv-ered to Sanlúcar de Barrameda, Puerto de Santa María, Cádiz, Sevilla, Valen-cia, Barcelona, and Palma de Mallorca.[87]

In addition to slaves captured during conquest or "just war," many were taken illegally throughout the conflict by raiders and conquistadors alike. Even former allies found themselves enslaved. Case in point, in 1493 Lugo enslaved a minimum of forty-two natives of La Palma, at first claiming he had captured them during the conquest. However, in the ensuing court case (brought forward by the Palmeses in Sevilla) officials discovered that Lugo lied about the timing of their capture, and that they were enslaved after the end of the war. Nor were the Palmeses taken during an ensuing rebellion.[88] Lugo replicated his behavior after the conquest of Tenerife, enslaving bap-tized and peaceful Guanches across the island, often through trickery. In one instance he invited a group of two hundred Guanches to a church service, but once they were inside, he locked the building, took them captive, and delivered them as slaves to Valencia and Barcelona. It is estimated that at least one thousand Guanches were enslaved illegally in the wake of the conquest of Tenerife.[89]

In addition to the Guanches taken, the Spanish enslaved many free and allied Canarians illegally in the wake of hostilities in Tenerife. Following Gran Canaria's surrender to the Spanish in 1483, many Canarians participated as Spanish allies in the conquest of Tenerife. Yet they too suffered slavery at the end of the conquest of the island. Many Canarians understood this possibility and feared participating in the conquest of other islands. To avoid enslavement many hid, avoiding transfer to Tenerife. However, this option was not foolproof as the refusal to serve with the Spanish was considered rebellious behavior. This is shown in the case of the Canarians Juana and her husband. In fear of being enslaved, despite their conversion to Christianity, Juana and her husband hid from the Spanish to avoid serving during the conquest of Tenerife. However, the two were discovered, enslaved, and sold in Jerez de la Frontera because of their actions. They appear on the record suing for their freedom in Sevilla in 1491 under the defense that they were captured illegally, after having converted to Christianity and while at peace with Spain.[90]

Concurrent with the slave trade emanating from the Canary Islands was the growing slave trade involving Portuguese merchants and explorers along the coast of Africa. While slavery was a common practice in the late Middle Ages across the Mediterranean world, expansion into the Atlantic made slavery into a bigger business, especially for the Portuguese who early on fulfilled the European demand for African slaves. Europeans considered African captives to be legitimate slaves because they had been enslaved during war between sovereign African kingdoms. Therefore, the Europeans could purchase African slaves captured in "just war," like Guanche and Canarian slaves, without having to enslave anyone themselves.[91] By the end of the fifteenth century, African and Canarian slaves arrived in the ports of southern Spain in high numbers.[92] There they sold for similar prices, with customers paying more for women than their male counterparts, largely because many of them were destined to be concubines.[93] By the 1490s there was a small Canarian quarter inhabited by Guanche and Canarian servants and slaves in Sevilla, the very city that became the center of the New World enterprise.[94]

Mirroring the inextricable links between the Canary Islands and Iberia, and particularly Andalucía, the Canary Islands also became tightly connected to the Americas. From Columbus forward, nearly all expeditions of conquest, colonization, or resupply stopped in the Canaries on the way to the Americas. But the connections do not stop there. An excellent example of the ties between the enterprise of the Indies and that of the Canaries is seen in Francisco de Riberol, a Genovese banker and merchant. He helped to fund the conquest of both La Palma and Tenerife, working closely with Alonso de

Lugo, beginning in 1492. As part of his investment, Riberol received Guanche slaves from Lugo in 1497.[95] He also had ties and connections with Columbus and helped to fund the admiral's fourth voyage. Riberol went on to send at least two ships to the Americas in 1501, loaded with goods for the colonies without permission from the Crown. One wonders whether these contraband goods included slaves from the Canary Islands.[96]

It is plausible that Riberol's ship carried enslaved Canary Islanders, among other goods and products from the Canary Islands (like sugar cane), as there is evidence of Canarian slaves in the Americas during the early years of conquest.[97] The few documents that point to the presence of enslaved Canary Islanders in the Americas remark on their physical abilities, especially their talent for swimming. In 1514 the governor of Panama, Lope de Sosa, wrote to the Crown requesting permission to transport fifty Canarian slaves from Gran Canaria to Panama, where they would be put to work on the coastal pearl islands. The letter specifically references the Canarians' aquatic abilities.[98] As late as the 1520s, slaves from the Canary Islands are mentioned in Caribbean sources. Slave ordinances, passed in 1522 on Española, included Canarian slaves as a separate category of enslaved person, underscoring that the laws applied to black, white, and Canarian slaves.[99] The explicit inclusion of Canarian slaves makes it clear that there were still Canarian or Guanche slaves in the Indies three decades after initial colonization. Additionally, there were also still white, likely Moorish, slaves present.[100]

Iberian experiences in the slave trade both in Africa and on the Canary Islands helped to inspire the soon-flourishing Indian slave trade of the Americas from 1492 onward. Columbus also used his personal experiences in Africa and the Canary Islands to shape his model for colonization and profit in the Americas, the basis of which was slavery. Just as the Europeans used the taking of slaves to fund their expeditions of conquest in the Atlantic Islands, Columbus soon turned to slave trading to subsidize his American enterprise.

CHAPTER 2

Two Worlds Collide

The Rise of the Indian Slave Trade

Recent experiences in the Canary Islands and the Reconquista influenced Spanish responses to the Americas and its inhabitants. Many of the institutions imposed on the islands of the Caribbean, and later the mainland of North, South, and Central America, can be traced to fifteenth-century Spain, for example, the *encomienda*. One of the most influential practices brought to the New World was that of slavery: not only the system itself, but also the laws surrounding when, how, and why someone could be enslaved. While the legality governing slavery evolved over the first decades of colonization, the basic ideas came with the European explorers. With recent slaving expeditions on both the Canary Islands and along the African coast in mind, it is no wonder that as early as 1493 Columbus planned to make a profit by enslaving the Indians of the Caribbean.

While the Spanish court debated Columbus's proposal for enslaving the peoples of the Americas in the last decade of the fifteenth century, the lack of clear laws surrounding the trade inspired many entrepreneurs to bring hundreds of Indian captives from the Caribbean to the Iberian Peninsula. The numbers of indigenous captives transported to Spain swelled following early indigenous revolts and conflicts on Española. But the Indian slave trade did not explode until Isabela, and later Ferdinand, declared it legal to enslave all Carib Indians and Indians residing on "useless" islands (those lacking in gold). By the end of the second decade of colonization, the growing indigenous slave trade engulfed the Lucayos Islands, Puerto Rico, the Lesser Antilles, and much of the coastline of present-day Venezuela and Brazil. These slaves were put to work alongside the diminishing Taínos of Española (and later Cuba and Puerto Rico) in gold mines, on cattle ranches, and at sugar plantations. Here were the beginnings of the Indian slave trade, accelerating and amplifying the interisland connections and relationships present in the pre-contact Americas.

At first, the influx of foreign Indians into Española helped mask the massive depopulation of the island, but only slightly. It was the decline in Taínos alongside the visible violence of the indigenous slave trade that inspired religious officials to rebuke Spanish authorities in the Caribbean. However, their efforts helped little, and the early slave trade only increased, expanding beyond the Caribbean to include lands as distant as Mexico and present-day South Carolina. These legal and illegal raids, wars, and exchanges fill the colonial records. From Columbus's first proposal to enslave Indians to the height of the slave trade in the 1530s, the search for and profit from Indian captives was central to the development of Spanish colonial institutions. The indigenous slave trade was especially influential in the evolution of colonial law. This chapter explores the creation of the circum-Caribbean indigenous slave trade, in particular how specific events, ideas, and legislation propelled the trade throughout the first three decades of colonization.

Columbus's First Captives

With three ships and a few hundred men, Columbus set sail from southern Spain on August 3, 1492. The group sailed for thirty-three days before making landfall on one of the Bahamas or Lucayos Islands on October 12, 1492.[1] Columbus and his men spent several days reconnoitering the island and exchanging goods with the Indians.[2] While the initial interactions between the Lucayans and the Spanish were purportedly peaceful, prior to continuing with their explorations, Columbus ordered the capture of seven Indians who would act as guides in their search for Cipango, or Japan. Following this service Columbus planned to take the Indians to Spain where they would be instructed in Spanish and Catholicism. They would then serve the Europeans as interpreters and intermediaries in return voyages of colonization to the Indies.[3] Here Columbus was following the model used by Franciscan friars in the Canary Islands and by the Portuguese along the coast of Africa.[4] Though these men were not slaves per se, Columbus and his colleagues saw nothing wrong with their capture and forced removal from their homes. He also commented on their quick wit and docile natures, remarking that these characteristics would make them ideal servants.[5] His

comments served as foreshadowing of Columbus's future indigenous policies. It also could reflect common European ideas regarding inhabitants of
the lower latitudes. Many Europeans, including Columbus, believed that
they would find either very "childish" or "monstrous" populations along
with a plethora of gold when they entered the "torrid zone." These inhabitants, like the supposedly simple natives of the Lucayos, were justifiably
enslavable.[6]

Following exploration of the Lucayos Islands, Columbus and his group
traveled to Cuba and Española. Throughout their journey they captured more
Indian guides or slaves. When Columbus began his return journey to Europe,
he possessed around twelve Indian captives hailing from the Lucayos, Cuba,
and Española.[7] Of the Indians taken from Española, two survived the journey
to return with Columbus the following year after they were baptized in Spain.[8]
Four others survived long enough for Columbus to present them alongside
his other discoveries at both the Portuguese and Castilian courts. In Lisbon,
Portugal, during the interrogation of King Don Juan II, the Europeans learned
the extent of indigenous knowledge of Caribbean geography and navigation.
The Portuguese were incredibly interested in the geography of the newly discovered lands, perhaps because they believed they might have a claim to the
islands. Two of the Indians excelled at the test, constructing crude maps of the
Caribbean by using painted beans. On the maps they showed the positions
of Española, Cuba, Jamaica, the Lucayos, and many of the Lesser Antilles.
Columbus used this knowledge to guide him to the Lesser Antilles in search
of Caribs at the start of his second voyage to the New World.[9]

After the interrogation in Lisbon, Columbus and his entourage traveled
to the Spanish court and presented the Indians alongside his other discoveries and curiosities. Initiating the "spiritual conquest" of the Americas, all
of the surviving six Indians were baptized in Barcelona with the king and
his son, Prince Juan, serving as their godfathers.[10] During the baptismal
ceremonies each of the Indians received a new name, creating a religious
bond between the godparent and his charge. The baptismal ceremony in
many ways mirrored the Taíno tradition of exchanging names when forming reciprocal alliances and bonds of kinship. So perhaps the Indians
understood the ceremony and exchanging of names as formalizing reciprocal, even equal, bonds between themselves and the Spanish rulers. Unfortunately, we can never know exactly how the Indians perceived the ritual of
baptism, but it is likely that they witnessed and understood it within their
own cosmology.

Creating the Carib Trope and Legitimizing
the Indian Slave Trade

Columbus traveled back to the Caribbean in October 1493, this time heading for the islands southeast of Española.[11] On the islands of Guadalupe and
Dominica, Columbus and his men first encountered Carib Indians.[12] The
royal physician from Sevilla, Diego Alvaréz Chanca, described discovering
four or five human arm and leg bones in an abandoned hut on the island
of Dominica. Because there were no large animals in the Caribbean before
the arrival of the Spanish, the large bones had to be human, proving to the
travelers that the island's inhabitants were indeed the fearsome Caribs per
the Taínos of Española. From this encounter forward, the Spaniards used
the practice of cannibalism as an excuse to justify the enslavement of anyone labeled a Carib.[13] Nor did the Europeans have to prove consumption of
human flesh to bestow this title.[14]

Regardless of whether cannibalism was practiced by the Caribs, Columbus and his men greatly exaggerated the custom to promote their own objec-
tives. Likewise, they amplified the conflict between the Caribs and the Taínos
of the Greater Antilles likely without fully understanding the Taíno/Carib
dynamic. The Caribs and Taínos had a complex and evolving relationship
that included both peaceful political alliances and kinship networks as well as
violent raids to capture cemíes and women.

Why then did Columbus and other Europeans create such a clear dichotomy between the Caribs and the Taínos, with the Caribs playing the role of
villain? This can at least partially be explained by miscommunication. When
Columbus first met with Guacanagarí and the other Taínos of Española, the
Indians spoke of or gestured to an enemy that lived to the southeast that
they called "Caribs." In the Taíno language, "Caribe" or "canibale" means
"fierce, brave, strong person."[15] The Taínos may have used this descriptor
out of respect for the inhabitants of the Lesser Antilles. The Caribe could
have also been a purely mythological character, a creature of the realm of
the dead.[16] According to Columbus's writings, Guacanagarí described an
island called "Quari," which was "inhabited by a people who are regarded
in all the islands as very fierce and who eat human flesh. They have many
canoes with which they range through all the islands of India and pillage
and take as much as they can."[17] Columbus concluded, correctly or not, that
the Taínos feared these peoples and were at war with them. Columbus then
used the Taíno "fear" of the Caribs to paint himself as the protector of the
"good" and cooperative Taíno Indians. In this way Columbus justified both

the colonization of the Caribbean islands and the eventual enslavement of the "bad" Carib peoples.

Upon landing in Guadeloupe, the explorers found human bones, including a neck that was boiling in a pot and bones hung up around the houses.[18] These bones could have had a variety of meanings. For example, they could have served as a warning to enemies as they did in pre-contact Colombia. In 1514 in the province of Santa Marta, Vasco Nuñez de Balboa described human skulls posted at doors and necklaces made of human teeth. These served as human trophies and to warn any would-be interlopers.[19] Another possibility is that the bones were in the process of being treated prior to their burial or incorporation in ritual and religious objects—such as cemíes that often contained bones. Not understanding the other uses of bones in indigenous cultures, the Europeans assumed they were proof of cannibalism. This horrified the Europeans, especially as this was their first contact with possible cannibals. Neither Africans nor the Guanches and Canarians practiced cannibalism. So, while the Iberians were familiar with a wide range of cultures, this was their first encounter with possible cannibalism.

Despite the Caribs' bellicose reputation, Columbus's men met very few Indians on Guadeloupe because most had fled to the mountains when they saw the Europeans approaching. Still, the group was able to capture eight men. Of these, they reported that six were Taínos from Puerto Rico (Boriquen). In addition to the eight men, the party took twelve women and some children, all of whom they assumed to be captives of the Caribs. Chanca even speculated that the women's husbands had been eaten by the Caribs of Guadeloupe.[20] Another chronicler, a friend of Columbus's named Michael Cuneo, described the captive women as being "very beautiful and fat, between the ages of fifteen and sixteen."[21] It appeared then that these women were well treated by the inhabitants of Guadeloupe, whether or not they were concubines, wives, or slaves.[22] Throughout the eight days that Columbus and his men remained on Guadeloupe they encountered both Taínos and Caribs, taking many by force, though some came with them willingly. Of note is that the Europeans could tell the two groups apart only by hairstyle, with the Caribs wearing their hair very long while the Taínos preferred a shorter, boblike haircut.[23]

How did the women and men of Puerto Rico come to be on Guadalupe in 1493? Were they truly slaves captured during raids with the men and then destined to be eaten? And, if so, why were they still alive and allowed their freedom on the island? Or had they served as gifts to solidify recent alliances between the Taínos of Puerto Rico and the Indians of Guadalupe as archaeological evidence suggests? Whether or not these men, women, and children were from Guadalupe, were visiting the island, or were in fact slaves or captives of the Caribs as the Europeans assumed, Columbus sent them all to Spain where they would serve as examples of Caribs or Carib prisoners.[24]

Only a few days after sailing from Guadeloupe, a canoe carrying many Caribs attacked the European vessels with arrows. In response Columbus and his men captured the canoe, killing several Indians and taking the rest hostage.[25] There is no specific further account of these captives. But it is likely that they were sent to Spain with Antonio Torres in February 1494 when he returned to gather supplies for the nascent colony of La Isabela. By the time of Torres's return trip to Spain, on which he carried a report by Columbus to the monarchs, the admiral had formulated a plan and rationale to enslave the Caribs. First, some of the Indians would serve as interpreters and guides for the eventual conquest of all the Carib islands. Second, most Carib slaves would be put to work in Spain or the Canary Islands. To collect sufficient slaves for both purposes, Columbus advocated that the Crown send several caravels to the Caribbean to hunt and capture Caribs. The Caribs were the perfect target of slavers, due to their natural strength and temperament paired with their inhumane practice of cannibalism.[26] The profit from the slaves could be used to purchase supplies and food for the colonists.[27] Columbus adopted the same design after the Taínos of Española turned against the Europeans.

As Columbus developed a plan for an Atlantic indigenous slave trade, Queen Isabela questioned the practice and its morality. In 1495 she postponed the sale of the five hundred Indians that Columbus shipped to Spain, waiting to confer with scholars and theologians to determine whether they were legal slaves. She also sought a more complete description as to how the Indians were enslaved and why they were sent to Spain.[28] A full year later Isabela was still undecided. While little documentation exists to determine the fate of most of these Indians, at least fifty were sold to Juan de Lezcano to serve as galley slaves.[29] Another, named Francisco, was sold to the widow Inés Rodríguez in Sevilla for three thousand *maravedíes* by two Genoese mariners in 1497.[30]

A few years later the queen finally came to a decision and declared the Indians of the Americas to be free persons and subjects and vassals of the Spanish Crown. As vassals to the Crown, the laws of Spain extended to the Indians of the Caribbean and, in theory, prevented their abuse at the hands of Spanish colonists. Isabela even went so far as to order the return of all the surviving Indians whom Columbus had shipped to Spain.[31] By the summer of 1501 only twenty-one of the original five hundred were still in the possession of Torres, and one of them was too sick to travel.[32] The other twenty were to be escorted home by the first large contingent of Franciscan friars to journey to the Americas in 1502.

In addition to the Indians already in Spain, Isabela also tried to protect those in the colonies. In her 1501 instructions to the new governor of Española, Fray Nicolás de Ovando, she made it clear that while the Indians of the Caribbean were to serve the Spaniards they were not in fact their slaves, but vassals of the Crown.[33] The Indians also had to be converted to Catholicism and treated well. Ovando and the other colonists were to be especially respectful of caciques who would make sure that their subjects obeyed Crown orders.[34] Nevertheless, there still existed two ways to obtain an indigenous slave legally: if he or she was already declared a slave (and there existed proof of this status) or through warfare. So Spaniards could still legally purchase or trade for pre-contact indigenous slaves in the Caribbean, as well as enslave any Indians captured during warfare. Though there were still avenues to enslaving Indians, the restrictions limited Columbus's dream of indiscriminate enslaving throughout the Caribbean.

Isabela's royal policy did slow down the Indian slave trade as intended, but it did not stop it entirely. Nor did colonists, merchants, and raiders respect the constraints imposed by Isabela's laws. For the three years that the enslavement of most Indians was forbidden, from June 1500 until August 1503, an illegal slave trade thrived in the Caribbean. For example, in 1501 Cristóbal de Guerra engaged in legally questionable rescate, acquiring large amounts of pearls, brazilwood, and Indian slaves, from the Pearl Islands of Cumaná and Cuchina.[35] He then went on to the island of Bonaire where he encountered some indigenous resistance and took more slaves during the conflict. He transported all the slaves taken in the coastal raids first to Española and then on to Sevilla, Cádiz, and Córdoba, selling them along the way.[36] However, in Jerez de la Frontera, Gonzalo Gómez de Cervantes, a local judge, uncovered Guerra's actions. As the Indian slave trade had recently been declared illegal, the Crown ordered Guerra to provide records of all the Indians he sold so that those who had purchased the slaves could be found and refunded their money in exchange for the ill-begotten Indian slaves. The Indians were to be entrusted to comendador Lares, who was to return them to their homelands as soon as possible. While the Indians were under the care of Lares, Guerra was to pay their expenses. He also had to pay a fine for his crimes. While the destiny of most of Guerra's slaves remains unknown, six of them were in Córdoba.[37] They were the property of Pedro Hernández de Córdoba who relinquished the Indians directly to the corregidor Cervantes in Sevilla to be returned to their native territory. Whether or not they survived to journey back to the Caribbean is unknown.

Only two years after her initial decree, Isabela made even more exceptions to her ruling against the enslavement of the Indians of the Caribbean. In 1503 she made it legal to enslave all Caribs or other Indians who violently resisted Spanish governance and Catholic conversion.[38] This change in legislation opened Pandora's box, allowing for unscrupulous colonists and merchants to deem any "unpacified" Indian as a Carib. As a result, many Taínos, along with other indigenous groups of the mainland, were wrongly designated as Carib, accused of cannibalism, and carried off as slaves to Española.[39]

In 1503 Isabela designated the islands of San Bernardo, Fuerte, and Bara, the ports of Cartagena, the Venezuelan coastline, and "anywhere where the cannibals are" as Carib lands.[40] Demonstrating the purely economic character of the designation, none of these lands corresponded with reports of cannibalism. Instead the territories marked as Carib were those close to areas the Spanish believed held mineral wealth.[41] Between 1509 and 1512 the rest of the Lesser Antilles and much of Tierra Firme were added to the list.[42] Any method used to capture the Carib slaves was legal, from rescate to extreme violence. From the sale of these slaves the Crown expected to receive a fifth of the profits, becoming openly involved in the indigenous slave trade.[43] The merchant Juan de la Coosa commanded one of the first assaults against the Caribs, attacking the island of Codego located at the mouth of the port of Cartagena in the summer of 1503. During the raid Coosa captured six hundred Carib Indians, many of whom were women and children.[44] Small slaving expeditions continued to capture Carib Indians from 1503 forward, and as the Taíno population continued to fall, efforts to replenish the islands' labor force only increased the number of expeditions setting sail for Carib lands. One such group embarked in 1508 with a license to raid and enslave the Caramarai Indians near the gulf of Cartagena and on the islands of Saint Bernabe and Fuerte. The men, led by Diego de Nicuesa and Alonso de Hojeda, also had permission to capture up to four hundred Indians from neighboring Carib islands. They were then instructed to bring the indigenous slaves back to Española. Upon their sale, the Crown would receive a fifth of the profits, though the four hundred Indians from Carib islands were kept separate as they were already marked for work in the Crown's gold mines.[45] To help the rest of the colonists of Española, the Crown issued a decree in June 1510, allowing all residents of the island to take slaves from the islands to their north, essentially the Lucayos that were labeled as "useless."[46]

In 1511 the Crown expanded the list of Carib lands, legalizing war on the Indians of Dominica, Martinique, Santa Lucía, San Vicente, La Asención, Los Barbados, Tabaco, Mayo, and Trinidad. The royal order labeled most of the inhabitants of the Lesser Antilles as Caribs, legalizing their capture, transportation to, and enslavement in Española and Puerto Rico.[47] Per a royal order issued in July 1511, all Caribs introduced as slaves to Española and Puerto Rico had to be branded as such on either their legs or arms.[48] Though the brand continued to change, the earliest model was that of an F for King Ferdinand. Additionally, while merchants previously had to pay the royal fifth on sales of Carib Indians, they no longer did as of 1511. Now profits from Caribs as well as naborías, those hailing from the "useless islands," were tax free.[49] By 1511 the Indian slave trade was on the rise, encompassing much of both the Greater and Lesser Antilles. However, some key islands were still exempt from slave raiding, including Guadeloupe and Santa Cruz, sites of burgeoning Crown colonies since 1508. This changed by the end of 1511 as the result of one of the largest cross-island indigenous rebellions.

In the late summer of 1510, up to thirty caciques in Puerto Rico met secretly to plot a rebellion against the Spaniards. Despite warnings of danger, encomendero Cristóbal de Sotomayor journeyed to cacique Agueybana's (Agueybana II) territory and demanded guides and translators to accompany him to the island's central mountain range.[50] Though the cacique initially agreed to Sotomayor's demands, upon his departure from Agueybana's cacicazgo, Agueybana and a small squadron attacked Sotomayor and his men. During the assault the Indians killed the encomendero and his four companions.[51] Next, Agueybana and three thousand Indians attacked and burned down the new town of Aguada. This began a general uprising that lasted for several years. Throughout the conflict the Crown licensed the governor of Puerto Rico, Juan Cerón, to enslave all Indians taken during the fighting and brand them with an F on their leg or arm. They were then sold in the markets of Española.[52]

But the violence was not limited to the Taínos of Puerto Rico. According to officials, Caribs from the neighboring islands of Santa Cruz and Guadeloupe joined the Taínos of Puerto Rico in their uprising.[53] By 1513 there was concrete evidence that a coalition of Taínos from Puerto Rico with Indians (Caribs) from the Leeward Islands worked together to burn the northern settlement of Caparra, killing eighteen Spaniards.[54] Juan Gonzaléz Ponce de León, one of the leaders of the Spanish offensive against Agueybana, underscored the number of Caribs involved in the conflict. In his writings to the governor, as well as in testimony years later, he described his indigenous opponents as three distinct groups fighting as one: "*indios, principales/*

caciques, and *Caribs*."[55] Other witnesses echoed his account, claiming that thousands of Caribs were aligned with Agueybana. The Spanish faced some of their fiercest battles at sea due to the indigenous use of Carib *piraguas* (large canoes) and the Indians' ability to swim. In an attempt to impede the indigenous war effort, the Spanish confiscated all the canoes they could find, thereby limiting indigenous mobility.[56] In the end the Spanish, with the help of some allied caciques, were able to defeat the indigenous coalition, reportedly killing thousands in battle and taking many thousands more captive.[57] Some of the captives were shipped to Santo Domingo as slaves, while others, presumably leaders, were executed by hanging or drowning.[58]

Taínos from Puerto Rico also sought refuge in Santa Cruz, Guadeloupe, and as far south as Trinidad and the Windward Islands throughout and after the conflict.[59] In 1511 Spaniards encountered Taínos in Dominica, Matinino (Martinique), St. Lucia, Ascencion, Barbados, and Tobago.[60] By 1513 they may have traveled even farther, perhaps to Florida or the mainland of South America.[61] And the Spanish chased the fleeing Taínos. After defeating Agueybana near the town of San Germán, Ponce de León chased a group of Taínos and Caribs from Puerto Rico to a nearby island, Virgen Gorda. There, Juan Gonzalez captured eighty-eight Taínos from Puerto Rico and seventy-seven Caribs. He also found Spanish weapons and items from the Caparra church that the indigenous rebels stole months earlier.[62] Here is some of the best evidence of pre-contact ties between Taínos and Caribs surviving into the colonial era; these ties continued to fuel the Indian slave trade.

Agueybana's rebellion prompted the government in Española to issue a royal order at the end of 1511 that declared general war on Caribs and called for their immediate enslavement and relocation to Española or other islands with mines.[63] No taxes had to be paid on the slaves taken during these expeditions.[64] The Crown wanted nothing more than to destroy the Caribs to gain control of the burgeoning empire. By the summer of 1512, officials organized two large armadas to punish the Caribs and engage in rescate for slaves and pearls in Dominica and the Virgin Islands. All the Indians captured on these ventures were taken to Santo Domingo and were branded and registered.[65] Afterward two-thirds of the Indian slaves were divided between Spanish leaders of La Vega, San Juan de la Maguana, and Buenaventura, all of whom had invested in the armadas sent to enslave the Caribs. The last third was distributed between the soldiers of the expedition.[66]

Then, in 1514, King Ferdinand went beyond authorizing slaving expeditions across the Caribbean and ordered a royal armada to attack the "caribes" living in Trinidad, Dominica, Guadeloupe, Santa Lucia, Barbados, and

Table 1. Estimates of Numbers of Indians Taken from Carib and "Useless" Lands, 1503–1516

Slaver	Year	Captured in	Taken to	Estimate of number
Juan de la Coosa	1503	Codego	Santo Domingo	600
Various	1510	Lucayos	Santo Domingo and Puerto Plata	25,000
Gaspar de Epinosa	1515	Panama	Santo Domingo	Unknown
Various	1515	Guadeloupe	Santo Domingo	1,200
Various	1516	Pearl Islands	San Juan and San Germán	55
				Total known: 26,855

San Vincente specifically to capture slaves to sell on Española.[67] In response, thirty-nine royal armadas attacked and enslaved "caribes" across the region from 1515 to 1520, each capturing dozens to hundreds of Indian slaves.[68] Additionally, many private expeditions set out to raid the Lesser Antilles.[69] Dominican friars later claimed that the raids led to the complete depopulation of forty islands belonging to the Lucayos chain, as well as three more (present-day Aruba, Bonaire, and Curaçao) populated by "giants."[70] Adding insult to injury, most of the "giant" Indians transported to Española died within a few months, many from eating a poisonous fruit. The officials of the island attributed the high attrition rate of the "giants" to their unfamiliarity with the island and homesickness. Apparently these same problems did not affect the Carib or Lucayan slaves, leading officials of Española to promote their capture over the "giants."[71] Again highlighting pre-contact connections between the islands, 70 percent of the 1,200 slaves captured on Guadeloupe in 1515 were Taínos from Puerto Rico. Additionally, the majority were women and children. These individuals had likely sought refuge in Guadeloupe, taking advantage of kinship ties in the southern Lesser Antilles during the war with Agueybana.[72] See Table 1 for estimates of how many Indian slaves were taken during the campaigns against Caribs or "useless" islands based upon records found in the Archivo General de Indias in Seville, Spain.

"Just War" as a Slaving Rationale

The rebellion of Agueybana, and the ensuing war against Caribs, reveals another legal justification for the capture and transport of indigenous slaves:

"just war." Per the definition of "just war" in the Siete Partidas, previously employed in the Canary Islands and during the Reconquista, Spaniards could use violence to enforce the dominion of the Spanish Crown and the Catholic Church. The failure to accept Christianity justified enslavement.[73] "Just war" also allowed enslavement of the losing party and confiscation of their goods.[74] But the war in Puerto Rico was not the first time the Spanish employed this rationale in the Americas. Beginning with Columbus's second voyage to the Caribbean, colonists faced indigenous resistance, first enveloping the island of Española in violence. Only a few weeks after the founding of Isabela, Columbus sent a group into the interior of the island, the Cibao, in search of rumored gold mines.[75] After finding evidence of gold, Columbus organized a much larger expedition of over four hundred men who marched south and established a fort called Santo Tomás in March 1494.[76]

Nearly as soon as Spaniards broke ground, the ruling cacique closest to Santo Tomás began to threaten the settlement. In addition to the threats, Indians began to desert their villages surrounding the new fort.[77] Unknown to the Spanish, the fort lay at the heart of the territory overseen by cacique Caonabó, one of the most powerful rulers on the island. In response to Caonabó's attacks, Columbus sent another four hundred men led by Alonso de Hojeda to reinforce the nascent settlement.[78] With Hojeda's forces he sent instructions on how to deal with Caonabó and his people. Columbus's orders offer insight into his plans for the Taínos and their "pacification." Columbus's very first command was to ensure that no one should harm an innocent Indian to prevent an uprising. In the very next sentence Columbus prescribed that any Indian caught stealing be punished by the removal of their ears and nose: "And if you find any of them stealing the punishment should be to cut off their noses and ears since these are body parts that they cannot hide so that all the people of the island will engage in rescate and understand what will be done to any other Indians."[79] Though Hojeda and his men carried some provisions with them, Columbus instructed them to acquire the majority of their food through trade with the Indians of the Cibao. In exchange for food, the soldiers were to give the Taínos trinkets, including silver hawks' bells and glass beads. If they refused to trade, a likelihood as the Taínos did not have enough surplus food for the four hundred Spaniards, Columbus gave permission to the group to take anything they needed by force.[80] This quickly led to conflict. A group of five Indians conscripted as porters for the Spanish stole a bundle of clothing while fording a stream, taking advantage of the Spaniards' vulnerability in the water. In retaliation Hojeda captured the cacique of the Indians in question and sent him in chains to La Isabela. Hojeda then chopped the ears off one of the cacique's relatives to ensure cooperation from the rest of the Indians during the march inland.[81] But the imprisonment and torture of the Indians had the opposite effect. Within a few days, a group of Indians organized an attack on the Spanish expedition, leading to a battle in which dozens of Indians were killed and many more wounded.[82] The Taínos of Española refused to be easily conquered.

Despite the attacks and threats against Santo Tomás, Columbus still sought to make an alliance with the paramount cacique of the region, Caonabó, or at least to gain his surrender to the church and the Crown. Thus, he ordered Pedro Margarite (the leader of the fort) to choose eleven "discreet" men to deliver gifts to Caonabó in the hopes that the demonstration of good will and friendship would seal an alliance and an avenue to indigenous stores of gold.[83] But Columbus also added that if the cacique refused to meet with the delegation or did not respond favorably, Margarite had permission to capture Caonabó using any means necessary.[84] After dealing with Caonabó, Margarite was to leave Santo Tomás to explore and pacify the rest of the island, leaving Hojeda in charge of the fort.[85]

Neither Margarite nor Hojeda followed Columbus's orders and instead abandoned their post at Santo Tomás, returning to La Isabela. Margarite went even further, sailing back to Spain along with many other dissatisfied Spaniards.[86] Las Casas related that the men Margarite left behind quickly spread across the island, wreaking havoc on the indigenous population. Not only did the soldiers seek large quantities of food, which the Taínos did not have, but they also violated hundreds of Indians.[87] In particular Las Casas claimed that the men raped and stole any Taíno women whom they found attractive, regardless of age or marital status.[88]

The behavior of the colonists was undoubtedly horrible, but the number of Spaniards was still small and their impact isolated and temporary as they traveled around the island. With most Spaniards having left his cacicazgo and Fort Santo Tomás essentially abandoned, Caonabó likely did not view the Spanish as a serious threat. However, upon Columbus's return to La Isabela at the end of September 1494, he sent another small envoy, led by Hojeda, to visit Caonabó. They were to deliver gifts and invite him to La Isabela to meet with Columbus. Caonabó, as a paramount cacique of a powerful cacicazgo and the largest settlement on the island, likely felt that Columbus should come to his territory if he wanted to negotiate an alliance.[89] Thus he refused to accompany the Spaniards back to La Isabela, instead communicating that the admiral should come to La Maguana. The Spaniards then enacted a new plan to capture Caonabó, through trickery.

To remove the cacique from the center of his village, isolating him, the Spanish told Caonabó that they possessed one final gift for him, a gift of "turey." The Taínos referred to Spanish metals of brass, silver, and gold as "turey" and understood their significance to the Spanish.[90] Hojeda promised to deliver the gift to Caonabó while he bathed by the nearby river, which he did often, usually in the company of only a few servants. As Caonabó more than likely did not view the small group of Spaniards as a threat, he proceeded with his normal routine, heading to the river at the appointed time for his bath and to receive the gift. Hojeda then presented Caonabó with a pair of shiny, silver handcuffs. Having never seen anything like it, Caonabó gladly accepted his "offering" as well as Hojeda's help in putting on the "jewelry." Hojeda then offered the cacique a horse, a symbol of great power and prestige even this early in the process of colonization. With Caonabó indisposed, the rest of the Spaniards quickly mounted their horses and galloped for La Isabela, their trap a success.[91]

The captivity of such a powerful cacique instigated the first full-scale war against the Europeans. The Macorix cacique named Guatiguará began the violence, attacking the sparsely populated fort of Magdalena in late 1494. During the assault, between ten and forty Spaniards were killed.[92] In retaliation, Columbus organized an attack on Guatiguará. During the conflict they captured over a thousand Indians, marching them to La Isabela in February 1495. Because these Indians had assaulted a Spanish settlement, they were legally taken as slaves in "just war."[93] Columbus chose "the best" 500 of the 1,600 captives to send to Spain, possibly along with Caonabó, partitioning the rest to Spanish colonists.[94] Of the five hundred slaves sent to Spain, two hundred died during the journey. The surviving three hundred were sold in the slave markets of southern Spain.[95] Columbus also divided an undetermined number of slaves taken from Española between his family members and friends.[96] The official, legal Indian slave trade had begun.

Meanwhile on Espanola the uprising had spread from Magdalena and the Macorix. Within a few weeks of Caonabó's capture and Guatiguará's assault, the remaining most powerful caciques (Behechio, Guarionex, and Higuanamá) on the island formed an alliance against the encroaching Europeans.[97] Faced with the specter of further attacks, Columbus and his brother Bartolomé marched a force of two hundred Spanish soldiers, twenty horsemen, attack dogs, and three thousand Indian allies led by Guacanagarí into the Cibao to face the league of caciques.[98] Upon reaching the central valley, the Europeans set up a small palisade atop one of the highest mountains. The mountain overlooks the entire Cibao Valley with views extending almost to the Atlantic Ocean.

It was also located very close to Guarionex's largest settlement, Maguá, the target of Columbus's force. The Taínos, numbering anywhere from five thousand to one hundred thousand, depending on the account, soon attacked Columbus and his men.[99] After a day of ferocious fighting, the Spanish had to retreat to their mountaintop camp, and it seemed as if they would have to surrender. However, the following morning they awoke to find the valley deserted. Columbus believed this signified the submission of the Taínos, with many attributing the "miraculous" victory to the Virgin of Las Mercedes. As a result, they named the mountain Santo Cerro, its name to this day. Taking advantage of his "victory," Columbus conducted a surprise attack on Maguá in the middle of the night during which he was able to capture Guarionex. He then negotiated a treaty with the cacique to gain another indigenous ally (beyond Guacanagarí).[100]

Why the Taíno warriors actually abandoned the battle is a question left unanswered.[101] One of the best hypotheses regarding the surrender is that of a double misunderstanding.[102] It is possible that the Taíno warriors and caciques believed that the battle was over when the Europeans retreated in disarray back to their base at Santo Cerro. Therefore, they returned to their respective cacicazgos after what they believed to be a victory, sure that the Europeans would soon leave. With his allies and support gone from Maguá, combined with the surprise nocturnal attack, Guarionex likely felt vulnerable and that his best option was to negotiate an alliance with Columbus. Regardless of the reasons why, this was the beginning of Columbus's tribute system that required a fixed amount of gold dust sent to the Spanish Crown every three months.[103]

From the start few Taínos could fulfill Columbus's tribute demands, leading to renewed conflict and rebellions. Each outbreak of violence was labeled as "just war," providing a constant supply of Taíno slaves. By 1497, Guarionex revolted against Spanish authority. Columbus's brother Bartolomé quickly defeated the uprising, with large Taíno casualties, and captured Guarionex. But the Spanish almost immediately freed the cacique in an effort to regain his alliance so that they could maintain power over the Indians of the Cibao. It was only through Guarionex that the Spanish could guarantee the cooperation of the Taínos, including the delivery of tribute. But Guarionex was done cooperating with the Spanish, at least with the Columbus government.

Within months of his release, Guarionex entered an alliance with the Spanish rebel Francisco Roldán against the Columbus government. Roldán rose against the Spanish government when Bartolomé prepared to move the capital from La Isabela to Santo Domingo. In exchange for Roldán's protection, the cacique housed and supported the rebel group in Maguá. Roldán promised Guarionex and any Indians who joined him that they would no longer have to pay tribute to the Spanish government.[104] The lack of tribute making its way to Isabela quickly brought the alliance to the attention of Columbus in 1498 when he returned from an exploratory voyage. Columbus's return also pushed Roldán to flee even farther from the central Spanish settlements to the Jaragua cacicazgo, leaving Guarionex vulnerable.

When Guarionex realized the dangerous position he was in, he fled the Cibao and found shelter with the Macorix cacique Mayobanex in the north of the island. This alliance only further motivated Columbus to attack Guarionex, compelling him to lead a force into the northern mountains to capture both caciques along with their followers. The Spanish labeled all these Taínos and Macorixs as slaves.[105] Five ships transported the eight hundred Taíno slaves, taken in "just war," to Spain in fall 1498.[106] In an accompanying letter, Columbus's intentions to create an Indian slave trade were clear. He wrote, "In the name of Saint Trinidad I send all of these slaves that can be sold along with brazil wood; of these if the information I possess is correct we can sell at least 4,000 . . . and because in Castile and Portugal and Aragón and Italy and Sicily and the Islands of Portugal and of Aragón and of the Canaries many slaves are used up, and I believe that fewer are coming from Guinea, these Indian slaves can be sold for three times the price."[107] Later in the letter Columbus also mentioned that in addition to the Indians of Española, there were many more Indians who could be enslaved, especially the Caribs, on neighboring islands. In Columbus's opinion until larger sources of gold were found, the key to economic success in the Indies would be the Indian slave trade. While Columbus advocated his plan, others, including Hojeda, the same captain who captured Caonabó, and the Italian Amerigo Vespucci, were already engaged in the trade. Both of these men sold over two hundred slaves from Española and the coast of Venezuela in the port city of Cádiz in 1498 and 1499.[108] See Table 2 that lists slaves captured by Columbus and others during the first years of colonization.

Conflict with Guarionex and Roldán was one of many problems faced by the Columbus government, all of which resulted in the admiral's arrest and removal to Spain in 1500.[109] In order to gain control of the island, his replacement, Nicolás de Ovando, employed ruthless policies, including "just war," across the island. The first cacique to rise against Ovando's labor and tribute demands was Cotubanamá, a lesser cacique of the Higuey cacicazgo located in the southeast corner of the island. First, many of the caciques of Higuey told the Spaniards that they could pay only a third of the tribute owed. During

Table 2. Indian Slaves Captured by Columbus and Other Early Explorers

Slaver	Year	Captured in	Taken to	Estimate of number
Christopher Columbus	1495	Española	Spain	500
Christopher Columbus	1497	Española	Spain	30
Christopher Columbus	1498	Española	Spain	800
Alonso Hojeda and Amerigo Vespucci	1498–1499	Española and Tierra Firme	Cádiz, Spain	200
Cristóbal de Guerra	1501	Pearl Islands	Cádiz, Sevilla, and Córdoba, Spain	Unknown
			Total known: 1,530	

ensuing negotiations, a Spanish attack dog killed a lower cacique. To avenge his death, and possibly to avoid paying any more tribute to the Spaniards, all the Taínos of Higuey rose up.[110] Under the leadership of Cotubanamá, the Indians killed eight Spaniards.

Upon learning of the uprising, Ovando sent four hundred to five hundred Spaniards to punish the cacique and his people.[111] According to Las Casas, what followed was a massacre in which hundreds of Taínos perished, including the cacique Cotubanamá, who was hanged along with another thirteen men.[112] The Spaniards took many more as slaves to sell in Santo Domingo, though some were still destined for Spain.[113] Notarial records show the sale of dozens of Taíno slaves, mostly children, in Sevilla in 1503.[114] Each Spanish soldier led between ten and twenty Indian slaves in chains back to Santo Domingo.[115] If this accounting is accurate, the Spaniards took a minimum of four thousand slaves from Higuey.

Soon after the attack on Higuey, Ovando led another expedition into the heretofore largely untouched cacicazgo of Jaragua in southwest Española. While the previous cacique Behechio agreed to provide Bartolomé Columbus with cotton in 1496, after his death the Spanish government stopped receiving tribute. This is likely because Behechio's successor, the *cacica* Anacaona, formed an alliance with the rebel Roldán, whose followers found refuge in Jaragua after the capture of Guarionex.[116] Why would she pay tribute to the Spaniards at Santo Domingo when she supported and believed herself to be under the protection of Roldán?

Either due to the lack of tribute or Anacaona's alliance with Roldán, Ovando along with three hundred soldiers marched into Jaragua in July 1503.

Even though Anacaona greeted the Spanish entourage with ceremony, welcoming them, Ovando responded with violence. During the attack Ovando set fire to Anacaona's royal house, killing eighty-four of her elite subjects.[117] The Spaniards then hanged Anacaona, demonstrating her status as paramount cacica.[118] With this massacre Ovando succeeded in neutralizing one of the last powerful indigenous rulers of the Caribbean. As in Higuey, the Spanish enslaved hundreds of Indians. However, in Jaragua many were able to escape, fleeing to Cuba and other nearby islands or to the mountains of Bahoruco.[119]

Legal Institutions of Indian Slavery

Until June 1500 there were few if any restrictions or laws controlling the nascent indigenous slave trade in the circum-Caribbean. Then, in 1500 Queen Isabela declared the trade illegal and all indigenous peoples free. The order did little to halt raiders, merchants, and colonists already operating in the Americas, but it did prevent the trade from growing. That is, it did so until 1503 when Isabela reversed her previous decree, making it legal to enslave all cannibals or Carib Indians. Concurrent with this legislation was the renewal of the taking of Taínos in "just war" on Española. While Isabela's ruling still nominally prohibited the enslavement of peaceful Indians in the Americas, the provision allowed for the enslavement of all rebellious subjects. In addition, she decreed that Indians had to labor for Spanish colonists to construct towns, extract gold, and provide food and other goods. The Spanish were to arrange the labor schedule with the island's caciques and pay every Indian a small salary. If the Indians refused to work, they could be forced to complete specific tasks, but always as free men, not as slaves.[120] The contradictory nature of these laws was immediately apparent. Nor were the laws permanent. Over the ensuing decade, laws controlling the Indian slave trade changed nearly every year in response to various economic, religious, or political developments, leaving loopholes for slave raiders, colonists, and conquistadors across the Americas.[121] The loopholes both allowed for massive numbers of illegal, or somewhat legal slave raids, and prevented any documentation of said slaving.

As the slave trade grew, Ovando, the new governor of Española, tried to implement Isabela's orders. By December 1503 he realized that the Taínos of Española were not going to willingly move from their ancestral lands to labor in newly created Spanish towns per Isabela's decrees. This realization brought about the creation of the very controversial encomienda, an institution that formally subjected the Americas' native peoples to Spanish colonists. The Crown commended a certain number of Indians (living within certain boundaries or in a specific territory) to a single Spaniard known as an encomendero. The encomendero collected all tribute from his commended Indians, usually through the help of their cacique, and gave the Crown their royal fifth. In exchange for the tribute, the encomendero was charged with ensuring that his Indians were converted to the Catholic faith and that they were well treated. The Indians serving in an encomienda, except the caciques and their families, were known as naborías. This term comes directly from the Taíno word for "commoner" or "worker." Naborías could not be sold or inherited and were not considered property, unlike the Indian slaves taken from Carib lands or in "just war."[122] Nitaínos, caciques, and their families were legally exempt from tribute and given special privileges such as finer Spanish clothing and access to horses.

In theory then, an encomendero would provide his Indians with food, Spanish clothing, an education, and legal protection, as they worked with their cacique to gather tribute for the Crown. In reality the encomienda system worked quite differently. With few authorities monitoring the treatment of Indians by their encomenderos, abuse was endemic. In many cases the lives of Española's naborías were only marginally different from that of slaves. Conditions only deteriorated further as the population of native Taínos fell, with encomenderos expecting the same amount of labor or tribute from fewer Indians. For example, if one cacique governed two hundred Indians in one year and fifty died while laboring for their encomendero, the following year the encomendero still expected the cacique to provide him with the same number of workers or amount of tribute (in gold or cotton, for example), regardless of the population loss.[123] Many caciques faced this scenario as the implementation of the encomienda system led to a precipitous decline in the native population of Española. The fall in population can be explained by many factors, including wars and attacks like those of Santo Cerro and Higuey, the spread of diseases,[124] famine,[125] overwork and exhaustion in the island's gold mines,[126] and suicide.[127] As the island's population fell, colonists and the Crown alike tried to find new sources of labor, including through the legal expansion of the Indian slave trade.[128]

Growth of the Indian slave trade allowed the Crown to replace the diminishing Taíno population, facilitating the extraction of gold as well as the growth of other industries in the nascent Spanish Empire.[129] The Crown's policy shift toward supporting an indigenous slave trade was pragmatic. And King Ferdinand went far beyond allowing the existing slave trade, which, in

1508, was limited to taking Caribs and Indians during active war, by creating new ways to expand the industry. As noted earlier, after Isabela's death, King Ferdinand authorized the enslaving of Indians from all "useless islands" (*islas inútiles*), meaning those lacking gold mines. Beyond the economic benefit of relocating the Indians, the Spanish also argued that the residents of the "useless islands" would benefit from closer proximity to Christians to help in their conversion to Catholicism since their islands were "filled with sinful Indian idolaters."[130] Although the Indians taken from the "useless" Lucayos Islands were legally categorized as naborías, not slaves like the Caribs, they were not afforded the same legal protections as native, commended Taíno naborías. Instead they were *naborías perpetuos* (perpetual naborías), meaning they worked year-round and received no protection from a local cacique. Most were destined to labor in Crown gold mines. And if they resisted the demands of their encomendero they could be declared slaves and legally sold.[131] The legal division between naborías and Indian slaves was shrinking rapidly by 1509.

In September 1509 the king sent orders to Ovando to "capture and bring as many Indians from outside Española as possible."[132] The demand for indigenous labor combined with the Crown's new allowances sparked a huge rise in slaving expeditions from late 1509 into 1510. The exact number of voyages and how many Indians captured by each merchant remains unclear. The lack of records surrounding these missions can be explained by the fact that the slavers did not have to pay taxes on profits gained from Indians classified as naborías.[133] Perhaps this is because the profits were so slim. Or this may speak to the moral and legal gray area in which the trade operated, where neither slavers nor officials were certain when they should report an expedition or sale. Another option is that the arrival of Indian slaves in Española was so commonplace that it seemed unimportant to note. Whether all or one of these was the cause, the lack of records makes it difficult to estimate the size of the trade or even to ascertain which traders and raiders traveled to "useless" islands or Carib lands to capture their merchandise.

However, estimates from various officials and chroniclers do exist for these years. In 1510 alone, approximately 25,760 Indians (whether slaves or naborías) disembarked at the ports of Puerto de Plata and Puerto Real on Española's northern coast.[134] While the records do not clearly state the identities of these Indians, the fact that they arrived on the island's northern coast suggests that they hailed from the Lucayos. In 1518 an official, Alonso de Zuazo, estimated that over fifteen thousand Indians from the Lucayos were brought to Española, with at least three thousand dying upon arrival on the island due to hunger.[135] Lucayan numbers helped to mask the rapidly decreasing native population on the island, but only slightly. It is likely that only a small percentage of those captured survived the journey and their initial days on Española due to slavers' treatment. Many died of hunger or wounds received from Spanish enslavers before they ever made it to the Greater Antilles.[136] Merchants did not expend money caring for the Indians as each sold for an average of only four pesos.[137] At this point the Spaniards viewed the supply of Indians in the Caribbean islands as practically inexhaustible. For the Lucayan Indians who survived the journey, it is possible that the transition to life on Española was not too difficult. Due to widespread kin linkages throughout the islands (especially the Greater Antilles), the Lucayan Indians were likely able to assimilate to life with the Taínos of Española. In fact, Spanish officials reported that the Indians of Española quickly incorporated the Lucayans into their society as if they were already one people.[138]

After years of unrestrained slave raiding, at the latest by 1520, the Lucayos Islands were depopulated. Las Casas estimated that up to forty thousand Lucayan Indians were sold in Española during the height of the trade in Indians from "useless islands."[139] Many of these Indians were sent to the Pearl Islands after 1514. In later years, the value of Lucayan Indians soared as the Spanish recognized their ability to dive for pearls. Their price rose to between 50 and 150 pesos each. This increase in possible profit led to even more slave raids of the islands, despite the dwindling numbers of inhabitants. Eventually these raids led to the "discovery" of present-day Florida and South Carolina. Perhaps because of their nautical skills Lucayan slaves were treated better, with records indicating the survival of Lucayans in the pearl fisheries of Cubagua and Margarita as late as 1527.[140]

As indigenous populations dwindled, and in response to early complaints by religious officials concerned with the well-being of the Americas' indigenous peoples, the Crown instituted a new practice in 1514: the reading of the *requerimiento*, or requirement.[141] This document required the indigenous peoples of the New World to submit religiously and politically to the Crown of Spain and the Catholic Church.[142] Before attacking Indians, or enslaving them, Spanish soldiers had to read the requerimiento publicly, giving the native peoples an opportunity to submit peacefully to the new religion and authority. If the Indians failed to submit or refused to accept Christianity, they could legally be attacked by Spanish soldiers and enslaved.[143] However, the requerimiento, as with many other laws and policies, did little to change the actions of Spaniards on the ground. Not only was it usually read to indigenous populations who could not understand the speech, but the Spanish often read the requerimiento from onboard their ship or in the middle of the night to an audience of trees and empty huts.[144]

With the new requerimiento in hand, ship after ship set out to attack Caribs, engage in rescate in the Pearl Islands and coast of Tierra Firme, and collect any more Indians living on "useless islands." Pedrarías Dávila was the first Spaniard to use the requerimiento in an expedition to Santa Marta in 1514. Two caciques of the province of Cenú responded to the document with incredulity, asserting that the pope had given land that was never his to give nor did they want or need another leader.[145] Because the Indians did not respond favorably to the requerimiento, they were reduced to slavery.[146] By 1515 the circum-Caribbean witnessed a full-scale Indian slave trade. Within only three months at least four armadas left from Puerto Rico, sailing for Guadeloupe, Santa Cruz, and other Carib islands to capture slaves.[147] One to Trinidad, led by Juan Bono, captured 180 Carib slaves.[148] In 1516 at least eight armadas assaulted the Pearl Islands, all sailing from Puerto Rico's two main ports: San Juan and San Germán. Only two of these armadas recorded the number of slaves taken; one returned with fifteen Indians from Cariaco and the other with forty Indians from an unknown territory.[149]

Beyond the areas where the Spanish could legally take slaves, merchants also traveled to Central America and Florida as the need for Indian laborers inspired missions of exploration. In 1515 Gaspar de Espinosa captured many slaves from the province of Comogre in Panama.[150] And Espinosa was not alone. Shortly after his expedition, Bishop Juan de Quevedo of Panamanian Darien complained to the Crown about the harmful effects of taking slaves from Panama. According to Quevedo the slavers were not only depopulating his lands but also causing all the Indians of the region to mistrust the Spaniards, running away from them on sight. Thus, the slave trade was preventing the conversion of these Indians to Catholicism.[151]

With the indigenous population still falling and some officials questioning or criticizing indigenous slave raiding, the Crown instituted a much larger-scale restructuring of the colonial enterprise known as the Repartimiento of Albuquerque, the redivision and relocation of surviving Taíno residents, or the first reducción. Executed in 1514, this legislation redistributed approximately 22,000 Indians (not counting children and the aged who could not work) across Española, radically changing the social and political landscape of the island.[152] Through the Repartimiento, the Spanish Crown tried to rein in the power of the local colonial government by taking the right to grant encomiendas away from the governor of Española and limiting how many Indians any one encomendero could possess. The Repartimiento also relocated Indians to towns located closer to the island's gold mines and burgeoning sugar plantations, increasing Crown revenue.[153]

Whatever the intent, the Repartimiento did not begin to address the issues with the recently escalating Indian slave trade. This is because slaves were considered personal property and thus were not subject to the laws of the Repartimiento. Nor did the legislation actually give preference to Spaniards present on the island, with the largest number of Indians going to the Crown or Crown officials living in Spain. The greatest numbers of Taínos were allotted to Lopes Conchillos (the king's secretary) and the king himself, who received 1,430 Indians.[154] This led to a massive exodus from the island for those without Indians. The majority moved on to explore South and Central America in search of new labor pools.[155]

Once enacted, the Repartimiento completely altered the population distribution of the island. Prior to 1514 the bulk of the native population resided in the western half of the island. But with the Crown seeking laborers for developing sugar plantations, located near Santo Domingo, and gold mines in the central mountain range, the Repartimiento transferred the majority of the Taínos to these regions. The move left only a fifth of the original Taíno population in the western portion of the island, near their ancestral homes.[156] Amplifying the turmoil caused by physical displacement, the Repartimiento often combined two or more chiefdoms to account for a decrease in population. This forced as many as four caciques to live and work together, decreasing the power of each cacique and causing internal divisions within the new settlements.[157]

Spaniards found it necessary to combine cacicazgos due to the island's sharp decline in population, which diminished once-populous indigenous settlements to as few as ten residents. Additionally, a shocking 43 percent of Taínos did not have children per encomienda lists.[158] In fact, only nine of the forty-three cacicazgos counted more than two hundred Indians in 1514, and the majority contained around forty inhabitants.[159] Even larger cacicazgos were broken up and joined with unaffiliated chiefdoms, pointing to other motivations for reorganizing indigenous cacicazgos in the Repartimiento. Though the policy was not explicitly articulated, it is probable that Spanish officials dissolved cacicazgos to diminish the power of any one cacique, thereby increasing the power of the encomendero over all the Indians in his encomienda. Instead of relying on one cacique, the encomendero could pit various caciques against one another.

Adding to the personal, geographic, and social displacement for native Taínos of the island was the growing presence of foreign Indian slaves arriving daily to Española. Just as the division of cacicazgos undermined the authority of Taíno caciques, the growing number of foreign slaves further reduced the power that the caciques once possessed both in their own indigenous settlements and in negotiations with the Spanish. While foreign Indians were not listed as such in the Repartimiento, their presence is hinted at within one category. Throughout the Repartimiento all Indians owing fealty to a Taíno cacique received the label of *indios de servicio* (Indians of working age). They were listed directly below the name of the cacique to whom they were related. Following the number of Indian laborers came a list of Indians who were not of service, meaning they were children or elderly. These Indians still likely owed allegiance to a cacique and were native to the island. After these Taínos came the listing of any naborías that a Spaniard was to receive. As they did not belong to any of the island's cacicazgos, and were not related to a local cacique, it is very likely that the naborías listed were recent arrivals from the Lucayos. These Indians, unlike Caribs, were designated as naborías, essentially indentured servants for their Spanish masters. Many entries of naborías also included the name of the Spaniard who registered them, alluding to their recent arrival to the island.[160] The highest numbers of commended naborías appear in the Repartimientos of settlements located on the northern coast of the island, like Puerto Real, Puerto Plata, and Santiago, reflecting the status of these ports as entry points for Lucayan Indians.[161]

*   *   *

The laws and institutions of the circum-Caribbean indigenous slave trade developed from the very beginning of the colonial enterprise. The Spanish used a variety of old and new rationales to legitimize the enslavement of various indigenous populations, beginning with accusations of cannibalism and progressing to "just war" or rebellion. As the legal framework of the indigenous slave trade developed, causing intermittent explosions in the trade of Indians, so did the larger colonial infrastructure on Española. Key to this infrastructure were institutions of labor that included not only slavery but also the encomienda system and the Repartimiento of Albuquerque.

With the islands in upheaval by the middle of the third decade of colonization, and the slave trade spiraling out of control, many began to register complaints about Crown policy and colonial practices. Here we see some of the early arguments against the slave trade and its impacts on the native peoples of the Caribbean. These calls, made by religious and some secular officials, brought about concerted efforts to reform both the Indian slave trade and the general treatment of the Americas' indigenous peoples. However, despite efforts by the Crown and religious orders, the Indian slave trade only grew, especially as more and more Taínos perished in the first smallpox epidemic in 1518.

CHAPTER 3

The Ties That Bind

Religious Orders and Indian Caciques
on Española, 1500–1534

"Are these not men? Are we not bound, in our dealings with them, by the rules of charity and justice? Do they not own their lands? Have they not their natural lords and lordships? Have they done us any injury? Are we not required to preach the law of Christ and to strive to convert them to it? How has it come that this great multitude of people who, as we are told, lived in this island, have in fifteen or sixteen years so miserably perished?"[1]

With these words, Dominican friar Antonio de Montesinos condemned the actions of Spanish colonists on the morning of December 21, 1511. Following the sermon, which many identify as the first call for reform in the Americas, controversy enveloped Española and incited a debate on the humanity of America's indigenous peoples that continued for nearly half a century. Among the many issues addressed by Montesinos's sermon was the recent dramatic increase and expansion of the indigenous slave trade, precipitated by the decline in the native population of Española. By the third decade of colonization, one of the most profitable and fastest-growing economies of the early Spanish Caribbean was the Indian slave trade. Early fights that consumed the friars, the Crown, Spanish colonists, and Indians of the Americas all reveal the importance of the Indian slave trade. While Queen Isabela (and later Cardinal Cisneros) tried to impede the development of the Indian slave trade, by the 1520s, King Charles V decided against the religious orders in favor of Spanish slavers and secular officials by legalizing the Indian slave trade along much of the coast of Tierra Firme.

This decision showed the limits of the Crown's commitment to the "spiritual conquest" of the Americas.[2] Ultimately, economic or military conquests took precedence over the spiritual even though the two were meant to work hand in hand. Most early modern Iberians (including the Crown and the pope) would not have separated the two conquests, and Spain's earliest claims to the Americas rested on papal bulls. Thus, the Crown actively supported missionary activity in the New World from 1493 forward. Nor did Iberians separate spiritual from military conquest, as one of the goals of war and pacification (and even slavery) was the conversion of the conquered people.[3] In other words, the Sword was to enable the victory of the Cross.[4] Economic exploitation was also linked to the Christianization of the Americas' native peoples in the purportedly reciprocal institutions of the encomienda and the Repartimiento. Many abused these systems, but the revenue collected from indigenous labor also served to fuel the continuance of the "spiritual conquest." Franciscan monasteries, for example, held large numbers of commended Indians, arguing that their charges possessed the easiest path to conversion.

Placing the history of the indigenous slave trade within the larger lens of the "spiritual conquest" allows us to view how power and law operated (or did not) in the burgeoning Spanish Empire. The disparity between royal provisions and instructions and what actually occurred throughout the Americas is striking. Many factors contributed to the failure or limitations of various reform schemes proposed and attempted by religious orders in both Spain and the Caribbean. Perhaps the largest obstacle standing in the way of meaningful change was greed. Secular leaders, officials, and residents of the colonies fought with all their might to maintain their right to extract labor and tribute from both the Caribbean land and its peoples. The opposition presented by secular powers thwarted the best plans made by religious clergy, who did not possess the power to enforce new guidelines for the treatment of Indians. However, impediments to reform originated not solely from secular corners, but from the competition between the different religious groups themselves. In-fighting among religious orders only undermined an already difficult process, enabling the clergy's opponents to persist in their exploitation of native peoples for decades more.

When Montesinos and the other fourteen Dominican friars arrived in Española in 1510, they joined the nearly twenty Franciscan friars who had been working and living with the Taínos for eight years. Although the Franciscans supported many of the calls for reform articulated by the Dominicans, they concentrated more on the everyday interactions and relationships with the Caribbean's indigenous peoples. On the other hand, the Dominicans focused more on the legal realm, debating Crown policy. These two distinct strategies produced different results on the ground, and the competition between the two groups also undermined their individual successes. The situation grew more complicated with the arrival of the Jeronymites in 1517. Even though they were sent to resolve the growing conflicts between the Franciscans, Dominicans, and secular officials on Española, in the end they settled nothing. As debates raged in both the Caribbean and Spain, both commended and enslaved indigenous populations continued to be exploited in gold mines and sugar plantations. Additionally, and despite calls from both Franciscans and Dominicans, the Indian slave trade was not only allowed to continue but also underwent several periods of legal expansion in the following decades.

While the "spiritual conquest" was central to the creation and legitimization of the Spanish Empire, the colonial elite could not afford to place religious goals above those of the struggling colonies, especially as conditions deteriorated in Española, Cuba, and Puerto Rico near the end of the third decade of colonization. As death and disease stalked the native inhabitants of the Caribbean, the need for Indian slaves could not be ignored, even by religious leaders like the Jeronymites. While evangelization continued at the core of the empire, frontier missions and indigenous populations were often sacrificed. Economic and political goals won over spiritual at the edges of the Spanish Empire. Ultimately, the Indian slave trade impeded the earliest efforts of the "spiritual conquest."

The Foundation of the "Spiritual Conquest" in Española

On Columbus's second voyage in 1493, he brought the first Franciscans to the Americas: Fray Juan de la Deule, Fray Juan de Cosin, and Rodrigo Pérez.[5] Accompanying the Franciscans was a Jeronymite friar, Ramón Pané.[6] During his first year on the island, Pané lived in the Spanish fortress Magdalena, located in the Macorix chiefdom led by cacique Mabiatué. The inhabitants of the region spoke Macorix, a dialect of the Arawak tongue used by the majority of the island's inhabitants.[7] Matching his hopes to pacify the Cibao region, Columbus ordered Pané to move to Maguá, Guarionex's cacicazgo, in late 1494.[8] From April 1495 until the fall of 1496, Pané resided in Magua, learning the language and customs of the island's majority Arawak/Taíno population. Pané's relocation makes sense in 1495 due to the recent conclusion of the first war between Europeans and Taínos.

While Pané was in the cacicazgo of Guarionex at la Vega, Deule visited him and they worked together to promote the conversion of Guarionex and his followers.[9] The first Indian who received baptism was Juan Mateo, a Macorix Indian of Magdalena where Pané began his work in 1494.[10] Pané and

Juan Mateo remained with Guarionex for nearly two years, moving to the nearby cacicazgo of Mabiatué in the spring of 1497 after Guarionex attacked Taíno Christians in the fall of that same year.[11] The cacique might have viewed the converts as traitors, or the assault could have been a symptom of Guarionex's larger discontent with Spanish demands.

Despite Juan Mateo's death and Guarionex's rejection of Christianity, Pané still presented his time with the natives of Española as a success when Columbus returned to the island in 1498. From these experiences, Pané wrote the first ethnography of the Taíno, entitled *Relación acerca de las antiguedades de los indios*, in which he details their religious beliefs, rituals, and medical practices. Pané's writings were widely read, influencing the works of Las Casas and helping other Franciscans and Dominicans support their arguments for the freedom and humanity of the indigenous inhabitants of the Americas.

By the second decade of colonization, the very limited religious presence and program of individuals like Pané and Deule expanded into the much larger "spiritual conquest." In 1500 seven Franciscans traveled to Española with two sets of instructions. First, they were to construct the necessary institutions to convert the Taíno population. Second, they were charged with returning the Indians who had been brought to Spain after Columbus's first two voyages since Isabela declared them subjects of the Crown. How many slaves were returned is uncertain, though it is likely that two Indians baptized in the Franciscan monastery at Guadalupe in Spain were among the group. These two *criados* (personal servants), having risen from their initial position as slaves, were baptized in the Real Monasterio de Santa María de Guadalupe on July 29, 1496, in the presence of Columbus.[12]

Within a few months of their arrival in the Americas, the Franciscans claimed to have baptized up to three thousand Indians.[13] Excited by this apparent success, King Ferdinand sent another twelve Franciscans to Española in 1502.[14] In addition to the missionaries, the expedition also brought the first royally appointed governor of the Indies, Fray Nicólas de Ovando, along with two thousand settlers.[15] Ovando was responsible for carrying out the full military and political conquest of the Caribbean, something that Columbus failed to accomplish during his tenure. Meanwhile, the Franciscans were charged with initiating the religious conquest of the New World. The military and spiritual conquests were inseparable.

Upon their arrival in Española, the Franciscans separated into smaller contingents of three to four friars, each assigned with building a small community alongside larger Taíno settlements. Each settlement was to include a cathedral and monastery for the friars. The two largest groups of clergymen, four each, settled in the areas with the most Spanish colonists: Santo Domingo and Concepción de la Vega. These were also the centers of the islands' economy due to their proximity to the best harbor and gold mines, respectively. The Franciscan monastery at Concepción de la Vega was the most powerful of the Americas, and thus it housed the leader of the order, Alonso de Espinal.[16] Two to three priests traveled to Jaragua and began their mission in the nascent village of Santa María de Vera Paz.[17] It is here that the small group built the monastery that eventually housed the first school for native leaders.[18]

As the number of Franciscan friars in Española grew, the native population steadily fell due to disease, overwork, and abuse at the hands of the rising populace of Spanish colonists. Despite the legal restrictions and duties inherent in the institution of the encomienda, Spanish encomenderos focused on personal gain rather than following Crown policy. As colonists attempted to amass as much wealth as possible, the exploitation and abuse of the native population worsened. Meanwhile, the Franciscan clergy remained preoccupied with working in indigenous population centers, spreading themselves thinly across the island and often ignoring the actions and policies of secular leaders.

In 1510, almost two decades after the first Franciscans traveled to the Caribbean, a group of fifteen Dominican friars landed in Santo Domingo. Unlike the Franciscans, the Dominicans focused on the spirituality of the Spanish residents of Española, specifically those living in the central Spanish settlement, Concepción de la Vega.[19] So, the Franciscans' monopoly on indigenous conversion remained largely intact. The Dominicans, led by Fray Pedro de Córdoba, soon began witnessing how Spanish encomenderos treated their commended Indians, which they described as being worse than livestock. After several weeks of observation, the Dominicans decided to challenge the residents of Santo Domingo. The confrontation took place on the morning of December 21, 1511, during the Advent sermon in the partially constructed Catedral Primada. For an image of the oldest cathedral in the Americas, Catedral Primada, see Figure 2.

In his speech, Montesinos condemned the encomenderos' actions and questioned their very right to wage war on or enslave the Indians of the Americas.[20] "You are in mortal sin, that you live and die in, for the cruelty and tyranny you use in dealing with these innocent people. Tell me, by what right or justice do you keep these Indians in such cruel and horrible servitude? On what authority have you waged detestable wars against these people who dwelt quietly and peacefully in their own land?"[21] While Montesinos and his fellow Dominicans criticized the encomenderos for their abuse of the Indians, it is important to understand that Montesinos did not question the

Figure 2. Catedral Primada, Santo Domingo. Photo by author.

Spaniards' right to rule over the natives and to collect tribute and labor from them. His main contention was *how* they reigned over the Taíno. Montesinos also emphasized the right of the Taínos to be converted on the grounds of their humanity, and he accused the encomenderos of preventing conversion by overworking and enslaving them.[22]

The encomenderos did not react positively to Montesinos's condemnations. The very night of the sermon, the leaders of the colony met at the governor's home and decided to confront the friars, hoping to convince them to retract their statements. However, neither Córdoba nor Montesinos renounced the sermon, claiming that it simply represented their beliefs and service to God and the king. In response, the residents of Concepción de la Vega withdrew all food and support from the Dominican friars and sent a letter and account of the sermon to the king, convinced he would see Montesinos's words as treasonous.[23]

The man who delivered the message to the Spanish court was none other than the Franciscan friar Alonso de Espinal, the leader of the twelve Franciscans who had arrived in 1502. The very fact that a priest also dedicated to the conversion of the indigenous peoples of the Americas would agree to denounce Montesinos's sermon demonstrates the tension, and even animosity, between the two orders. The sermon, and Espinal's support of the encomenderos in its aftermath, also divided the Franciscan order into two factions: the moderate group (represented by Espinal) and the more radical idealists, whose views were similar to those of Montesinos and the Dominicans.[24] Above saving the souls of the Taínos, Espinal wanted the Franciscan order to maintain their monopoly in the Americas and not be replaced by the vocal Dominicans. Espinal also sought to keep the encomiendas that supported the Franciscan monasteries.

The Laws of Burgos

The split between the Dominicans and Franciscans became clear in the debates inspired by Montesinos's sermon. Dominicans, Franciscans, and encomenderos all took part in the debates in Burgos from 1512 to 1513.[25] Montesinos traveled back to Spain to argue for the salvation and freedom of the Indians, but his arguments were largely ignored. Instead the Crown sided with the more moderate Franciscans who sought amelioration for the Taínos within preexisting Spanish structures on the island, including the encomienda system. To address the suffering of the Indians, the Laws of Burgos attempted to improve working conditions in the mines, limit the number of Indians that any encomendero could possess, and ensure that the Indians received sufficient food, clothing, and religious instruction.[26] For example, order XXIV stated, "We order and command that no person or persons shall dare to beat any Indians with sticks, or whip him, or call him dog, or address him by any name other than his proper name alone." The laws also tried to ensure better treatment for caciques, with the indigenous leaders receiving a lighter workload and better clothing, along with schooling for their children.[27]

But the laws also validated the institution of the encomienda and the legal Crown exploitation of the native peoples of the Americas. While attempting to help the natives of Española, the laws simultaneously confirmed the status of foreign Indian slaves. Whereas naborías and Taínos of the island had to be converted to Christianity and treated with "love and gentleness," any Indian declared a slave could be "treated by their owner as he pleases."[28] The laws may have pushed many Spanish colonists toward expanding the Indian slave trade, not limiting it. The Laws of Burgos, while the first step in reforming Indian policy, were riddled with inconsistencies and limitations, and ultimately they did little to change the situation of America's native peoples.

Despite their differences, both Dominicans and Franciscans harshly criticized the law code, with many instead turning their hopes to the creation of separate religious communities at the edge of the Spanish Caribbean. The

Dominicans in particular, led by Córdoba, turned their attention to helping and converting indigenous peoples far from the centers of Spanish settlement. They believed that conversion to the Catholic faith was nearly impossible within the bounds of the encomienda system. Searching for a territory suitable for the creation of the first religious communities, the Dominicans' gaze turned to the coast of Tierra Firme, more specifically present-day Venezuela. As of 1513, the coast of Tierra Firme remained relatively isolated from the growing Spanish Empire and its "scandalizing" settlers.[29] Here the friars hoped their efforts would not be undermined by secular Spanish colonists and officials. But it was not meant to be.

Instead, secular leaders, officials, and residents of the colonies fought to maintain their rights and privileges to extract labor from the indigenous peoples of the Caribbean. Of utmost importance during this period was the increasingly profitable circum-Caribbean Indian slave trade, and many viewed Tierra Firme as one of the best sources for this trade.[30] Flotillas and squadrons constantly attacked the coastline and its nearby islands, capturing and enslaving as many Carib Indians as they could find. In one such expedition slavers captured Don Alonso, an allied cacique from Cumaná. His capture inspired a revolt that led to the murders of all the Dominican friars in mid-1515 and the end of their nascent community in Tierra Firme.[31]

The mission on the Venezuelan coast was only one part of a larger Crown policy to increase missionary efforts in the Americas. To this end Ferdinand charged Franciscan Alonso de Espinal (the same friar who represented the encomenderos' case against the Dominicans) with leading forty more Franciscans to the Americas. These friars and priests were sent to Tierra Firme, Cuba, Jamaica, and Puerto Rico where they were to begin evangelizing local populations.[32] The Crown also ordered the officials of Española to pay the costs incurred by Espinal and the other Franciscans. This included their passage from Española to mission sites and all necessary supplies from blankets and pans to wax.[33] The treasurer, Sancho de Matienzo, also had to provide Espinal with clothing for his Indian servant.[34] Many of the Franciscans may have been destined to work in the newly forming schools for *hijos de caciques* (the sons of native leaders).

The School for Hijos de Caciques

While the Laws of Burgos did little to ameliorate the daily suffering of the Taínos of Española, they did inspire one significant development: schools for hijos de caciques. Specifically the Laws of Burgos required that "all of the sons of caciques on the island of Española, now and in the future, thirteen years of age or younger be given to the friars of the Order of Saint Francis so that the friars show them how to read and write and the ways of our faith."[35] To fulfill these instructions, in 1513 Bachiller Hernán Súarez received twenty grammar books, several reams of paper, and other books with which he was to begin a school for the hijos de caciques at the Monastery of Verapaz on Española.[36] For this work Súarez received a salary of 33,000 maravedíes.[37] The school was attached to the monastery established in 1502, but reinforced in 1512 with the arrival of three additional Franciscan friars.[38] These friars brought with them twenty copies of Antonio de Nebrija's *Artes de gramática*, the work that became the basis for translations across the Americas. Just one year later another thirty copies of the text were sent to Santo Domingo.[39] This was not a small educational endeavor. Together the monastery and school, the first of its kind in the New World, were charged with educating the island's future leaders in Catholicism and the Spanish language, perhaps even to create a group of native clergy.

While the school closed within a decade, it first produced at least one famous alumnus, cacique Enrique. He wrote the only documents ever penned by a Taíno Indian, and he also carried out a fourteen-year (successful) rebellion against the Spanish Crown.[40] Enrique also maintained close relationships with his former instructor, Fray Remigio de Mejía, and demonstrated his commitment to Catholicism even while in rebellion, meeting multiple times with Catholic clergy to receive communion and placing crosses on the doors of every structure in his runaway settlement.[41] Enrique also had many of his followers, including cacique Tamayo, baptized while living in the mountains.[42] Whether or not these actions were the result of a true conversion to Christianity is difficult to ascertain. Enrique might have used Catholic symbols and rituals as political tools. However, it is possible that Enrique truly embraced the Catholic faith.

Regardless of its success, in 1520 the school and the monastery and larger settlement of Verapaz were abandoned, with its friars and residents relocating to Santa María del Puerto de Yaguana. In many ways the opening of this school, following the construction of cathedrals and monasteries in both Concepción de la Vega and Santo Domingo, represented the high point of the Franciscan experiment in Española. Because of the success of the first school, others were soon created, first in Concepción de la Vega in 1517 and then in Santo Domingo in 1523. In 1517 encomendero Rodrigo de Figueroa placed two of his commended caciques, Don Diego and Don Henríquez, under the tutelage of the Franciscans at the monastery of Concepción de la Vega. Beyond these two caciques Las Casas recorded that several other hijos de caciques lived within the larger Franciscan monastery where they learned reading and writing in addition to their religious education.[43] This was likely an attempt to fulfill the Crown's order to create another *casa para enseñanza* (house of learning) on the island to teach the native children to read and write.[44]

Then in 1523, a school for hijos de caciques opened in Santo Domingo under the leadership of instructor Aquilés Holden. For his work Holden was to receive thirty thousand maravedíes annually.[45] There was even a plan for some indigenous leaders to study in Spain. In 1526 the Crown asked the officials of Cuba and Española to select and send twelve of the most promising sons of indigenous leaders to Sevilla. In Spain these youths would receive instructions about the Catholic faith and how to live "in order and reason." After several years they would return to the Indies where they could relay their knowledge and serve as examples of Spanish acculturation.[46] Whether or not this plan came to fruition is unknown, but we do know that after the conquests of Mexico, Peru, and Florida (among other territories), schools for the indigenous elite were established. In 1536, following the conquest of Mexico, Franciscans from Española opened a school for native leaders in Tlatelolco. One leader was Friar Pedro Melgarejo de Urrea, Hernán Cortés's chaplain during the conquest of Mexico, who first served at the monastery of Concepción de la Vega.[47] While it is difficult to ascertain how much his experience in Española influenced the school of Tlatelolco, we do know that the new school relied on Córdoba's *Doctrina*. Pedro Menéndez de Avilés also established a Jesuit school for principal indigenous children in Havana, Cuba, to serve both surviving Taínos and the youths of Florida. Some of the first pupils hailed from the Tecuesta chiefdom of southwest Florida in 1566.[48]

The Repartimiento of 1514 and Its Consequences

While the Laws of Burgos and schools for hijos de caciques were some of the Crown's first responses to the Dominicans' denunciations, they were not the last. In the coming decades the Crown, along with religious clergy, engaged in debates regarding the rights and humanity of the Americas' native peoples. These discussions resulted in numerous changes of the laws regulating Indian labor and enslavement. Within a few short years authorities carried out a rapid succession of policies, laws, and experiments meant to ameliorate the suffering of the Caribbean's native populations. One of the most comprehensive of these policies was the Repartimiento of Albuquerque, the large-scale restructuring of the colonial enterprise that divided and relocated all surviving Taíno residents on Española. As seen in Chapter 2, the legislation had economic, social, political, and religious goals. In particular, the legislation tried to ensure that encomenderos followed the Laws of Burgos, including such provisions as favoring married couples and those actually living in the Caribbean over single, absent encomenderos.[49] These changes were to allow for more efficient conversion of surviving Taínos to Catholicism. However, the legislation satisfied neither the Franciscans nor Dominicans.

Despite all the hope and promise represented by nascent Franciscan monasteries and schools for hijos de caciques opening across the island, much of their influence was undermined by the Repartimiento of 1514. Many even closed. For example, the school in Verapaz lost many of its students, including Enrique, following the Repartimiento.[50] This separated indigenous leaders from their Franciscan instructors while also transferring them from their ancestral lands and yucca fields. As previously discussed, the reducción also often combined various caciques into one encomienda. Only adding to the social and political tensions within the new settlements, many Indians, especially those assigned to Crown gold mines, also faced harsher work conditions, leading to a further diminution of the native population. Conditions pushed many natives of the island to flee their assigned settlements, the majority returning to their ancestral lands. The physical and political displacement, only exacerbated by the growing presence of foreign Indian slaves, pushed some caciques to rebel. As the Spanish colonists faced an ever-decreasing indigenous labor pool, they searched for more sources of slaves and for new leaders and policies to alleviate the hemorrhaging island economy.

The Jeronymite Intervention: From Hope to Catastrophe

Dissatisfaction with the limitations of the Laws of Burgos, the havoc wrought by the Repartimiento of 1514, and the growing clamor for change within religious circles all led to an in-depth examination into how to reform the governance of Española in 1517. This investigation and intervention was led by a most unlikely party, neither secular officials nor the already-involved Franciscans and Dominicans but a small group of Jeronymite friars. In January 1516 King Ferdinand died, leaving power to the regent of Castile, Cardinal Francisco Jimenéz de Cisneros (until Ferdinand's grandson Charles came of age). Cisneros appointed the group of Jeronymites to serve as an impartial religious government in Española.[51] Even though Cisneros was a member of the Franciscan order, he decided that he had to choose an impartial judge or party or at least a group with less extreme ideas. In his discussions with Las Casas, Cisneros revealed that while he believed that the Indians were inherently free, they still needed guidance (both religious and political) before they could live in a civilized manner. While the Indians were receiving this education, Cisneros believed that they could be required to serve the Spanish, just not as slaves.[52] Additionally, the Franciscans and Dominicans were still embroiled in conflict with one another. Cisneros likely felt that he had to appoint a group not previously involved in the conflict. The Jeronymites, a completely cloistered group who had remained separate from all politics, seemed like the perfect choice.[53]

Cisneros tasked the Jeronymites with investigating and then reforming the government of the Indies, with the goal being the salvation of the land's native peoples and the resurrection of the island's failing economy. To achieve these lofty ambitions, the Jeronymites planned to slowly replace the faltering and labor-intensive gold-mining industry with sugar production. They also sought to substitute indigenous labor with African slaves. The Jeronymites then needed to decide the fate of the much-criticized encomienda system. If they decided to dismantle the encomiendas, the next step was to pick between the creation of completely free Indian towns or towns governed jointly by clergy and a cacique (*pueblos tutelados* or *pueblos indios*). Finally, the Jeronymites were challenged with relieving tensions between the different religious and secular factions in Española, something that the Repartimiento had exacerbated.[54]

Upon arriving in Española in January 1517, the Jeronymites interviewed the fourteen most powerful officials and encomenderos on the island. Most described the Indians as "lazy," "enemies of work," "liars," "drunkards," and "inclined only to vices not virtue," arguing that the Indians did not possess the capacity to govern themselves in a civilized manner.[55] While some of the Spaniards may have honestly held these beliefs regarding the Taínos, it is likely that they were more interested in protecting their economic interests. Only two officials believed that at least some of the island's Indians had the capacity to live freely. The first, Pedro Romero, was married to a Taíno woman and possessed an encomienda in the southwest corner of the island, in Jaragua. He testified that only "exceptional" Indians could and should live freely and independently from the Spanish. What he meant by this is up for interpretation, though it is likely he believed the "exceptional" Indians were the most Hispanicized, or *ladino*, Indians.[56] The term "ladino," or

"Latinized," came from the African slave trade where Africans (slave or free) were divided into two groups: ladino and *bozal*. Ladinos were "European-ized," meaning they likely spoke Spanish or Portuguese, were Catholic, and may have lived on either the Iberian Peninsula or in the Canary Islands prior to their residence in the New World. Bozal slaves came from the interior of Africa and had little contact with or knowledge of Europeans prior to their enslavement.[57]

The other defender of Indian liberty who was interviewed was more pre-dictably a Dominican friar. He argued that all Indians had the ability to live in complete freedom, though some would have to be trained in pueblos tutela-dos first. The rest of those interviewed all agreed categorically that the Indians were innately unfit to govern themselves, including at least one Franciscan friar.[58] Because of these reports, and a fear that dismantling the encomien-das would provoke a rebellion on the island, the Jeronymites advocated the maintenance of the encomienda system for an undetermined period of time. It is important to note that all these decisions were made without interview-ing any Taíno Indians.

Though they defended, at least initially, the encomienda system, the Jeronymites immediately prohibited the Indian slave trade on the coast of Tierra Firme. With the threat of slavers reduced and the support of both Cisneros and the Jeronymites, another group of Dominican friars decided to give missions on the coast of Venezuela another chance. This time both Córdoba and Montesinos accompanied the group in founding the mission Santa Fe in Chichiriviche.[59] In addition to facilitating the conversion of the indigenous population of present-day Venezuela, Cisneros also charged the Jeronymites with securing the entire coastline from both Spanish colonists and Carib Indians.[60] With the wide powers given to the friars and an end to the *legal* slave trade in Tierra Firme, the missions seemed to have a much better chance of success in 1517.

However, two problems soon presented themselves. First was the basic inability of the small groups of friars to police the huge expanse of territory when hundreds of Spanish merchants still sought to engage in all types of exchanges with the Indians of Tierra Firme. Second, and perhaps more unex-pectedly, many indigenous groups of Tierra Firme were dissatisfied with the arrangement. Not only were they forbidden to trade with multiple Spaniards, using competition to gain the best product or price, but they also could no longer legally sell Indian slaves. Indigenous slavery predated the Spanish in Tierra Firme and slavery was a common outcome of Arawak warfare.[61] In fact, many wars were fought for the purpose of gathering slaves, perhaps even to exact vengeance on a community that had enslaved members of one's own town. While indigenous groups did not want their own people to be enslaved, they had no problem with the institution itself or with the profit they gained from selling "Caribs" to Spanish merchants.[62] Neither the Indians of Tierra Firme nor the Spanish slavers wanted the slave trade to end, leaving the few missionaries fighting an uphill battle.

Within months after their return to Tierra Firme, the friars began to complain about new slaving expeditions to nearby Trinidad and even into Paria, territory supposedly controlled by the religious orders and exempt from slaving.[63] By early 1518 the region was fully under assault by slave traders, including the valley of Chichiriviche; the provinces of Cumaná, Paria, Cariaco, and Maracapana; and part of Castilla del Oro (present-day Colombia).[64] Slavers frequented virtually the entire territory governed by the friars. Whether or not the merchants obtained their slaves through peaceful or violent methods, the removal of indigenous peoples from Tierra Firme left the region generally unsettled as the demand for Indian captives provoked conflict between indigenous groups. Because these expeditions were illegal, very little documentation exists regarding them. Thus, it is difficult to estimate the number of assaults or how many Indians were taken to Santo Domingo among other ports. At the very least the slaving was substantial enough to preoccupy the friars and other officials throughout 1517 and into 1518. When Alonso de Zuazo, a *licenciado* (judge), landed in Española in early 1518, he remarked on the number of indigenous slaves sent to Santo Domingo from diverse regions of the Caribbean, including the Lucayos and Venezuela, many of them dying of hunger or illness soon after their arrival.[65]

After addressing the indigenous slave trade, or trying to, the Jeronymites next removed all Indians from encomiendas where owners were absent, finally fulfilling the Laws of Burgos. These Indians, of which there were approximately three thousand, with the majority belonging to the Crown, were the first to move to pueblos tutelados.[66] The first of these settlements were in the Cibao where Indians continued to work eight months out of the year in gold mines. However, instead of the profit from this work going to the Crown, or encomenderos, the Indians themselves reaped the benefits of their labor. The mined gold was used to buy the Indians clothing and food and to pay their religious mentors' salaries. In exchange the priests taught their indigenous charges religious and scholarly pursuits along with Spanish methods of farming.

For their brief existence the *indios depositados*, or those living in the pueblos tutelados, mined significantly more gold than their counterparts who remained in encomiendas. From early 1518 until 1519, Indians under the Jeronymites' supervision mined 9,960 pesos of gold. The *indios encomendados*, or those belonging to encomiendas, mined only 7,520 pesos.[67] The contrast is especially extraordinary when one considers that the number of Indians living in the pueblos tutelados was only about 9 percent of the island's indigenous population. The Jeronymites attributed this difference to the positive effects of just and fair treatment.[68]

While the settlements were overseen by both religious clergy and secular authorities, the Jeronymites also tried to maintain the pre-Hispanic eminence of the native caciques by giving them better clothing, fewer work hours, and an opportunity to assist in governing the pueblos tutelados. In the Jeronymites' plan these caciques would eventually lead completely free indigenous towns.[69] The early pueblos tutelados served as models for the Jeronymites' much larger-scale plan that they attempted in 1518: the creation of nearly thirty pueblos indios across the island and the complete end of the encomienda system. In many ways the Jeronymites were trying to return to the original social structure that Columbus tried to implement in Española in 1493 with the island's "natural lords" maintaining power and acting as intermediaries between their subjects and Spanish rulers.

Meanwhile, the Jeronymites advocated the importation of thousands of African slaves. The new workers were to aid in the shift to sugar production as the economic foundation of the island. To this end the Jeronymites petitioned Cisneros to provide Spanish residents willing to set up sugar *ingenios* with economic incentives, most importantly the ability to purchase African slaves without paying taxes in an effort to make the transition from indigenous to African slave labor smoother.[70] While the Jeronymites' emphasis on increased sugar production over gold mining did not ultimately help the Taínos, it did benefit Española's colonists. By the 1530s, Española shipped up to ninety thousand *arrobas* (just under three thousand pounds) of sugar annually to Spain from as many as forty ingenios.[71]

At the end of 1518 the Jeronymites decided to put their full plan in motion and began the process of creating pueblos tutelados across the island. Although they originally planned thirty towns, the number decreased to seventeen due to the loss of population during the early phases of the first smallpox epidemic to hit the Caribbean at the start of 1518. The Jeronymites planned to carry out their vision in two phases: first, by moving the most acculturated or ladino Indian caciques, and second, by supervising the voluntary relocation of the rest of the Indians. The Jeronymites firmly believed that once the caciques saw the benefits of living in pueblos tutelados they would choose to move to the elected sites.[72] In spite of all the Jeronymites' hopes, Española's Taínos did not view the second relocation in a positive light. While it is likely that most caciques wanted to be free from their encomenderos, they did not want to move yet again, especially not to locations even more distant from their ancestral cacicazgos.[73]

Before the Jeronymites could force all the Indians to move, or the encomenderos to release their Indians, the island faced the peak of the smallpox outbreak. According to island officials, the illness devastated the remaining indigenous population, killing up to a quarter of Española's Indians in a few months. The segment of the population most affected were the inhabitants of the infant pueblos tutelados.[74] Even the Indians who survived the epidemic suffered as they then faced abuse and exploitation in the pueblos tutelados now governed by secular administrators. After smallpox ravaged the island, there were simply not enough priests. The Jeronymites tried to prevent mistreatment by paying salaries to the town's administrators, but by late 1518 there were reports of widespread abuse by the towns' overseers, who forced the Indians to work overtime and then even stole their yucca.[75] The Indians then fled the pueblos tutelados to escape disease and abuse and to return to their homelands. Despite the Jeronymites' best intentions, all the towns were deserted by 1530.[76] As the experiment of the pueblos indios or pueblos tutelados deteriorated, so did the Jeronymites' determination. By the end of 1519 they also gave up on dismantling the encomiendas, agreeing that the Taínos could continue to live under the practices of the Repartimiento system.[77]

Prior to the failure of the pueblos tutelados (and other attempts at ending the Repartimiento system), the Jeronymites turned their attention to finding laborers to replace the Taínos of the island. From the beginning the Jeronymites promoted the use of African slave labor over indigenous, even outlawing the Indian slave trade when they first arrived in the Caribbean. But they needed to do more. In early 1518 they began executing their plan, issuing a decree that allowed for the purchase and transportation of bozal African slaves to the island of Española.[78] However, it took years for African slaves to arrive in the Caribbean in large numbers. So leaders looked elsewhere to solve the labor shortage on Española, specifically to the importation of *both* African and Indian slaves. Only one year after the Jeronymites made the Indian slave trade illegal, they repealed the prohibition on trading for slaves from the Pearl Islands and Tierra Firme.[79] To justify their policy, the Jeronymites labeled the majority of Indians living on the coast of Tierra Firme as "Caribs" or cannibals, making their capture and enslavement legal per laws dating from 1503. One of the earliest beneficiaries of the Jeronymites' new policy was the treasurer Miguel de Pasamonte, who received a license to enslave Caribs in Tierra Firme, as long as they labored in his burgeoning sugar mill.[80] The Jeronymites even sponsored some slaving expeditions, including one led by Diego de Caballero, which captured between 150 and 200 Indians from the peninsula of Paria.[81] From June to October 1519 more than five hundred Indian slaves (over half women) were recorded and branded in Santo Domingo.[82] The Jeronymites even issued licenses for the residents of Española to purchase Indian slaves, specifically Caribs, from Portuguese traders in Brazil.[83] By 1520 Rodrigo de Figueroa, a judge of the royal court in Santo Domingo, reported that the majority of ships docking in Santo Domingo carried Carib slaves from Tierra Firme.[84] Alonso de Zuazo confirmed Figueroa's observations, claiming that up to fifteen thousand Indians had been captured and enslaved from the Lesser Antilles and the coast of Tierra Firme in 1518 alone.[85] To distinguish these slaves easily from the naborías or from free Taínos, they were branded with a large C for Carib on their upper arms.[86] After their branding they were sold publicly for thirteen pesos each.[87] In the end, despite their goals and rhetoric, when the very basic survival of the Spanish enterprise in the Caribbean was in question, the Jeronymites had to focus on secular and economic concerns, pushing the "spiritual conquest" to the side.

The Legal Definition of Carib Lands and the Consequent Growth of the Slave Trade

As more Carib slaves arrived in Española's ports, many questioned whether those labeled as Caribs were actually cannibals or even enemies of the Spanish. In 1520 King Charles I (who took the Crown upon Cisneros's death in late 1517) ordered the newly appointed justice of Española, Rodrigo de Figueroa, to conduct an ethnographic inquiry into the inhabitants of the Caribbean. He was to resolve the "Carib" issue and decide who could be enslaved. In particular, in an official report to the Crown, Figueroa described the goal of this project: "to indicate in which territories Carib Indians live and as such can and should be taken as slaves by the Christians."[88] While he was supposed to tour the lands himself, he instead based his report solely on interviews with "pilots, captains, and sailors, and other persons who are accustomed to travel to the islands and coast of Tierra Firme."[89] Essentially, Figueroa's sources were slavers or traders who, while familiar with the territories in question, would benefit from the expansion of, not a reduction of, the legal definition of Carib lands. Additionally, Figueroa's investigations coincided with a point when Española's labor supply was reaching a new low, following the smallpox epidemic of 1518 as well as the turmoil caused by both the Repartimiento of Albuquerque and the Jeronymites' pueblos tutelados. After the loss of indigenous labor, and with it profits, colonists began to flee Española, searching for opportunities on other islands or the mainland, abandoning many towns.[90] As colonists left and profits from both gold mines and sugar plantations dwindled, everyone from the Crown down to small landholders experienced a drop in revenue.

In this context Figueroa's wider designation of Carib lands makes sense and could have been what the Crown intended. Figueroa's report declared that all islands in the Caribbean not inhabited by Christians, other than Trinidad, Barbuda, the Lucayos, Los Gigantes, and Margarita, were Carib lands.[91] Most of these were uninhabited islands or already depopulated; therefore, to open them to slave raids was inconsequential. In addition to the islands, much of the coast and interior of Tierra Firme were also defined as Carib. Here were some of the most densely populated regions, most of which had yet to be fully explored. Slaving licenses to these areas served a double purpose: to supply labor to the Greater Antilles, and to instigate and fund new exploratory ventures. From all of the lands inhabited by Caribs, licensed Christians could "enter and take, seize and capture, and make war and hold and possess and trade as slaves those Indians who in the designated islands, lands, and provinces are judged as caribes, being permitted to do so in whatever manner, so long as they are first given permission by the justices and officials of your Majesty."[92]

After Figueroa published his report, the number of slaving licenses, already on the rise after the Jeronymites' change in legislation in 1518, grew rapidly. Zuazo (who had always argued that the enslavement of Caribs was necessary to save the Arawak Spanish allies of Tierra Firme) was at the center of much of the reinvigorated slaving operations. He issued licenses, organized armadas, and worked with many prominent merchants and pilots to obtain slaves and pearls from Tierra Firme.[93] He was not the only elite colonial official to engage directly in the indigenous slave trade. Sometimes entire communities or cities came together to organize slaving expeditions. By August 1520 Lucas Vázquez de Ayllón, Juan Ortiz de Matienzo, Marcelo de Villalobos, Rodrigo de Bastidas, García Hernández, Miguel de Pasamonte, and Diego Caballero had all received licenses to conduct both rescate and slave raiding in Carib territories.[94] In addition to licenses issued to individuals, the Crown also supported the organization of larger slaving armadas. Juan de

Cardenás, a resident of Sevilla, received one such license in August 1520 that allowed him to prepare and arm two caravels in Santo Domingo. The ships were then to travel to Barbados, Isla Verde, Trinidad, and the province of Paria to conduct rescate for gold, pearls, precious stones, and Carib slaves. These slaves were to be branded and sold in the markets of Santo Domingo.[95]

With slave raiding on the rise, the friars working in the missions on the Venezuelan coast pleaded for an end to *all* legal slaving of the region, but instead officials ordered that Spanish expeditions focus on enslaving *only Caribs*. For example, Juan de Ampiés, the royal treasurer, issued a proclamation prohibiting slavers from assaulting peaceful indigenous groups who resided along the coast forty leagues east of the Gulf of Venezuela.[96] Indians caught outside of this region could be legally enslaved. Because of these ambiguous prohibitions, which were nearly impossible to enforce since officials relied on the slavers to ascertain where they encountered and captured Indians, slaving continued. Even soldiers ostensibly sent to help and protect the friars, including a group sent by Bartolomé de Las Casas to reinforce the Franciscans near Cumaná in July 1520, participated in slaving.[97] After they arrived in Venezuela, the soldiers deserted the Franciscan missions. Instead the soldiers traveled to Paria, even though the peninsula was part of Las Casas's grant of 270 leagues, to conduct slave raids along the coast.[98] The friars had lost any control they may have had in Tierra Firme and by late 1520 the constant slave raids took their toll.

On September 3, 1520, cacique Maraguey entered the Dominican monastery as the friars were conducting mass. Maraguey was a neighbor of the mission and had had friendly relations with the friars. On this day though, Maraguey brought with him many Indians from both his own territory and nearby Tagares. Inside the church they killed two friars, then moved on to the monastery where they murdered nine others, including one Indian translator.[99] Next the Indians robbed the monastery, stole all the religious ornaments valued up to one thousand pesos, and finally burned down the monastery itself. Only one Indian, a servant of the friars from the coast of Tierra Firme, survived the attack. The survivor traveled to Cubagua, where he reported the attack to Antonio Flores, the governor of the island.[100] Simultaneous with the assault on the monastery were several other attacks against secular Spanish traders throughout the region from Maracapana to Cuanta and Cumaná.[101] Then in early 1521 the Indians of Tierra Firme attacked the Franciscan monastery at Cumaná. Not only did the Indians kill two friars, along with five or six Indian servants taken from Española, but they did so again while the friars were in the middle of celebrating mass.[102] After murdering the friars and servants, the

Indians robbed the church, stealing all the religious ornaments including the friars' robes and chalices. They then burned down the friars' huts (*bohios*) and the storehouse with all of the mission's supplies and weaponry.[103] Finally, they broke the church's bell and killed the friars' horses and one mule.[104] The Indians were rejecting all links to the Spanish, even their livestock.

Whether these attacks were orchestrated or isolated incidents is uncertain, but their similarities are striking. And as the indigenous attacks had much in common, so did Spanish responses to them. Once Spanish officials received word of the series of rebellions, the governor of Cubagua gathered five ships with forty men to journey to Santa Fe to punish the Indians. Then in January 1521 the royal court of Santo Domingo organized a much larger expedition, led by Captain Gonzalo de Ocampo, to attack the Indians of Cumaná, Santa Fe, Tagares, and Maracapana.[105] Ocampo was specifically ordered to locate and capture the cacique Maraguey and his brother. But the instructions did not end with Maraguey. Ocampo and his men were also permitted to make war on and enslave any Indian who resisted their advances.[106] Though Las Casas tried to stop Ocampo's mission, the captain refused to recognize Las Casas's control over the region.[107] Instead, Ocampo sailed to Maracapana where he and his crew attacked and enslaved Indians all along the coastline. The fate of Maraguey and the other rebellious caciques is unclear; however, within two months of Ocampo's expedition, at least six hundred Indian slaves from Tierra Firme were sold in Santo Domingo.[108] Presumably at least some of the culpable Indians were among the captives.

By 1522 all the religious communities had failed in the wake of indigenous insurrection and slave raiding. The Dominicans' and Franciscans' dreams were over as the military and economic conquests overruled the spiritual goals of the Spanish. At this point Tierra Firme began its journey toward becoming a harvesting ground for Carib Indians. Indigenous resistance and rebellion only solidified Spanish legal and political designations, transforming any Indian who opposed the Spanish into a Carib.[109] Slave raiding continued well into the 1520s with perhaps hundreds of expeditions launched against the Caribs of Tierra Firme. Unfortunately, it is nearly impossible to calculate the exact number of Indian slaves brought to Española during the period due to a lack of documentation. The only specific cases for which documents exist involve disputes or illegal activity that made their way to the courtroom. For example, in 1523 an armada funded by the city of Concepción de la Vega and Juan de Logroño captured 190 Venezuelan Indians. While the expedition's license was issued legally, it allowed only for the purchase of slaves through rescate. Though the slavers claimed they followed the conditions of their license, under further investigation by Judge Figueroa, he discovered that of the 190 Indians only sixteen were acquired through rescate. The remainder were taken by force.[110] In another case in 1524 a group of 130 slavers led by Martín Baso Zabala and Diego de Yllescas penetrated Venezuela with a license to attack and capture Carib Indians. However, instead of enslaving Caribs, the expedition captured 120 Indians allied with the Spanish. Among those taken were several relatives of local caciques, including the daughter of cacique Manaure and nephews of cacique Baltasar. These Indians were taken to Española and sold as slaves, regardless of their legal designation.[111]

*   *   *

While the Jeronymites' decision to reopen, and even expand, the Indian slave trade was partially instituted to help the Taíno population of Española, the extension of slaving expeditions increased the suffering of both native residents of the island and newly arrived captives. Most of the newly enslaved were brought to new reducciones created in the 1514 Repartimiento of Albuquerque. The introduction of more foreign Indians to newly formed communities reduced Taíno caciques' power even more. Then the decline in population following the 1518 smallpox epidemic caused the Spaniards to increase the importation of foreign Indian slaves. With new Jeronymite legislation and Figueroa's report permitting large slaving expeditions, the residents of Española, along with those on other islands like Cuba and Puerto Rico, expanded the Indian slave trade throughout the 1520s. The increase in Indian slaves influenced how the Spaniards viewed Española's indigenous peoples. By the 1530s the Spanish began referring to indigenous slaves as piezas, or pieces, denying them their humanity and grouping them in with increasing numbers of African slaves.

Even though the Jeronymite government came to a quick end, its policies had long-lasting consequences. Almost all the legislation enacted by the Jeronymites, from the expansion of the Indian slave trade to the maintenance of the encomienda system, directly contradicted what both the Dominicans and Franciscans advocated, as well as what the Jeronymites had initially intended. In fact, the only Jeronymite policies that seemed to work were the augmentation of the African slave trade (though slowly) and the promotion of sugar plantations. For all these reasons, Las Casas traveled to Spain in 1519 to denounce the Jeronymites' reforms and to ask for their removal from the island. He believed that almost any secular government would be preferable to their ineffective reign. The king did in fact recall the two remaining Jeronymite friars from Española at the end of 1519, leaving their reforms incomplete, the Taínos of the island largely unprotected, and Española in a state of general disorder.[112] This first part of the "spiritual conquest" in many ways failed, while the Indian slave trade was only growing.

Though most of the efforts at spiritual and political reform failed, or had very limited success, their historical impact both in the Caribbean and for future colonial ventures was paramount. The lessons learned by both secular and religious officials in Española influenced the development of economic, social, and religious institutions and practices across the Americas. While the early reforms did not halt the abuse and enslavement of Indians in the Americas, they did change the way in which religious operations were funded, justified, and at times hindered. Echoes of the religious debates can be seen in the discourse and laws that allowed for the continuation (and at times expansion) of the Indian slave trade in the late 1520s into the 1530s.

CHAPTER 4

The Search for Slaves Inspires
New World Exploration

By the second and third decades of the Spanish colonial experiment, conditions on Española, Cuba, and Puerto Rico all propelled increases in the circum-Caribbean indigenous slave trade. Despite frenzied slaving in the Bahamas and throughout the many "Carib" islands, residents of Caribbean colonies still faced a lack of laborers. The labor shortage, compounded by the first epidemic of smallpox, inspired a new push in the hunt for native populations. The search for indigenous captives across the Americas led directly to missions of exploration during the third decade of conquest. These ventures went past the known ports of call, heading north and west into territories like present-day Florida and Mexico. The first European explorations of Central and North America were slaving missions.[1]

It is true that Spanish explorers hoped to locate new, more plentiful sources of mineral wealth, but one of the most important motivations for these journeys was the search for Indian slaves to serve on sugar plantations in Española and in the gold mines of Cuba. Most of the financiers and leaders of these expeditions sought indigenous laborers both to work on their own properties and to sell. Even when the central goal of a mission was to find gold or pearls or new routes, expeditions took the opportunity to enslave Indians.[2] Exploration and indigenous enslavement were inextricably connected throughout the first half of the sixteenth century.

Despite the clearly stated goals of exploratory expeditions, historians have overlooked the role that the Indian slave trade played in spurring exploration and expansion in the circum-Caribbean, instead explaining exploration solely as a search for gold and silver. Of course, the Spanish sought pearls, precious metals, or spices, but only after they initially failed to locate large quantities of these items in the Antilles. Therefore, conquistadors focused

more on exploring to find new lands with new populations. These populations then served as sources of slaves or a quick profit. Patterns of conquest
and colonization in newly discovered territories reveal the centrality of
indigenous slavery to these processes. In the years just after the conquest of
central Mexico (despite the wealth of the Mexica Empire), the Yucatán, and
present-day Nicaragua and Honduras, served as temporary centers for the
Indian slave trade. The very act of military conquest provided the Spanish
with the legal rationale to take hundreds of thousands of Indians captive, as
an extension of "just war." In this way, the Indian slave trade directly influenced the growth and shape of the Spanish Empire.

Moreover, as conquistadors ventured farther into the interior of North
and South America, they relied more on indigenous captives for survival.
Indigenous slaves featured in the most elemental preparations for entradas
and were active participants in the ventures. While their participation was
usually involuntary, they nevertheless enabled Spanish forces to cover huge
swaths of territory by serving as guides, translators, porters, and servants.
Recently, historians have uncovered the role that Indian conquistadors played
in conquering the Americas, but little attention has been paid to the forced
allies or conscripts of Spanish conquistadors.[3] Not only were indigenous
slaves the impetus for many voyages of exploration, but they also played vital
roles in almost all exploratory ventures during the sixteenth century, allowing for the conquest and exploration of otherwise impenetrable territories.
Spanish explorers, conquistadors, and even friars all actively sought indigenous slaves whom they could mold into translators and intermediaries.[4]

As voyages of exploration neared their end, many conquistadors realized
that their dreams of locating fabulous wealth were not to be, inspiring them
to turn to another source for at least a small profit: indigenous slaves. Many
entradas ended with the capture of scores of indigenous slaves to serve as
compensation for the journey. In the 1520s and 1530s indigenous slaves were
one of the only ways to profit from an otherwise unsuccessful entrada. While
slaving was discouraged in areas where native peoples provided a sustainable labor force, at least by Crown officials, in lands with less acquiescent
populations or exploitable resources, slave raiding often served as the only
way to make a profit. Slaving then became tacitly, if not directly, supported
by all levels of the Spanish government. For example, many of the attempts
to find the mythical El Dorado in present-day Colombia led to the enslavement of thousands of Indians.[5] This pattern also held true for Trinidad, Venezuela, and the Yucatán Peninsula. Undergirding claims of exploration for
mineral wealth and religious conversion lay a pattern of conquest centered

on indigenous enslavement. In almost every armada or expedition from 1513 onward, there are records of Indian slaves, whether they were part of the initial force, the goal of the entire trip, or an afterthought that made a failed mission at least marginally profitable.

The Quest for Indian Slaves and the Discovery of Florida

While it is unknown exactly when the Spanish first "discovered" Florida, slaving expeditions frequented the territory many times prior to Juan Ponce de León's 1513 expedition. The peninsula appears on a Portuguese map as early as 1502, and many in Cuba, Puerto Rico, and Española (including Taínos) spoke generally of "lands to the North." One of the first Spaniards to encounter Florida's Indians was the slaver Diego de Miruelo, whose ship was thrown off course during a storm in early 1513. Miruelo's intended destination was not Florida, but the Lucayos Islands where he hoped to capture indigenous slaves. Upon his landing in Florida, Miruelo reported that he was well received by local Indians with whom he traded some items for a "few pieces of gold and silver" before sailing on to Cuba.[6] It is likely that other slavers and sailors also frequented the area, sharing their experiences with the territory's would-be conquerors, including Ponce de León and licenciado Lucás Vázquez de Ayllón.[7] It was not gold or precious metals that first attracted the Spanish to Florida, but the land's inhabitants, future slaves.

Though the draw of indigenous slaves initially attracted the Spanish to Florida, the territory's first prospective conqueror, Juan Ponce de León, sought more than slave raiding from the peninsula. When he set sail for Florida in 1513, he embarked on a mission of discovery, exploration, and settlement. Specifically he had royal license to "go to discover and settle the island of Bimini."[8] His *asiento*, or contract with the king, also gave Ponce de León permission to enslave any Indians who refused to accept the requerimiento.[9] These slaves would serve as an initial labor force for the colony. Enslavement played a role even in early missions of settlement and colonization. After leaving Puerto Rico in March 1513, Ponce de León's armada traveled through the Lucayos Islands and landed near present-day Cape Canaveral.[10] Not finding any indigenous people at this location, the expedition continued southwest, along the coast and then through the Florida Keys. Here Ponce de León found few inhabitants, and those that he did meet attacked his men when they went ashore to gather wood or water.[11] While it is possible that the Indians associated the Spaniards with previous armadas that had violently enslaved their people, it is also possible that Ponce de León and his men simply encountered a different group than Miruelo. He might have even come upon the Ais, an indigenous people who later attacked a group of shipwrecked Spaniards in 1566.[12]

Heading back north, he encountered a larger indigenous settlement, a group later known as the Calusa, and an Indian they believed to be a Taíno from the Greater Antilles.[13] Ponce de León and his crew came to this conclusion based on the Indian's ability to speak Spanish, though how he came to be on the west coast of Florida was a mystery.[14] It is possible that he escaped the Spanish during an earlier slave raid, or that he traveled there on his own following the Spanish conquest of Española or Cuba. After his arrival in Florida, it seems he was granted permission to remain with the Calusa, pointing to possible pre-contact connections between Cuba, Española, and Florida's indigenous peoples.[15] Prior to his flight he must have spent considerable time with the Spanish colonists in order to have learned Spanish this early in the conquest period. Here is an example of how Spanish conquistadors and slavers were already reshaping the political and social landscape of the Caribbean. Whether this Indian was forcibly removed from his homeland or chose to flee his native island, he was displaced within the first two decades of Spanish colonization.

Either way he likely intuited that the Spaniards' intentions were malicious, because he delayed the men from coming ashore for a full day, during which he promised Ponce de León that if they stayed overnight, the local cacique, Carlos, would bring pieces of gold.[16] Instead, after waiting for the cacique, the Spanish faced multiple escalating attacks. The violence prevented Ponce de León from going ashore and ultimately pushed him to return to Puerto Rico without erecting a settlement in Florida.[17] Here is an example of the power that Indians could harness during the uncertain and volatile encounters of exploration and conquest. It is likely that Ponce de León's journey would have had a different ending if not for the presence of the Taíno Indian and his influence on the Calusas' response to the Spanish expedition.

Following the failure of his colonization efforts, Ponce de León sailed back to Puerto Rico; however, not all his ships accompanied him. One of the three, piloted by Antón Alaminos, instead journeyed to the Lucayos Islands, though the purpose for the detour was not specifically stated.[18] The answer lies in what Alaminos's cargo held when it arrived in Añasco Bay in February 1514. The vessel carried four Indian men from Bimini and six Indians (two men, three women, and one woman with a young child) from other Lucayos Islands.[19] It is likely the ship sailed back to the Lucayos on a slaving mission to make a profit out of a failed expedition: a practice that became more common in the following years. Though Alaminos enslaved only a few Lucayan Indians during his 1513 voyage, the enterprise might have inspired his future, much larger, slaving ventures. In the following year he led a slaving trip back to Florida and then in 1517 participated in one of the first slaving armadas to the Yucatán Peninsula. Nor was Alaminos the only pilot to return to Florida to engage in slaving raids in between Ponce de León's first and second colonization attempts (between 1513 and 1521). Diego Miruelo engaged in slaving raids along the northern gulf coast in 1516 and Pedro de Salazar enslaved Indians along the Atlantic coast. In 1517 Ponce de León even brought a suit against the then governor of Cuba, Diego Velázquez, for capturing three hundred Indian slaves from Florida, later selling them in Cuba. Ponce de León argued that because Florida was still under his jurisdiction, per his agreement with the Crown, any raids or ventures to Florida without his permission were illegal.[20]

In the wake of Ponce de León's failed attempts to colonize the "land to the north," explorers and slavers from Puerto Rico and Española continued to frequent the territory, exploring new regions, to gather more indigenous slaves. Exploration of Florida and the indigenous slave trade remained intimately connected. One of these slavers, pilot Esteban Gómez, sailed from present-day Panama northward to the Florida coast. Gómez made port at multiple locations along the peninsula of Florida, taking as many Indians captive as he could at each juncture. He then sailed to Cuba with his slave cargo, off-loading some in the island and taking many more Indian slaves all the way to Castile, disobeying the laws against the transportation of indigenous slaves to Spain.[21] Other expeditions were even larger. In particular two influential and wealthy judges of Española, Lucás Vázquez de Ayllón and Juan Ortiz de Matienzo, both organized slaving journeys to the Lucayos, in the process finding a new land, La Chicora.[22] In the summer of 1521 Ayllón's and Matienzo's slaving missions encountered one another in the Lucayos Islands and together went on to discover what became the northern frontier of Spanish Florida (present-day South Carolina) several decades later.

Pilot Pedro de Quejo led one of the expeditions, with clearly stated goals: first to deliver merchandise to Cuba and then to move onward to the Bahamas to capture slaves for Española.[23] The other group, led by Francisco Gordillo, was simply instructed to gather slaves from the "useless" Lucayos Islands.[24] If Gordillo did not find Indians in the Lucayos, Ayllón ordered him to locate the source of Indians of "giant stature" that another slaver had found "at the end of a voyage to the north" at some point between 1514 and 1516.[25] Ayllón was one of the most prolific indigenous slavers at least partially because he required many laborers to work his multiple holdings on Española, which in 1520 included a large sugar mill on the northern coast near Puerto Plata. Ayllón already owned hundreds of slaves, even recently receiving his salary in the form of four hundred slaves. The ethnicity and origins of these slaves are unclear, but some records suggest that Ayllón owned at least two hundred indigenous slaves.[26]

Upon reaching the Lucayos, both Quejo and Gordillo found few Indians, which was not surprising. The islands' populations were already depleted after a decade or so of slave raiding beginning in 1508. The two pilots, finding themselves in the same predicament, resolved to sail together for either the territory of Florida or the land of "giant" Indians. On June 24, 1521, the two crews sighted land and soon after began exploring the area just south of present-day Myrtle Beach, South Carolina. There they encountered numerous indigenous villages, traded with the Indians, and took possession of the province in the name of their patrons.[27] After a few weeks of reconnaissance the group took advantage of the Indians' trust and invited them on their ship after which they proceeded to capture sixty of them to take as slaves to Santo Domingo.[28] To rationalize this action to the Audiencia of Santo Domingo, Quejo testified that the Indians "ate human flesh," were lazy sodomites, and lacked the ability to speak without inciting horror. Here is a continuation of the Carib/cannibal trope created by Columbus to justify the enslavement of indigenous peoples.

Among the group of natives was the Indian Francisco, or *el Chicorano*, a nickname meaning something between "little frog" and "frog boy," who became the basis of the myth of La Chicora.[29] The Chicora myth centered on Florida's amazing agricultural and mineral potential, as a land that was simply waiting to be settled and exploited by the Spanish.[30]

In addition to his role in the creation of the Chicora myth, Chicorano both orchestrated Ayllón's attempted colonization of Florida and destroyed the nascent settlement. After Chicorano's arrival in Santo Domingo, he became Ayllón's personal servant. In this role he befriended Ayllón, learning Spanish and sharing his knowledge of his homeland with the judge. After two years with Ayllón in the islands, Chicorano journeyed with him to Spain where he was baptized at the royal court as Francisco de Chicora. While at court Francisco regaled the king with tales of the bounty of his homeland. He especially highlighted the availability of pearls and copper in his territory. He also extolled the virtues of his people, describing how skilled they were in hunting, medicine, and tailoring, while also depicting them as morally righteous and sexually chaste.[31] Essentially, Francisco presented La Chicora as a paradise, perhaps to inspire the king to fund an expedition during which he could return to his birthplace. If this was indeed Francisco's plan, it worked. He and Ayllón returned to the Caribbean in 1525, after Ayllón received the governorship of La Chicora.

The rest of the fifty-nine Indians captured by Quejo and Gordillo were not as lucky as Francisco Chicorano. Upon their arrival in Española, the financial supporters of the expeditions divided up the Indians. Matienzo's indigenous slaves likely went to work on his cattle ranch located five leagues outside of Santo Domingo, while Ayllón's share either were sent to labor on his new sugar ingenio near Azua or to his older mining holdings located close to Concepción de la Vega.[32] Regardless of where the Indians found themselves working, nearly all of them died within a few months due to starvation, disease, or general "mistreatment" per Matienzo. In fact, only one of the captured Indians was alive in 1526, and he was working in a pearl fishery in Cubagua.[33] Preparations for Ayllón's mission of colonization to La Chicora revealed the fate of those enslaved with Chicorano. Although Ayllón already had Chicorano to serve as an intermediary, he sought more porters, guides, and translators familiar with the territory. Unfortunately for Ayllón, he failed to locate any more surviving and accessible Indians from Chicora.

In the spring of 1526, accompanied by Francisco Chicorano, Ayllón sailed for present-day South Carolina to create a permanent settlement.[34] This was not a slaving voyage, but the conqueror was still allowed to trade native peoples for slaves.[35] Indians who were enslaved by other Indians could still be legally purchased or bartered for (taken via rescate) and sent back to Española. Additionally, Ayllón and his fellow colonists were not required to pay taxes on the profit garnered from selling these slaves.[36] However, likely due to the controversy over the original sixty slaves taken from Chicora, Ayllón was under strict instructions to treat any future Indian slaves well, supplying them with both wages and religious instruction.[37]

Despite these precautions the expedition ended in complete failure with the town San Miguel del Gualdape abandoned by mid-November 1526. Hardship for the new settlement began immediately with the loss of one of the group's three ships (along with many of its supplies and food), which ran aground and sank at the mouth of the Rio Jordán at the point of Santa Elena.[38] Next, Ayllón and the Spanish lost their most valuable tool, the Indian ally Francisco Chicorano. Within only a few days of his return, Francisco fled the Spanish. Perhaps this was the fulfillment of his plan or maybe he simply took advantage of his situation. Following Francisco's flight, the Spaniards, nearly six hundred colonists at the start of the enterprise, were left with few supplies in an unfriendly land without native assistance.

Soon the group faced starvation and widespread illness, culminating with Ayllón's death on October 18, 1526. Making matters worse, Gualdape faced multiple attacks by the region's native population, perhaps led by none other than Chicorano.[39] It remains unclear from the documentation whether the Indian assaults were large, organized attacks on the actual settlement, or more disparate harassments of smaller groups of Spaniards out hunting for food. Regardless of the size of the indigenous strikes, they led to many Spanish deaths and helped to bring about the settlement's abandonment. While indigenous allies did help the Spanish, they could also sabotage a new settlement. Both despite and because of Francisco's time as a Spanish slave, he was able to orchestrate his return to his homeland and expel his former captors.

A group of ladino African slaves also attacked the Spanish at Gualdape, burning down several buildings, at the same time as the Indians assaulted the settlement. Of the many dwellings set ablaze by the African slaves, the majority of whom were household servants or artisans, was the house of Ayllón's self-appointed successor, Ginés Doncel.[40] The fire led to the almost complete destruction of the settlement and was the first slave revolt in North America. These two attacks, in combination with Ayllón's death, led to the failure of the colony and its abandonment within four months of its foundation. By the time of Gualdape's desertion, only 150 of the original six hundred colonists escaped with their lives.[41]

The "Discovery" of Mexico and the Expansion of the Indian Slave Trade

Just as the Spanish were initially drawn to Florida in their search for indigenous slaves, slave traders were also the first to interact with Mexico's Indians. Prior to the Spaniards' official arrival on the Yucatán Peninsula, slavers frequented the islands off of Central America, namely the Guanaxas Islands along the coast of Honduras. As early as 1515 the governor of Cuba, Diego Velázquez, began sending slaving missions to the Guanaxas. His interest in the area was piqued after receiving reports from Cuban caciques describing the arrival of Indians in large canoes, hailing from a territory almost due west. These Indians, traveling five or six days to reach Cuba, brought a variety of goods and were large in stature. More than likely these mysterious Indians were the Maya, who possessed advanced seafaring technology and whose canoes were sighted by Columbus during his voyage to the Gulf of Honduras.[42]

While the goods and stature of Guanaxas Indians were enticing, they were also some of the most belligerent indigenous groups that the Spanish dealt with. Even with the number of slaving voyages and raids throughout the first decades of Spanish colonization, there are few records of onboard mutinies. Of the few cases, two involved Indians taken from the Guanaxas Islands. First, in 1515, a group of Indian captives from the Guanaxas seized the ship when many Spanish sailors went onshore for water along the coast of southern Cuba. The slaves succeeded in sailing the ship back to their homeland. Here is an incredible example of resistance, as well as a demonstration of the depth of geographic knowledge that indigenous groups of the Caribbean possessed. Despite the loss of their slaves and ship in 1515, Velázquez ordered another slaving mission to the Guanaxas only one year later.[43] This expedition was part of a larger royally funded armada; its goals were to attack all islands inhabited by Caribs and to enslave rebellious Indians from the Honduran province of Higueras.[44] This mission discovered the fate of the first group of mutinous Guanaxas Indians. Upon their arrival in the islands in 1516 the Spaniards chanced upon the wreckage of the ship run aground. Beyond locating the ship, the second expedition to the Guanaxas captured up to five hundred Indians. But the Spanish raiders again suffered a mutiny, this time while at sea prior to arriving in Cuba. Because this mutiny occurred with the Spanish crew onboard, heavy fighting ensued, during which several sailors were killed. The Spaniards did manage to regain control of the ship and bring four hundred indigenous slaves back to Cuba.[45]

Although Spanish slavers approached the Yucatán Peninsula in both 1515 and 1516, they did not actually "discover" the mainland of New Spain until a voyage led by Francisco Hernández de Córdova. Córdova, accompanied by pilot Antón de Alaminos, future chronicler Bernal Díaz del Castillo, and one hundred men, sailed from Havana in February 1517.[46] The expedition had orders from Governor Velázquez to travel to the Guanaxas Islands to enslave Indians to sell in Cuba.[47] Córdova was returning to a familiar slaving area, so he should have had little difficulty navigating the way. Yet Córdova and his crew instead sailed past the islands, to the coast of the Yucatán Peninsula. Alaminos, a prominent slaver, may have inspired this change in plans. It is also possible that the sailors altered their destination due to statements from recently captured slaves who spoke of a rich land farther to the northwest beyond the Guanaxas.[48] Another explanation comes from

Díaz's chronicle, in which he claims that the expedition never intended on fulfilling Velázquez's slaving instructions since they "knew that what Diego Velázquez asked of us was not just."[49] While it is possible that some of the men involved in the expedition opposed Indian slavery, this claim was more likely employed to defend the crew's deviation from their superior's instructions. Either way, the men diverged from their initial slaving endeavor and instead sighted the Yucatán Peninsula.[50]

During their exploration of the Yucatán Peninsula, Córdova and his crew encountered vast evidence of a highly advanced indigenous culture along with many impressive cities, including Campeche and Champotón. The voyage also took two Indian captives, later baptized as Julian and Melchior, destined to serve as guides and translators for future expeditions. The venture sparked the imagination of dozens of men in both Cuba and Española, leading to the 1518 journey of Hernán Cortés and the conquest of New Spain from the Mexica.[51]

The discovery of Mexico, and subsequent territories throughout Central and South America, dramatically expanded the slave trade. Even before the actual surrender of Tenochtitlan, Cortés and his fellow conquistadors began taking indigenous slaves, with permission from the Crown.[52] As early as 1519, after the attack on the city of Cholula, Cortés authorized the taking and branding of slaves by his men. The slaves taken during combat received a branding of G, for *guerra*, or war, on their faces.[53] The enslavement of defeated combatants, and distribution among the victors, was a Spanish practice, but it also fell within pre-Hispanic indigenous structures. The Spanish allies, the Tlaxcalans, actively participated in enslaving former enemy combatants, including the Cholulans and later opponents from the province of Tepeaca.[54] In Cortés's second letter to the Crown, he explained why so many Tepeaca, Zapotec, and Mixe Indians were enslaved. In his correspondence he described them as refusing peace (the requerimiento) and eating human flesh.[55] At the time of Cortés's death, one of his estates included 94 African slaves and 193 indigenous slaves hailing from diverse regions of Mexico, including Tlaxcala, Oaxaca, and Tepexi. And this was just one of many Cortés holdings that spanned across central Mexico, including several properties in Tenochtitlan itself.[56] Cortés was likely one of the largest holders of indigenous slaves in Mexico.

Nor were slaves taken only during the conquest of Mexico. Slaves played a role from the beginning of the conflict. Spaniards brought hundreds of Taíno slaves and servants (commended Indians) with them from Cuba to serve as porters and laborers.[57] And each successive Spanish armada that sailed for

Mexico brought more Indians, both enslaved and commended. Pánfilo de Narváez alone took over one thousand Indians from Cuba on his mission to arrest Cortés in 1520. Multiple officials in both Cuba and Española complained to the Crown of the damage caused by the loss of Indians, especially so soon after the smallpox outbreak. Many feared the lack of Indians inspired more Spaniards to abandon the islands for more lucrative opportunities.[58] While their fears had merit, soon after the conquest of Tenochtitlan in 1521, the flow of indigenous slaves leaving Cuba and Española was reversed with hundreds, and later thousands, of enslaved Indians disembarking in the Caribbean islands.

Though some captives taken during the wars of conquest served Spaniards in New Spain, the majority were shipped to the labor-starved Caribbean islands. From January 1521 until May 1522, a few months before and immediately after the fall of Tenochtitlan, Spaniards registered and paid taxes on nearly eight thousand indigenous slaves.[59] At least some of these slaves later crossed the Atlantic to form part of conquistadors' retinues in Spain. In fact, the possession of at least a few indigenous slaves or servants soon became a status symbol.[60] Female and child slaves were especially prized.[61] One Indian slave, Ana, who appears in Spain in 1543 as one of hundreds of indigenous slaves who gained their freedom during the Crown-ordered Inspection of Gregorio López, was purchased in 1525 in Havana by the ship captain Ginés de Carrión.[62] But Ana had been enslaved two years earlier, during an initial entrada into the province of Pánuco. Not only was Ana a victim of conquest, but she was also "doubly displaced," suffering removal first from Pánuco to Cuba, and then across the Atlantic Ocean to Spain.[63]

Thousands more indigenous slaves were taken from areas around Tenochtitlan in the ensuing conquests of present-day Guatemala, Honduras, Nicaragua, and northwest Mexico.[64] Already in January 1524, a Spanish company led by Pedro de Alvarado (supported by hundreds of indigenous allies from central Mexico) moved south and east to conquer numerous Maya population centers. Faced with early resistance from the K'iche, Alvarado and his companions quickly resorted to violence, including capturing slaves and razing villages. Harsh treatment during the entradas led to years of indigenous revolts, culminating in thousands of lost Maya lives. Las Casas claims that the Alvarado brothers and their colleagues killed four million native Guatemalans during the 1520s and 1530s. How many were enslaved is unknown.[65] The farther south that the expeditions of conquest moved, into present-day Nicaragua, Honduras, El Salvador, and Panama, the more slaves they gathered as part of the conquest repertoire. Rebellions in the wake of violent conquests, such as that in western Honduras that involved up to thirty thousand Indians in the early 1530s, only supported the taking of even more indigenous slaves.[66]

Nor did the end of formal conquest and rebellion always mean the end of slave taking. Instead leaders of nascent colonies often continued slave raiding until more profitable businesses could be consolidated. Many officials also accepted slaves in place of tribute when caciques could not fulfill their obligations in gold, silver, or cotton. In December 1525, only a few years after the conquest of central Mexico, Rodrigo Albornoz, an accountant, reported that many encomenderos were collecting one hundred to two hundred indigenous slaves when their commended caciques could not provide gold. In order to gather enough indigenous slaves, many caciques included free Indians (those who were not previously enslaved through war). Some even admitted turning their children over to conquistadors or whipping free Indians until they submitted to slavery.[67] Pedro de Rios and Diego López, governors of Panama and Honduras, respectively, enslaved at least two hundred Indians in Nicaragua, whom they sold in Panama. The two officials made two thousand pesos from the sale.[68]

Pedrarias Dávila, the governor of Nicaragua, began a lucrative slave trade in his territory just after conquest in 1526. Nearly all indigenous slaves captured by Dávila were sent to Panama (Castillo de Oro), where he had previously served as governor before his appointment to Nicaragua. In 1527 the governor of Honduras, Diego López de Salcedo, joined Dávila and other slavers in Nicaragua. His mission was to quell an indigenous revolt in the valley of Comayagua, where many indigenous villages had risen against the Spanish, burning their towns and fleeing to the mountains. During his campaign, Salcedo captured nearly three thousand Indian slaves, many of whom were caciques and principal Indians.[69] However, by the time he arrived in León, where he intended to sell his merchandise, only one hundred Indians remained alive.[70] Salcedo became infamous for this expedition and his general treatment of indigenous peoples in Central America, whom he reportedly punished with death or mutilation for the smallest infractions.[71] And Salcedo was not alone. The bishop of Honduras claimed that Alvarado's expedition to conquer Honduras resulted in the death or enslavement of six thousand Indians, at least three thousand of whom were sold either in Guatemala or the Caribbean islands.[72] Indigenous resistance and conquest were still the most common excuses used to enslave large numbers of indigenous people across the Americas, as had been the case since 1493.

By 1528 the trade in Indian slaves was the most profitable business in Nicaragua, and five ships were engaged exclusively in the transport of slaves to Panama and the Caribbean islands. Each ship normally carried approximately 350 slaves, with overcrowding leading to high death rates among the captives. For example, in 1535, an overcrowded vessel, with more than four hundred slaves aboard initially, completed its journey to Panama with only fifty surviving indigenous souls.[73] Because most slaving vessels did not have to travel far, as in the transatlantic passage, the small, crowded crafts used to transport indigenous slaves usually lacked even basic provisions, like water. Tropical heat amplified the suffering of indigenous slaves. And at times calm winds stranded the vessels for days, leading to high sickness and death rates. Some contemporaries put the mortality rate on these voyages at between 25 and 50 percent.[74]

The constant taking of slaves from Nicaragua, either via war or simply raiding, led to the near depopulation of the province by the 1540s. In 1544 one estimate of the indigenous population of Nicaragua was as low as thirty thousand. Las Casas claimed five hundred thousand slaves were removed from Nicaragua from 1526 to 1542, while the chronicler Oviedo counted four hundred thousand.[75] Nicaragua was a popular slaving territory due to its proximity to the mines of Peru.[76] While these numbers might be high, they are plausible. They also likely include Indians taken from southern Guatemala and Honduras who may have been sold with Indians from Nicaragua in Panama, Peru, and the Greater Antilles. By 1538 the Spanish had taken so many Indians from Honduras that the Crown passed an order limiting the number of Indians taken from the territory. Five years later, it was forbidden to take any indigenous persons from the region.[77] With fewer Indians available in Central America and the Caribbean, prices rose from around two pesos for an Indian slave in the 1520s to as high as thirty-three pesos in the mid-1530s. It is important to note that only slaves skilled in European trades (metal working, pearl diving, etc.) fetched such high prices.[78]

The conquest of Mexico, including the provinces of Guatemala, Honduras, and Nicaragua, pushed the circum-Caribbean indigenous slave trade to new heights. By the late 1520s hundreds of thousands of Indian slaves, many taken during the search for and conquest of new lands, were captured and shipped across the Americas. The need for indigenous slaves pushed and inspired exploration. The subsequent conquest of new lands then supplied the conquistadors with captives to sell. The indigenous slave trade provided one of the earliest ways to secure a profit in the Spanish Empire. But the taking of Indian slaves as inspiration for and part of expeditions of conquest and exploration was not the only link between the Indian slave trade and exploration.

Slaves as Consolation Prizes in the Hunt for El Dorado

The discovery and conquests of Mexico and Peru not only pushed the indigenous slave trade to new levels, but also gave hope to would-be conquistadors
that they too could chance upon their own Inca or Mexica Empire. The search
for indigenous slaves still helped to inspire voyages, but by the 1530s slaves
were no longer the primary focus of explorers. These men sought cities of
gold, silver mines, and pearl beds. In their minds slaves taken during conquest
would only add to larger profits from mineral wealth. But not every conquest
was successful: for example, the disastrous voyages deep into South America in
search of El Dorado. On these entradas Indian slaves served both as forced collaborators during the missions and as consolation prizes afterward. Instead of
leaving surviving captives and conscripts behind, the explorers, conquistadors,
and plunderers of Nueva Granada (Colombia) and Venezuela kept their Indian
slaves with them, selling them to make a slim profit out of a failed venture.

If explorers did not have many slaves at the conclusion of their journey,
which was common due to high death rates suffered by Indians and Spaniards alike on these lengthy entradas, they often captured dozens as they
approached Spanish settlements. Upon reaching a port city the Indian slaves
were sold with the claim either that they were captured during "just war" or
that they were Caribs. Here Indians became consolation prizes for expeditions that did not locate new sources of mineral wealth. In some cases, Indian
slaves even served as foot soldiers' salaries.

Residents of the Pearl Islands, Trinidad, and the Greater Antilles all participated in slave raids and missions of exploration into the interior of Tierra
Firme, especially after the region was declared as majority "Carib" by Judge
Figueroa in 1520. But the transformation of Indian slaves into consolation
prizes can best be witnessed in the entradas of a series of German colonists
and conquistadors from the late 1520s into the early 1540s. While German conquistadors, along with some of their Spanish counterparts in Nueva Granada,
learned to view Indian slaves as consolation prizes, in their first expeditions
into the interior of Venezuela they refrained from engaging in slave raiding as
an end unto itself. Conquistadors did capture hundreds of Indians to serve as
guides, porters, and translators (as had most Spanish explorers before them in
other regions), but at the culmination of their entradas they returned with few
if any Indian slaves.

At this point then, early in the penetration of the continent when the
Spanish still sustained hope for discovering a new wealthy civilization, the
benefit of taking huge numbers of Indian slaves was not enough to defray

the consequences of either disrupting indigenous settlements or disobeying Crown orders. Following decades of experience in establishing colonies in the Americas, the Spanish understood that the enslavement of hundreds of people often led to unrest, rebellion, or depopulation of a region, essentially ruining the area for future Spanish settlement. Thus, if there was hope to profit from a region using the area's native peoples as a sustainable labor force, the removal of its indigenous population through the slave trade was discouraged, especially by Crown officials. The Crown actively attempted to curtail the transport of enslaved Indians from the province of Venezuela in 1531. That did not prevent the residents of Venezuela from enslaving Indians completely, however.

Instead, Venezuelan officials used loopholes in Crown laws and ordinances to carry on a limited indigenous slave trade from the very beginning of the colony. The Germans gained a foothold in Spanish America through the powerful and wealthy Welser family, who first dealt in goods and trade with the Orient, but in 1526 expanded to the New World by opening a factory in Santo Domingo.[79] In 1528 the king of Spain awarded the Welsers a contract to conquer and settle the territory of Venezuela.[80] As part of this contract, the first German governor, Antonio de Alfinger, possessed a license permitting the enslavement of any Indians who refused the requerimiento and those purchased publicly from licensed indigenous slave traders. However, the provision included a small caveat: that these indigenous slaves were to be employed only *within* Venezuela, for example, in the very important entradas into the interior.[81] Conquistador Nicolás Féderman soon exploited and ignored this legal loophole.

During his seven-month voyage, in search of El Dorado, Féderman took dozens to a hundred Indians from each settlement that he passed to serve as porters and guides. When the servants were willingly given to him, Féderman rewarded indigenous leaders by releasing their subjects after they reached a new province.[82] On the other hand, when the principal Indians or caciques disobeyed the conquistador, or in other words the requerimiento, he captured as many Indians as he could, especially favoring the detention of a cacique's female relatives.[83] Féderman then divided up the enslaved men and women among his men to serve them during their journey. If the slaves survived the expedition, they would supplement the soldiers' salaries.[84]

Toward the end of Féderman's entrada, he began capturing Indians for export alone. Following an altercation with the Indians of two towns, Paraguana and Tocayo, located to the southwest of Coro on Lake Maracaibo, all the "rebel" Indians fled to a series of small islands located in the center of the lake. These Indians were described by the Spanish as *rancheados*, meaning that they were isolated in these small camps or ranchos away from their homes and villages.[85] Any who left the islands risked immediate enslavement. With the Indians isolated on the islands, the Spanish freely looted their villages and settlements, taking all the gold and goods they could locate.[86] This incident destabilized the entire province, sending many indigenous groups into rebellion and drawing attention to Féderman. Conversely the rebellions provided the Spanish with more Indians to legally enslave and sell.

While the influx of Indian slaves for export temporarily buoyed Venezuela's nascent economy, the Crown and royal officials still hoped for much more from the province. Thus, they sought peaceful relationships with their indigenous neighbors. Féderman's cruelties were publicly denounced after his return to Coro, and he was exiled from the province for four years. At the same time the Crown issued a new order prohibiting the removal of *any* Indians from Venezuela, even on exploratory missions into the interior.[87] Additionally, a new policy made it illegal to take Indian slaves specifically from Paraguana. These Indians, known as *Caquetios* in contrast to their Carib neighbors, received special consideration as Spanish allies, otherwise known as *indios amigos*. The Caquetios then participated in Spanish and later German slave raids against other Indians designated as Caribs. In one such case the Indians designated as Caribs were a group known as the Jirajaras, an enemy of the Caquetios.[88] While the Spanish Crown tried to protect some Indians of Tierra Firme, their allies and conditions on the ground in Venezuela prevented justice for the majority of native peoples. The colonists, both Spanish and German, of Venezuela argued that they depended on the servitude of these Indians, especially when engaging in entradas into the interior. Thus, a local slave trade remained in effect, one that at least some indigenous groups supported and gained agency from.[89]

However, this soon changed. Within months of Féderman's denunciation, other German conquistadors began to turn to slaving as their central means of making a profit, especially as more entradas into the interior failed to discover great stores of gold or silver. From June 1531 to November 1533, Alfinger carried out a second expedition into the interior, ending in his death. Despite Crown policy and recent legislation, Alfinger used Indian slaves to supplement soldiers' meager salaries from the very start of the campaign. Upon reaching Maracaibo, a lake and settlement only forty leagues from Coro, Alfinger captured, branded, and arranged the transport of 222 Indian slaves to Santo Domingo.[90] This being the very beginning of his expedition, he only enslaved these Indians for a quick sale. They never served as conscripted porters or guides.

Alfinger also adopted Féderman's practices of assaulting and seques-
tering Indian villages to acquire both slaves and gold.[91] After attacking a
group called the Pacabueyes, Alfinger constructed a corral in the town of
Tamara where he imprisoned up to two hundred Indians, depriving them
of water and food until their relatives ransomed their release at a hefty price
of slaves and gold.[92] Alfinger's men continued to capture slaves throughout
the entrada, later branding and selling them in both Santo Domingo and
Jamaica, going directly against Crown policy prohibiting the removal of Indians from Welser Venezuela. The same man who shipped the 222 slaves to
Española, González de Leiva, also sold sixty-five Indians (for seven and a half
pesos each) captured during the venture in Jamaica in 1533.[93] For the sale of
these slaves, Leiva failed to pay the royal fifth (the quinto de esclavos), the
crime that the Crown punished him for.[94] As in many other cases, the Crown
was more concerned with payment of taxes than obedience.

Other larger shipments of Indian slaves taken during Alfinger's entrada
began arriving in Santo Domingo in April 1534, only a few months after
its conclusion. The Protector of the Indians, Bishop Bastidas, wrote to the
Crown reporting the arrival of many Indian slaves from the "government of
the Belzares." Bishop Bastidas questioned the legality of the Indians' capture,
but still allowed for their sale, albeit as naborías, not slaves. They each sold
for the very low price of six castellanos (a type of gold coin worth roughly the
same amount as a peso of gold) each. The modest price resulted from their
legal status of naborías, who could not be resold and were required to serve
their Spanish masters for only six years.[95]

The entradas of Alfinger and Féderman amplified the destabilization of
the interior of Venezuela, extending into Nueva Granada, but they were just
the beginning. Indians soon faced a double-pronged entrada conducted by
Nicolás Féderman and Georg Hohermuth von Speyer (Jorge Espira) from
1535 until 1539, the vying missions of Antonio Sedeño and Gerónimo de Ortal
from 1535 to 1536 into Paria and Meta, and the venture of Gonzalo Jiménez
de Quesada from April 1536 to early 1539 deep into Muisca territory.[96] All
these men enslaved hundreds, if not thousands, of indigenous peoples, both
to serve them during their expeditions and to sell afterward. Even Quesada, whose expedition was the most successful of the group, engaged in the
enslavement of Indians to serve as payment for his soldiers.[97] For example,
Quesada prepared an ambush on a group of Indians near present-day Bogotá,
in which they captured up to three hundred women and children who were
divided up among his soldiers.[98]

Féderman returned to Venezuela after the death of his opponent Alfinger, who had banished him from the colony after his first extralegal entrada in 1534. In 1537 he embarked on his second, completely illegal, entrada into the interior of Venezuela and Nueva Granada.[99] Féderman began the expedition by taking 174 Indians from Cabo de Santa Cruz y la San Antonio, shipping them to Santo Domingo. The Indians were branded and evaluated as being worth between eight and six pesos each, depending on their age and size.[100] These slaves could be legally sold, due to yet *another* change in Crown legislation in 1533–1534 that reversed the provision of 1531, reestablishing the legal removal of Indian slaves from Venezuela.[101] Operating within this milieu Féderman took slaves throughout his lengthy voyage into Nueva Granada; how many survived to sell at the end is unknown.[102]

In late 1538 multiple officials reported to King Charles that there were no Indians from which to create Repartimientos in the entire province of Venezuela.[103] According to Bishop Bastidas, the Welsers sold a total of 1,005 indigenous slaves, obtained through "just war," from 1529 forward. From the sale they earned 1,499 pesos.[104] In 1536–1538, when the Welser Company reported slaves obtained through rescate, the sale of 539 indigenous slaves brought in 3,713 pesos.[105] These numbers reflect only sales that were recorded, taxed, and considered legal. Many more were hidden, especially those where indios amigos were sold into slavery or where slave traders sought to avoid paying the quinto de esclavos. Only amplifying the impact of official entradas were the numerous licensed and unlicensed slave raids (originating from Cubagua, Española, Cuba, and Puerto Rico) attacking the coast of Tierra Firme. Exploration into the interior of Tierra Firme went hand in hand with the capture of Indian slaves, both providing compensation and forced collaborators.

Forced Collaborators

As seen in the two prior sections, Spanish explorers and conquistadors continuously dreamed about locating rumored lands of plenty. Each one of their voyages, especially those spanning years and hundreds of miles, necessitated the use of Indian labor. Missions of exploration sought both new sources of indigenous slaves to sell and employed captive Indians. Spanish explorers brought Indian slaves with them to serve as guides, translators, servants, or porters, and captured native peoples had to work as local guides or replace other slaves who had died. Although these men and women played invaluable roles in the conquest and exploration of territories, from Florida and Mexico to present-day Colombia and Venezuela, they were involuntary collaborators and as such received no part in the spoils of victory. In fact, other than stating their presence in many of these voyages, both historians and sixteenth-century Spaniards ignored their impact.

The transport of diverse indigenous slaves during missions of exploration and conquest throughout the 1520s and 1530s further illustrates the magnitude and complexity of the Indian slave trade and its connection to exploration and conquest. Indians were not simply brought from one location (be it Florida, the Lucayos Islands, or further afield) to labor in the central Caribbean islands; many were then taken to a third, perhaps even more distant location. This rapid movement around the Caribbean not only displaced thousands of indigenous peoples multiple times, but also, intriguingly, returned others to their homelands (like the aforementioned Francisco Chicorano).

The Crown understood, from the very beginning of the ventures, that indigenous slaves were indispensable for the maintenance of Spanish exploratory missions. Enslaved Indians were an integral tool and served as part of initial forces journeying to new lands.[106] The Spanish supplemented these unwilling intermediaries with captive local guides and translators. In recognition of the necessity of local slaves, the Crown gave conquistadors license to capture any Indians who defied the requerimiento, basically following the laws of "just war."[107] These slaves would serve as local guides.

And Florida was still inspiring explorers and adventurers to try their hand at the territory. Even though the slave trader and conquistador Ayllón's colonization attempt ended in disaster, others were still drawn to Florida. One such man was Hernando de Soto, a slave trader and owner of a slave ship operating in Central America, who hoped to locate another Inca Empire in North America.[108] Soto was interested not in colonizing Florida, but rather in seeing all that it had to offer. And his search was carried out on the backs of thousands of Indian slaves and unwilling allies. Soto's very first preparation for his endeavor was to secure Indian slaves from Florida to serve as his guides. Not finding any suitable candidates in Cuba or Española, Soto sent Juan de Añasco, Francisco Maldonado, and Juan López to Florida to capture two or three Indians.[109] In Cuba, the Indians were shown items of interest to the Spanish, including gold and corn, to see if they recognized them and could lead the explorers directly to the goods.[110] Nor was this unusual. In 1539 as part of regular voyage preparations into the interior of Tierra Firme, Pascual de Andagoya contacted officials of the Casa de la Contratación (the Sevillan headquarters for all colonial investment, taxes, and expeditions) to secure indigenous slaves from present-day Colombia. Fulfilling his request, the Casa de la Contratación located several slaves, paid their owners for their freedom, and delivered them to Andagoya.[111] These examples underscore the importance of Indian slaves to Spanish conquistadors both during their missions and while preparing for them.

In May 1539 Soto landed somewhere near Tampa Bay. Upon his arrival in Florida, Soto and his men marched inland, searching for the indigenous town of Apalache, intrigued by reports of its abundance from Cabeza de Vaca, one of the few survivors of the Narváez expedition.[112] As part of his royal contract Soto had a license to legally enslave Indians who opposed the requerimiento and also barter for those already held as slaves by indigenous leaders. But he exceeded these lawful avenues of indigenous enslavement by leaps and bounds throughout his time in Florida. Soto did not wait for indigenous provocation or the deterioration of peaceful negotiations. Nor did he only take Indian slaves that he absolutely needed for his expedition. Instead Soto began with violence, even in situations when an indigenous leader cooperated with him.[113]

The violence he perpetuated implies that he was not seeking slaves to sell at the end of his mission because he would accept nothing less than the discovery of a grand civilization. He was not thinking of small profits he could make by selling Indian slaves; he was simply using the captives as he acquired them. Even indigenous leaders who cooperated were not exempt from captivity and conscription. For example, the cacica of Cofitachequi gave Soto her best pearls (five or six kilos), all the food he requested, canoes to help his men cross the nearby river, shelter at her settlement, and instructions on how to reach the next town, but all that was not enough.[114] Following four or five days of residence in Cofitachequi, Soto and his men demanded hundreds of porters and slaves for the next leg of his journey.[115] The cacica was not willing to supply these men and women, leading her to flee to the nearby foothills.[116] Not willing to accept defeat, and needing the cacica to supply him with his unwilling allies, Soto and his men pursued the cacica, eventually taking her prisoner.[117]

The cacica still managed to regain her freedom, fleeing the group as they crossed the Appalachian Mountains, taking advantage of the Spaniards' disorganization and her familiarity with the rough terrain. Nor was she the only captive to do so. Following her escape, the cacica encountered a multiethnic group of slaves who also had deserted the Soto expedition. This group, illustrating the diversity of slavery in the early Spanish Empire, included a black slave by the name of Gómez, an Indian slave from Cuba, and a Moorish or Barbary slave. Together this motley crew returned to Cofitachequi from where the cacica and Gómez, whom she took as a lover, continued to govern the province.[118] At times expeditions of exploration provided opportunities for slaves to reclaim their freedom and agency.

Besides the cacica, Hernando de Soto conscripted and enslaved many more Indians, with some estimates in the thousands. He and his men required so many unwilling intermediaries because of the high mortality rate of those taken captive. While disease and starvation took many, the horrific treatment they endured, with some even being thrown to the dogs if they gave incorrect directions, resulted in the deaths of hundreds more. For example, early on in his journey Soto captured nearly 350 Indians from the indigenous settlement Aguacaleyquen. Despite this huge number, by the time Soto reached Cofitachequi in the spring of 1540, the majority had perished from exhaustion and exposure as a result of Soto's failure to provide the Indians from south Florida with suitable clothing for the winter in Georgia and the Carolinas.[119] Needing to replenish these lost porters and guides led to his conflict with the cacica of Cofitachequi. The pattern continued throughout Soto's reconnaissance of the present-day U.S. Southeast, with indigenous groups either fleeing from the Spanish or welcoming them into their settlements only to experience violence and enslavement in return. In the majority of Soto's expedition record, the explorers were silent as to how many Indians were taken from any one village, only saying that "they detained or were given many Indians."[120] In tales of battle, chroniclers gave clear numbers only of how many Indians were enslaved, not of those who were killed.

In the fall of 1540 a dearth of indigenous slaves and porters brought about one of Soto's most violent encounters at Mabila, near present-day Selma, Alabama.[121] Here, despite an initial friendly welcome from cacique Tascalusa, Soto's demands for Indian servants and slaves quickly produced tension between the two groups that exploded into an all-night battle.[122] Upon finding themselves trapped in a palisaded settlement, Soto and his men fled but soon returned, placing the village under siege and setting it ablaze. As the inhabitants of Mabila tried to escape the fire, the Spanish attacked them, killing the majority and enslaving others, including at least twenty women.[123] Some of these slaves, and others taken during the final months of the expedition, were sold in the slave markets of Pánuco and Mexico City. From there the slaves were taken to both Cuba and Guatemala. Here is an excellent example of the multidirectional character of the early Indian slave trade.[124]

By following the trail of terror produced by Soto and his men, the importance of possessing Indian slaves on lengthy expeditions of exploration, reconnaissance, and plundering is underscored. Soto needed them to carry his supplies, to guide his men through difficult territories, and to translate. Just because these men and women, for the most part, remain unnamed does not diminish the larger role they played in Soto's expedition. Without forced intermediaries Soto's expedition would have faltered much earlier.[125] Accounts of Soto's journey also show the Spanish dehumanization of America's indigenous populations. Despite the crucial roles played by his captive Indians, Soto treated them with the utmost cruelty, casting them off as soon as they lost their usefulness, replacing them with newly obtained captives. For Soto these Indian slaves were little more than tools or commodities, albeit ones of great importance.

For the few Indian and African slaves who were able to use the arduous journeys to gain their freedom, participation in missions of exploration was invaluable. While we possess concrete evidence of only a few Indians, and one African slave, achieving liberty during the Soto mission, it is likely that more succeeded in escaping the Spanish during exploratory ventures. The same upheaval that promoted the enslavement of thousands of Indians also created an opportunity in which a few lucky and motivated captives could attain freedom. In this case Soto's lack of care for his forced collaborators gave them opportunities to escape.

The best examples of Indian slaves gaining liberty through voyages of exploration include Francisco Chicorano and an Algonquin Indian named Luis. Luis, like Chicorano before him, lived and traveled extensively with the Spanish as a slave, becoming someone they perceived as their ally. Spanish slavers captured young Luis in 1559 or 1560 from Jacán, a territory encompassing the Chesapeake Bay. Following his capture, Luis was taken to New Spain where he met Pedro Menéndez de Avilés—the future conquistador of Florida—who was very interested in the boy as a guide and ally. In Mexico, he was baptized and received the name of Luis after the viceroy of New Spain, Luis de Velasco.[126] After his baptism Luis accompanied Menéndez to Spain in 1566 where he was presented to King Philip II. Within a year Luis returned to the New World and became an integral part of Menéndez's plan to settle the Chesapeake, which the conquistador believed would lead directly to the Pacific Ocean or the South Sea.

Menéndez's plans for settlement were usurped by those of the Jesuits, who also chose Luis's territory for a special religious settlement in February 1570.[127] By 1568 priests had already set up missions with the Calusa, Tequesta, Timucua, Ais, and Guale Indians of Florida.

However, the Jesuit priests continued to report that, regardless of their ardent efforts to convert Florida's natives, the Indians simply refused to renounce some of their most pagan customs. The Jesuits complained about the migratory nature of Florida's inhabitants, arguing that it prevented them from staying in contact with their native charges. The priests believed that if the Indians were forced to settle in towns, their preaching could then be effective. They also believed that these towns needed to be kept separate from secular colonists who, they argued, were bad influences.[128] To put this strategy to the test, a group of eight Jesuits journeyed to the Chesapeake Bay area (very close to the eventual site of the English colony of Jamestown and Powhatan's village) to establish another mission in September 1570.[129]

As with prior missions of settlement, the Jesuits brought with them an Indian slave, Luis, to serve as the group's guide and translator. Beyond Luis, the Jesuits brought little else to help them in case of conflict, even refusing Menéndez's offer of soldiers.[130] Once they arrived in Jacán the Jesuits discovered that their trust in Luis was misplaced, as had been Ayllón's faith in Chicorano. Upon his return to his native lands, Luis deserted the Jesuits, leaving them alone and without provisions. He returned to his people, perhaps explaining to them the Spanish predilection for native enslavement. Regardless of what he conveyed to his family, it resulted in hostile interactions between the natives of Jacán and the Jesuits. Don Luis's people refused to trade with the Jesuits, leaving them to search out other indigenous groups (often located much farther from their settlement) to barter copper and tin for corn and grain.[131] For a full year the Jesuits waited in vain for an expected Spanish supply ship and sent several messages to Luis begging him for his help and censuring him for abandoning his Christian ways.[132]

Meanwhile, Luis seemed to be plotting against the Jesuits. It appears that Luis wanted to prevent the formation of a permanent Spanish settlement in his territory, and with the Jesuits unable to leave, he and his family planned a brutal attack on their camp. On the morning of February 4, 1571, Luis and a large group of Indians assaulted the camp. They clubbed the Jesuits to death and beheaded others.[133] After the massacre, Luis divided up the Jesuits' clothing and sacramental objects, including bibles, crucifixes, and chalices, among the local Indians. Hence, when the first relief mission finally arrived in Jacán, the Spanish witnessed Indians wearing Jesuits' vestments. The silver chalice was given to solidify an alliance with another important cacique who resided several leagues farther inland.[134] The only survivor of the attack was a child, Alonso, who had helped the priests during their journey from Santa Elena to the Chesapeake. Though Alonso escaped the massacre, he was kept as a prisoner by Luis's uncle for over a year before being ransomed to the Spanish in July 1572. The boy was likely spared due to his youth, as it was customary for the Indians of the Chesapeake to adopt the children of their enemies following their defeat. Following Alonso's rescue, the Spanish learned the tragedy that had befallen the Jesuit settlement of Jacán.[135]

The massacre ended both the Spanish colony on the Chesapeake and the Jesuit presence in Florida.[136] A willing and loyal Indian ally could bring success to a Spanish mission, but a hostile intermediary could harness their agency to destroy a nascent colony. Luis and Chicorano used their knowledge of Spanish culture and practices, as well as the larger Atlantic system, to exact revenge on their former captors and to cause the failure of at least two Spanish colonies in North America. Nevertheless, and regardless of the risks involved, the Spanish depended on their unwilling collaborators for everything from information and guidance to carrying supplies. Despite the successes of a few actors (Chicorano, Luis, and the cacica of Cofitachequi), most of the Spaniards' forced intermediaries did not overpower their masters or secure their freedom. Spanish conquistadors explored the Americas on the backs of indigenous slaves and captives.

*   *   *

From their part in motivating voyages of exploration to new territories, to their presence in expeditions as guides, porters, and translators, and finally to their role as consolation prizes at the end of a failed expedition, one cannot underestimate the importance of Indian captives during the early years of conquest and colonization throughout the Americas. Indigenous slaves were inextricably connected to the processes of conquest and exploration. Their significance is highlighted, especially that of translators and guides, in the Spaniards' persistent return and use of enslaved Indians in missions of conquest and settlement, despite the dangers inherent in bringing these Indians back to their ancestral lands.

In a few cases some indigenous peoples were able to harness their power, using the Spanish not only to return to their lands, but also to exact revenge on their former captors. Previously enslaved Indians also shared their knowledge of the Spanish with other indigenous groups, for example, the Taíno Indian who helped to thwart Ponce de León's conquest of Florida by keeping the cacique of the Calusa from forming an alliance with the Spanish. In other cases, many Indian slaves simply used the trials and disorganization of journeys of exploration to escape their masters, finding refuge in foreign indigenous societies, as seen with the Soto entrada. Still others chose to minimally help the Spanish and, by allying with them, succeeded in escaping some of their worst abuses. Spanish voyages of discovery, and how Indian slaves at times succeeded in manipulating the journeys to their purposes, only add to the larger story of the Indian slave trade. While the tale is chiefly one of forced movement, migration, and displacement, it is also one of opportunity, survival, and empowerment for a few indigenous peoples.

It is still true that the majority of Indian slaves taken by the Spanish were unable to overcome their situation and suffered in unimaginable ways through incredibly lengthy treks across difficult terrain (or weeks at sea), during which they received little sustenance and were forced to carry heavy burdens of trade goods, corn, and other materials. Those who survived these trials often found only more suffering at the end of the journey, as they were sold into slavery far from their native lands, facing displacement and years of slave labor in distant and unfamiliar territories. Many Indians were displaced not once but twice through Spanish desires of conquest and exploration. For example, Indians enslaved in Mexico were taken to Cuba and then transported to Florida by the Narváez venture. In another instance Indians taken from the coast of present-day Virginia traveled all the way to Mexico, then Spain, and finally back to the New World. At times pre-contact trade or kinship networks made these migrations less traumatic, while other indigenous groups had no previous knowledge or contact with one another. This diversity in the experience of slavery further complicates the story of movement, displacement, and creation in the Indian slave trade.

CHAPTER 5

Granjerías de Indios

The Business of Indigenous Slavery

As initial conquest enterprises, from Cubagua's pearl fisheries to the gold mines of Española and Cuba, decreased in profitability, Spaniards searched for new lands, new opportunities, and new sources of labor. The indigenous slave trade helped inspire and promote the pursuit of new territories. As the trade evolved, encompassing new territories and peoples, it transformed into something new. By the late 1520s the Indian slave trade was an enterprise of its own. Many colonists viewed it as one of the few avenues to make a profit, albeit a limited one as most Indian slaves sold for very low prices. Most slaving armadas were organized and funded by elite members of colonial society who reserved half or a quarter of profits from each license or armada for themselves.[1] Others looked to the slave trade as a temporary occupation, something to sustain them until a better opportunity arose. In many ways this was an extension of the taking of slaves as "consolation prizes" in failed missions of conquest and discovery.

Like their predecessors, they too pushed the boundaries of empire in search of new sources of Indian slaves, in the process exploring the interiors of Mexico, Nicaragua, Honduras, Guatemala, Venezuela, Colombia, and other regions of Tierra Firme. These were not new discoveries, but the Spanish slavers and merchants had new interests when they returned to Tierra Firme in the 1520s and 1530s. In previous decades most slavers and slave voyages were sponsored by officials and wealthy landowners, like Lucás Vazquéz de Ayllón. These slavers received instructions to capture slaves for a particular island, mine, or fishery. By the late 1520s, slavers were no longer focused on the labor they (or their sponsors) could harness from captured Indians on sugar plantations or in gold mines or during missions of exploration. Instead, they were more concerned with the profits, though small, they would receive from selling the Indians in colonial markets.[2]

But where would these slaves go if the core areas of the early empire were faltering economically? Many were destined for the most recently encountered territories, especially after the Spanish located the fantastic wealth of the Inca Empire. Many of the captives taken from Central America were destined for the Andes. Others though were still meant for the islands of Española, Cuba, and Puerto Rico, where they were put to work on nascent sugar plantations. With a consistent demand for indigenous slaves across the empire, many merchants viewed the Indian slave trade as its own business. Slavers removed Indians from less profitable regions of the empire, sending them to newly vital areas where there was a demand for indigenous captives.

The growth of the indigenous slave trade as its own economic venture mirrored both the decline of some of the earliest colonial endeavors and the rise of new industries and colonies. By following the slave trade, one witnesses evolving colonial economies. In the 1520s the gold mines of Puerto Rico and Española were becoming less productive, with sugar plantations largely replacing the futile search for gold. In Cuba, copper mining was superseding gold extraction.[3] In the late 1520s cattle ranching also emerged on Española. Meanwhile, in the Pearl Islands, as older fisheries in Cubagua produced fewer pearls, new oyster beds were discovered in Coche, Margarita, and Cabo de la Vela. All these various discoveries and changes shifted the sources for and destinations of newly captured indigenous slaves.

These Indian slaves, wherever they were delivered, were both replacement laborers for rapidly diminishing Taíno populations of the Greater Antilles, and merchandise for new slaving entrepreneurs. In this economy, slavers and officials made profits by selling more than captured Indians. They could also sell slaving licenses to fellow colonists. The Crown even used slaving licenses as currency to pay administrators, including religious officials, throughout the Americas. Those involved in the inspection and sale of Indians also profited. For example, the official who declared an Indian to be a legal slave and branded them as such received one gold *tomín*.[4] As Indian slaves were increasingly commodified, Spaniards referred to their indigenous captives in new, less humane ways, as piezas. In earlier transactions Spaniards recorded their indigenous slaves as *indios esclavos*, as slaves, yes, but also as people. As the years went by, Spanish colonists referred to their Indian slaves more regularly as piezas.

The term "pieza," which originated during the African slave trade to Portugal, originally referred to one enslaved, healthy adult between the ages of fifteen and forty.[5] As the slave trade evolved, measuring or commodifying slaves as piezas, or units, allowed for merchants to distinguish between adult slaves and children or the infirm and elderly. Young or old slaves were partial piezas, a half or even a third.[6] "Pieza" was most often used when discussing cargos of slaves that included a substantial number of children. Because the indigenous slave trade included many children from the start, as they were preferred by Spanish colonists for household service, it makes sense that Iberian slavers quickly transferred the African terminology to the Caribbean trade in Indians.

Concurrent with the change in vocabulary was a decrease in the number of Indians taken as naborías, even perpetual naborías, with a correspondent rise in the branding of captured Indians as slaves. Because Indian slaves could be resold, they remained potential commodities or experienced terminal commodification, thereby impeding the process of resocializing, as naborías did upon entering an encomienda.[7] By the 1530s Indian slaves were treated more and more like African slaves, as property. In this new climate, traditional debates surrounding the morality of Indian slavery, which had occupied the Crown and officials throughout the second and third decades of colonization, began to fade. Instead, leaders focused on the legality of indigenous slavery, including issues regarding jurisdiction, the branding of slaves, and taxation. These conflicts help to reveal the chaotic nature of the Spanish colonial experiment in the early sixteenth century, where the line between legal and illegal was ambiguous and fluctuating.[8] The indigenous slave trade reveals the limits of the Spanish colonial government. This was not a lawless frontier, but a developing maritime periphery where power and legality were constantly changing.

Yet within the Indian slave trade we also witness the beginnings of the royal consolidation of power. In fact, the range and scope of both legal and illegal indigenous slaving raids implicate the Crown in many cases, at the very least for implicitly supporting the slaving armadas with legally questionable licenses. Here again the drive for profits trumped the moral imperative at the highest levels of Spanish colonial government. The Crown legislated against the Indian slave trade only when it negatively impacted their own proceeds. For example, the Crown outlawed the taking of indigenous slaves from New Spain in 1526, only after it became clear that the possibilities for wealth in New Spain greatly surpassed those of the smaller, less populated Caribbean islands.[9]

Competition over control of the indigenous slave trade, and the Indian slaves, was a central concern for merchants and officials as high as the Crown by the mid-sixteenth century. At this point most colonists and officials relied on Indian laborers and slaves, making the indigenous slave trade one of the largest businesses in the New World. The sale and transport of Indian slaves, an enterprise evolving since the fifteenth century, was central to the Spanish Empire by the 1520s and 1530s. To explore the intricacies of the trade, this chapter examines two detailed episodes, each involving the prosecution of high-level colonial officials for the enslavement of thousands of Indians. Each case delves into how the Indian slave trade functioned, revealing the limits of the enterprise and its relationship to both legal and political spheres.

Exchanging Indians for Livestock

After the surrender of Tenochtitlan, and much of the Mexica Empire, Cortés and his fellow conquistadors took indigenous slaves from across central Mexico, shipping the majority to the labor-starved Caribbean islands. Thousands more slaves were taken during the ensuing conquests of present-day Guatemala, Honduras, and Nicaragua. In addition to the slaves captured during war, Spaniards also purchased or traded for Indian slaves already held captive throughout the region. Through either method thousands of Indians were enslaved and removed from Central America from 1521 until the 1550s. Las Casas places the number as high as three million, though another Franciscan friar, Toribio de Benavente, gives a more modest estimate of two hundred thousand Indian slaves.[10] Given that as many as twenty thousand captives were removed from one town alone, Tlaxcala, in only one year, 1537, and that Cortés purchased one hundred Indian slaves in a single day, the higher estimates seem more accurate.[11]

Either way, the impact on the region was immense. Perhaps this explains why the king passed a mandate, or *real cédula*, making it illegal to capture any new slaves from New Spain in November 1526. The law also made it illegal to *herrar* (brand) and transport a slave outside of New Spain, even making the offense punishable by death or the confiscation of a person's wealth.[12] Finally the decree required that residents of New Spain bring their indigenous slaves to the royal court, to prove that they had been enslaved legally, returning those who were enslaved unjustly to their homelands. As with many other decrees issued by the faraway king of Spain, the new ordinance did little to curb actual practices on the ground in the Caribbean or New Spain, at least for the first several years. In 1529 the bishop of Mexico, Juan de Zumárraga, made one of the first attempts to enforce the law, bringing a case against two high-profile officials, Nuño de Guzmán (governor of the province of Pánuco and president of the royal court in Tenochtitlan) and licenciado Juan Ortiz de Matienzo (judge of the royal court in Tenochtitlan).[13] The bishop accused the two officials of granting licenses to enslave Indians in Pánuco well after the new law passed in 1526.[14]

The cases against Guzmán and Matienzo underscore the competitive nature of the Indian slave trade while also revealing tensions between conquistadors, royal officials, religious officials, and the Crown. While some slaving and transportation of Indians to the Greater Antilles was beneficial to the Crown's purse (in providing labor for developing sugar ingenios and cattle ranches, for example), the removal of too many indigenous peoples would impede the development of local industries in New Spain. Specifically, both the Crown and local leaders sought wealth from tribute provided by the region's huge indigenous population. In the case of Pánuco, officials in central New Spain wanted to limit the removal of Pánuco's indigenous populations to the Caribbean islands, since the province served as a source of enslaved Indians for Mexico City. Several residents of the settlement claimed that three to four thousand slaves were taken from Pánuco and delivered to Mexico City only days before Guzmán took up his post.[15] Beyond agricultural pursuits, these slaves were also likely employed in the search for mineral wealth.[16]

But local royal officials had more reasons to oppose Nuño de Guzmán than economic. Guzmán's appointment as governor of Pánuco effectively took power of the province from Cortés and his entourage in Mexico City. Pánuco was a stronghold for pro-Cortés sentiment and the arrival of a new, Crown-appointed leader threatened the region's traditional elite and power structure, much of which depended on personal favors from Cortés.[17] Most witnesses who later testified against Guzmán opposed both his leadership and slave raiding, citing how they had suffered, worst of all losing control of their encomiendas, during his reign in Pánuco. Only a few days after Guzmán assumed power in Santisteban (the capital and port city of Pánuco), he arrested official Lope de Sayavedra for mismanaging the estates of deceased persons.[18] Sayavedra later served as a vocal witness against Guzmán. Even Bishop Zumárraga, who prepared the accusations against Guzmán in 1529, was a well-known enemy of the governor, publicly claiming that Guzmán held a vendetta against Cortés from their time in Cuba together. According to Zumárraga, this animosity explained why Guzmán attacked supporters of Cortés, or those to whom he granted encomiendas.[19] It is possible the entire suit against Guzmán had little to do with his abuses of power or treatment of Pánuco's Indians, and much more to do with larger issues of economic and political competition in New Spain. Often these hidden motivations were the real impetus behind humanitarian legislation, despite the consistent veneer of moral arguments against Indian abuse. The case against Guzmán was a fight over control of indigenous labor and Indian slaves, not a fight for justice. Regardless, under Guzmán's leadership the indigenous slave trade in Pánuco exploded, sending Huastecs (the native inhabitants of Pánuco), Mexicans, Otomís, and Chichimecs (all neighboring indigenous groups) across the Caribbean.

While both the Crown and leaders in Tenochtitlan had reasons to limit the indigenous slave trade in Pánuco, the actual residents of the province had every reason to encourage it. The region possessed few natural resources and absolutely no mineral wealth. From the very beginning the only commodity readily available to residents of Pánuco was the province's Indian population (hence, the early transport and sale of Pánuco's indigenous slaves to Mexico City).[20] The idea of expanding the trade of Indians to the Caribbean, particularly in exchange for much-needed livestock, was appealing to many Spanish colonists in the region and perhaps was even suggested by them, as Guzmán claimed in his defense. Santisteban's small Spanish population, already faced with limited opportunities, likely found themselves in an even more perilous situation after Guzmán's initial attacks on the inhabitant's encomienda grants. They would have eagerly sought new ways to support themselves.

Upon his arrival in Pánuco, Guzmán removed all Indians from their encomenderos, placing them under his rule in the name of the Crown. He then explained that he would only return the Indians to their encomenderos after they provided documentation proving their legal claim to the encomiendas. To be legal the encomienda grants needed to come from the Crown; therefore, grants issued by Cortés would not be recognized. The majority of encomenderos in Pánuco either did not possess documentation for their encomiendas or held Cortés-appointed grants.[21] So most of Pánuco's residents lost their encomiendas along with their status and income. For example, Guzmán confiscated seventy commended Indians from Cristóbal de Quevedo, a *regidor* (an elected official). Soon thereafter, Quevedo lost all his property and was convicted for "crimes against the government."[22]

Guzmán then ordered all the province's caciques to gather in Santisteban and to bring gold, clothing, and Indian slaves as tribute for the Crown. At the meeting Guzmán made it clear that the caciques were not beholden to their encomenderos, at least for thirty days pending the demonstration of legal titles by their embattled encomenderos. Guzmán left the gathering with many indigenous slaves that he then sent to Española and Cuba. In exchange he received a shipment of cows, goats, and horses.[23] Horses and cattle were particularly valuable early on in colonization. In this case, fifteen Huastec slaves equaled one cow, and one horse was exchanged for twenty Indian slaves.[24]

This first transaction was one of the few legal shipments of indigenous slaves from Pánuco since the Indians sold were already held as slaves by their caciques. Spanish colonists could still legally purchase and trade for previously enslaved and branded Indians. A provision signed in Burgos in 1528 stated, "Of the new lands: Santa Marta, Tierra Firme, Higueras, Yucatan, Nueva Granada, Pánuco, Rio de Palmas you can traffic in Indian slaves already held by caciques as slaves."[25] And there were plenty of enslaved Indians in Mesoamerica as indigenous groups across the region practiced slavery. Indians were enslaved through war or as tribute fulfillment. Slavery was also a punishment for certain crimes, most commonly theft.[26] Slaves were distinguished from other members of society by their dress, hairstyle, the privileges they had, and their living conditions.[27] An exception was the Indians of Nicaragua who branded their slaves. They made cuts in the slaves' faces or arms and then rubbed charred and ground pine into the wounds. After the cuts healed, black scars remained.[28] The vagueness of indigenous slaving and branding made it easy for Spanish slavers to claim as a slave anyone who had previously been held as a slave, regardless of their actual legal status. The very existence of this loophole in slave law, nullifying part of the real cédula of 1526 that outlawed the removal of *any* indigenous slaves from New Spain, showed that the Crown was opposed only to indigenous slavery that endangered the royal purse. It also underscores the legal ambiguity of the indigenous slave trade.

Following the loading of his first ships of legally enslaved Indians, Guzmán issued slaving licenses to the residents of Santisteban. The licenses granted each colonist the authority to capture and sell between twenty and thirty slaves taken during an entrada into the interior of the province. The entrada's purpose was to attack the Chichimecs of Río de las Palmas, who had recently conducted multiple raids on Spanish settlements.[29] Colonists providing a horse for the expedition received larger licenses, allowing them to capture and sell up to thirty slaves, while those traveling on foot could take only twenty.[30] Guzmán also issued larger grants to higher-ranking members of Pánuco's society, allowing them to capture anywhere from three hundred to one thousand Indian slaves. Everyone was involved in the slaving business. The entrada into Rio de las Palmas lasted four to five months, ending with the capture of three hundred Indian slaves legitimized through the doctrine of "just war." Cristóbal de Quevedo witnessed the loading of the slaves into a small *pataje* (a small boat) with room only to stand. The pataje journeyed ninety leagues from Santisteban to Cuba.[31] The slaves in this one pataje were the only Indians legally captured and enslaved under Guzmán's governorship.

However, they were not the only slaves taken by Guzmán and the residents of Pánuco. Thousands more were enslaved through illegal slave raids. In the span of two years, sixteen or seventeen ships (though a witness, Lope de Sayavedra, puts the number as high as twenty-one) sailed from Santisteban filled with indigenous slaves.[32] Of these numerous vessels, at least two carried one thousand or more slaves, including those belonging to merchants Miguel de Ibarra and Juan de Urrutia.[33] Many others carried between one hundred and four hundred slaves each, including those belonging to Alonso Valiente (400), Juan de Cordero (120), Alonso de Zuazo (200), Cristóbal de Bezos (400), and Quintero (250). Of the slaves carried by these ships, Guzmán claimed one-third of the profits from their sale.[34] For other boats, Guzmán expected to take the profit from the entire cargo or at least half; for example, he claimed the entire profit from Sancho de Caniego's load of two hundred slaves. However, Guzmán did not hold a stake in all the cargos. Many other ships were operated by independent merchants, like the vessels belonging to Cuban residents Duero (200) and Comacho (350).[35] These slavers kept all the proceeds from the Indian slaves' sale. See Table 3 for a more complete list of slaves taken from Santisteban in 1528.

Table 3. Slaves Taken from Santisteban in 1528

Slaver	Estimate of number of Indians transported
Nuño de Guzmán (removes slaves from Pánuco encomiendas)	At least 70 Indian slaves exchanged for livestock in Española
Nuño de Guzmán (ships Chichimecs captured in "just war")	300 Indian slaves to Cuba
Miguel de Ibarra	1,000 Indian slaves
Juan de Urrutia	1,000 Indian slaves
Alonso Valiente	400 Indian slaves
Juan de Cordero	120 Indian slaves
Alonso de Zuazo	200 Indian slaves
Cristóbal de Bezos	400 Indian slaves
Quintero	250 Indian slaves
Duero	200 Indian slaves
Comacho	350 Indian slaves
	Total known: 4,290

Guzmán claimed that the Indians enslaved during his tenure were already branded as slaves by their respective caciques.[36] While these slaves could have been legally traded if they were indeed slaves before Guzmán's arrival, witnesses claimed that many caciques presented free Indians as slaves. In one such case a cacique of an interior village forced a free, young, female Indian to take the mantle of slavery. The Spaniards recognized the deception because Lope de Sayavedra had previously traded with the girl. Sayavedra explained this to Guzmán, telling him that she must have accepted the mark of slavery only under the threat of death. Despite Sayavedra's testimony, Guzmán proclaimed the girl to be a legal slave and she was sent to the islands alongside thousands of others.[37]

And she was not the only questionably taken Indian slave. Other caciques took advantage of the Spanish approach to capture slaves from enemy territories to sell to the Spanish. Some caciques even offered up other caciques as slaves for the Spaniards, removing many indigenous leaders from their territories.[38] Indigenous leaders conducting the raids benefited from the elimination of competitors, demonstrating how some Indians were able to take advantage of the Spanish presence (and conjunction of structures of the conquest period) to achieve their own goals and gain agency.

So how did these improperly obtained slaves get through the process of inspection before their sale? Here Guzmán is directly implicated. Under Guzmán the process of public inspections and interviews, which preceded the actual branding of a slave, failed or were conducted improperly. Guzmán, or his mayordomo Pérez de Gijón, handled most of the inspections and brandings, with both being accused of accepting bribes and ignoring testimony that contradicted enslavement.[39] Once declared a legal slave, the Indian was branded on the left side of their face with the letter R, standing for either *real marca* (royal mark) or rescate.[40] Those captured in war received a G for guerra. The process of branding transformed the Indians into commodities for the residents of Pánuco and the Greater Antilles.

As late as April 1529, only a few months before the start of the investigation into Guzmán's actions, several more ships laden with indigenous slaves departed Santisteban for Española and Cuba. One such vessel, owned by Alonso Valiente, carried 120 slaves while two other boats (belonging to Pedro de Mina and Miguel de Ibarra) each sailed with a cargo of three hundred. As with earlier shipments, Guzmán possessed a stake in many of the slave cargos, including three hundred of the 330 slaves that sailed on Juan Perez de Gijón's vessel. Other ships held larger numbers of slaves, including Juan de Urrutia's craft, which sailed with eight hundred souls aboard.[41] At least two

Table 4. Slave Shipments from Santisteban in April 1529

Slaver	Estimate of number of Indians transported
Alonso Valiente	150 Indian slaves
Pedro de Mina	300 Indian slaves
Miguel de Ibarra	300 Indian slaves
Juan Perez de Gijón	330 slaves to Santo Domingo
Juan de Urrutia	800 Indian slaves
	Total known: 1,880

witnesses testified to both seeing Urrutia's ship at dock in Santisteban filled with slaves and also observing the ship at its destination, Santo Domingo. One witness, Juan Pardo, was surprised to see that nearly half of the slaves had survived the journey.[42] Since he was surprised at the high survival rate, we can infer that it was normal for high numbers of slaves to die en route, even on a relatively short journey. Pardo also saw Matienzo in Santisteban filling two ships with slaves in April 1529. However, Matienzo's luck did not hold, as only one of the vessels made it to Santo Domingo; the other sank during the voyage and most of the slaves aboard drowned.[43] See Table 4 for a detailed list of slave shipments in April 1529.

At the end of his term in Pánuco, officials accused Guzmán of enslaving and transporting up to twelve thousand Indians, the majority of whom were enslaved illegally or at the very least questionably.[44] Bishop Zumárraga estimated that, by 1529, at the start of Guzmán's trial, approximately nine thousand Indian slaves had been removed from his jurisdiction in exchange for livestock.[45] With so many Indians being taken from the province in such a short time frame, the region suffered a huge decrease in its native population. Some witnesses stated that, as a result of the entradas carried out by Guzmán, there were few indigenous peoples left in the region, with remaining Indians fleeing to the mountains in fear after witnessing allied Indians being enslaved.[46]

This might or might not have been an exaggeration, as it is impossible to know exactly how many Indians were enslaved, legally or illegally, under Guzmán. Incomplete documentation presents a significant obstacle here. In this case, there was an eight-month gap in the registries of ships departing from Santisteban, for which one can only estimate the number of slaves and vessels that set sail for the Caribbean islands.[47] Also, the witnesses who accused Guzmán of transporting enslaved Indians from New Spain to the Caribbean provided a variety of estimates for the total number of captives exported, ranging from as low as 3,441 to as high as 12,000. While the real number likely lies somewhere in the middle, it is difficult to choose which witness to believe. Motivations of different witnesses and royal officials to either minimize or exaggerate Guzmán's actions make many testimonies problematic.

Digging deeper, it is clear that many had personal reasons to attack Guzmán. As discussed, Pánuco was a stronghold for pro-Cortés sentiment. So the arrival of a new Crown-appointed leader threatened the region's elite, many of whom depended on personal favors from Cortés.[48] This included Lope de Sayavedra, who was arrested for mismanaging estates of deceased persons, and he lost his Cortés-granted encomienda only days after Guzmán took power.[49] It is possible that some witnesses inflated the numbers of slaves taken in order to delegitimize Guzmán, perhaps even in an effort to regain their properties and commended Indians. But personal grievances do not change the facts that the indigenous slave trade exploded for a brief period in Pánuco and that the trade produced an influx of livestock to the area, including mules, horses, cattle, sheep, goats, and swine.[50] The entry of so much livestock prompted the growth of profitable cattle herds and ranches by the middle of the sixteenth century in northern Mexico.[51] The trade also produced a welcome surge of indigenous slaves for Cuba. Governor Manuel de Rojas was still referencing the arrangement five years later, in 1534, requesting its reestablishment as the island faced a dearth of slaves.[52]

While the consequences of these slaving expeditions were negative for many of Pánuco's residents, the fate of the slaves taken to the islands was even worse, as most of them died within their first year of residence if they survived the journey to the islands at all. According to the witness Diego de Padriera, many enslaved Indians died before reaching their final destinations, some even throwing themselves overboard and drowning prior to leaving Santisteban.[53] Here is one of the most visceral examples of how the indigenous slave trade impacted Indian captives. Some literally chose suicide by drowning over removal from their homeland and an uncertain future as a Spanish slave. One can only imagine the fear and pain that led to this decision.

Despite the upheaval that Guzmán's slaving expeditions caused in Pánuco, he did not have to pay for his misdeeds. Instead the Crown authorized him to assemble an army of conquest in May 1529 to pacify the province of Nueva Galicia.[54] Perhaps the Crown was willing to overlook his abuses of power in Pánuco in order to remove Cortés's influence from New Spain, as he had in Santisteban. Or it may have been in the Crown's interest to allow the removal of Indians from Pánuco, a province with no mines or other economic pursuits to employ the large indigenous population. Whatever the reason, Guzmán went on to serve as the first president of the Audiencia of Mexico from 1529 to 1533.[55] He also continued to questionably enslave thousands of Indians during his conquest and exploration of Nueva Galicia. He was eventually put on trial in Spain for his abuses in both Pánuco and Nueva Galicia, but he remained a presence at court until his death in 1551.[56] While the Crown never punished Guzmán, his actions in both Pánuco and Nueva Galicia became notorious even in distant areas of present-day Texas and northwestern Mexico. During Cabeza de Vaca's journey through these areas, he heard tales of the *mala cosa*, or "evil thing," whose description shares much in common with a Spanish soldier. The Indians who witnessed the mala cosa and escaped it often had scars similar to slave brands seared into their skin.[57]

Meanwhile the Crown revised its policies regarding the branding of Indian slaves both in New Spain and the larger empire to curb illegal enslavement of Indians during war and conquest.[58] First, in a provision from August 1529 the Crown limited the number of brands in its colonies. Then to further reduce the misuse of brands by a single corrupt official, the royal brand of each colony was to be kept locked in a chest that required three separate keys to be unlocked. Each of the top three royal officials (for example, the treasurer, governor, and bishop) of a given colony would hold one key, meaning that all three needed to be present to obtain access to the branding iron. In this way only Indians captured legitimately as slaves would be branded as such, in theory.[59]

Soon after the passage of the 1529 legislation that limited access to brands, conquistadors began to forge counterfeit royal irons. Others had so little regard for the law that they simply made their own personal irons, completely rejecting royal authority.[60] For example, when Vasco de Herrera, the regidor of Trujillo, headed south to Nicaragua to quell an indigenous rebellion in 1530, he brought with him the royal branding iron and two fabricated counterfeit irons. He used the royal brand on legally captured slaves, those caught through "just war," but he branded illegally begotten slaves with the counterfeit irons. These included nearly three hundred slaves from southern Honduras, Indians who were allied with the Spanish.[61] It seems that the profit from enslaving Indians was worth more than the risk of being caught and punished by the Crown.

Even after Guzmán exhausted Pánuco of its indigenous population, Indian slaves from New Spain continued to arrive in the Caribbean islands. For example, in 1530 many indigenous slaves from New Spain were sold in Cuba, though the exact number is not clearly documented. The "piezas" appear in the record only because of a dispute about taxation. Following the slaves' delivery to Cuba, residents registered numerous complaints about taxes that they paid on top of the slaves' purchase price. For each indigenous slave, the buyer paid an additional 7.5 percent, the same tax they would have paid for an African slave brought from Castille.[62] But after paying this *diezmo* (tax), the officials of Cuba became aware that residents of Española did not have to pay, or at the very least failed to pay, the same 7.5 percent on slaves from New Spain.[63] Officials Gonzalo de Guzmán and Diego Caballero both confirmed that in Española indigenous slaves purchased from New Spain, in addition to those from provinces such as Santa Marta (present-day Colombia), were not subject to the royal diezmo. Following this discovery, officials of Cuba began to petition for the return of taxes to those who purchased slaves from New Spain.[64] Note that the legality of the slaves was not in question; the concern was a matter of taxation.

Years later, after it was well known that Indian slaves were prohibited to be taken from New Spain, indigenous slaves from the region continued to appear in the ports of both Cuba and Española.[65] Officials did not know whether they could legally purchase the slaves or what they should exchange for the captives. Some thought the new slaves may have been a part of a renewed agreement, like that with Guzmán whereby they traded the slaves for livestock.[66] Others assumed they were coming from the Yucatán Peninsula as a result of its lengthy conquest by the Montejo family and thus were a product of "just war."[67] Regardless of their point of origin, the labor-starved residents of the Greater Antilles welcomed the slaves' arrival, though some more scrupulous officials did question the legality of their sale. And officials were pragmatic in questioning whether laws governing the indigenous slave trade had changed yet again, as in fact they had. In 1530 a royal provision made it illegal to enslave Indians through either rescate or "just war" *anywhere* in the Americas, due to abuses witnessed during the conquests of Mesoamerica and the Caribbean. Thus, only Caribs or Indian slaves enslaved by their own people could be purchased legally.[68] The legal slave trade shrunk precipitously, but not for long. Only four years later, in 1534 the Crown reversed the legislation, making it legal again to take Indians in warfare or through rescate.[69] Laws were quite malleable when it came to Indian slavery.

From Harvesting Pearls to Indians in Tierra Firme

Shortly after the discovery of Margarita, Coche, and Cubagua (known as the Pearl Islands), located off the coast of Venezuela, Spanish colonists established the first pearl fisheries.[70] The Spaniards employed Guaquerí Indians of Margarita and Lucayan Indians from the Bahamas in these early fisheries. The Spanish found that the local Indians were particularly useful in hunting for new pearl and oyster beds. Indians from the Bahamas were preferred divers due to their swimming skills, a necessity for harvesting pearls.[71] Because of their abilities, residents of Cubagua reportedly paid up to 150 pesos in gold for one Lucayan slave. This was an enormous sum when the majority of Indian slaves sold for fewer than twenty pesos and usually not for more than eight.[72] But there were not enough local or Lucayan Indians to fulfill the fisheries' demands, so Spaniards brought slaves from the nearby coast of Venezuela, the Lesser Antilles, and the Yucatán.[73] One of the first *rancherías de perlas* (pearl fisheries) opened in 1516 on the southern coast of Cubagua. By the 1520s there were over one hundred such fisheries.[74] In the fisheries' most lucrative years, during which they produced up to 1.2 billion pearls, it was illegal for Spaniards to conduct slaving armadas in the Pearl Islands or their adjacent coastlines. The Spanish Crown feared that slave raiding would destabilize the region and reduce the profitability of the pearl fisheries. It was even illegal both to trade for or purchase Indians already enslaved or to participate in rescate.[75] While these laws were not always followed, they did protect the islands' Indians from outside enslavement. The majority were still forced to work in the fisheries.

But the arrangement did not last. By the late 1520s the coast of Tierra Firme and even some of the Pearl Islands became harvesting grounds for Indian slaves. Residents from Española, Cuba, and Puerto Rico all flocked to the Pearl Islands and the surrounding coast of South America in search of indigenous slaves. In 1527 alone at least eighteen expeditions of rescate sailed from Española to various parts of coastal Tierra Firme. When each of the caravels returned, they all counted Indian slaves among their cargo.[76] But these were not only slaving expeditions; the merchants also traded for guanin and pearls on the voyages.[77]

Like slavers from the Caribbean islands, Pearl Island colonists had to expand their web to obtain enough slaves to complete the dangerous work of pearl collection. Some operations needed as many as forty Indian divers per day to collect the pearls. And this was perilous work, with many divers drowning or falling victim to shark attacks.[78] To fulfill these labor needs, residents of the Pearl Islands conducted more frequent raids into Tierra Firme.[79] As seen in earlier chapters, the most commonly raided areas prior to 1526 were those in a state of war or inhabited by Caribs as designated by Figueroa's 1520 report. The territory included the coastline between the peninsula of Araya to the Gulf of Cariaco, Santa Fe and Chichiriviche, and the area from

Neveri to Cumanagoto and Cabo Codera.[80] As Spaniards searched for new sources of Indian slaves, they expanded their raids to more distant coastal zones as well as into the interior of Tierra Firme.[81] The Crown supported the expansion of slaving zones, issuing more licenses to engage in trade and rescate along the coast of Tierra Firme in 1526. Some of these licenses, like that issued to Judge Alonso Zuazo, were annual.[82] In 1528 the number of licenses issued again multiplied, the majority going to the Caribbean elite, leading hundreds of slaving armadas to assault the coast of Tierra Firme.[83] After two years, these armadas left much of the coastline in ruin, along with hard-won alliances between the Spaniards of the Pearl Islands and Tierra Firme's indigenous inhabitants.[84]

While many colonists and colonial leaders sanctioned the slaving expeditions, slavers did occasionally face opposition from secular and religious officials who attempted to curb the raids, usually for pragmatic reasons. Most who tried to limit slavers' actions did not seek to end the slave trade. Instead, they sought to profit from selling Indian slaves themselves. Thus, their reform efforts were limited and often ignored. For example, in 1527 leaders Jacomé de Castellón (of Nueva Toledo or present-day Cumaná and the nearby coast of Venezuela) and Pedro Ortiz de Matienzo (of Santo Domingo) reached an agreement promising to desist from slaving in the Gulf of Cariaco to Santa Fe or Chichiriviche for forty days. The break from slaving was intended to allow the native inhabitants of the area time to recuperate. Following the forty-day respite, only small expeditions would be permitted to trade or practice rescate in the area, and these had a limit of two days each. Finally, all Indians purchased during the small trading expeditions could serve only as naborías, meaning they could not be sold as slaves or labor for more than six to eight years.[85] The agreement was quite detailed, but completely ineffective. First of all, the leaders agreed on only a forty-day lull instead of halting slaving expeditions entirely. Second, they incorporated multiple loopholes into the arrangement to still allow for some slaving after the forty days. The limitations of the contract highlight the importance of the indigenous slave trade to most Spanish colonial leaders.

Even more telling is that both officials ignored the treaty immediately after signing it. On the very same day that Matienzo signed the treaty, his substitute judge, Pedro de Barrionuevo, arranged an expedition of rescate destined for Cariaco. The voyage captured sixty Indian slaves.[86] Concurrent with Barrionuevo's illegal trip to the Gulf of Cariaco were voyages of rescate to Cupira, Piritu, Maracapana, and Paria.[87] The Crown even supported the slaving mission to Paria, which took between 170 and 180 slaves.[88] Again the

Crown enforced its laws regarding Indian enslavement only when it benefited the royal purse, not to benefit indigenous populations.[89]

The expeditions of rescate and raiding from 1526 to 1528 gave birth to a
new phenomenon, *granjerías de indios* (ranches or farms of Indian slaves).
From these so-called ranches, which encompassed much of Tierra Firme,
Spaniards gathered and harvested thousands of Indian slaves for the next
decade. At first indigenous leaders were voluntary participants in the trade.
Slavery was not a new concept for the native peoples of South America. Captivity was a common result of war and was a part of regular trade. Slaves were
often exchanged for goods such as salt. With the arrival of the Spanish, the
goods changed, but at first the practice was all too familiar to the Indians of
Tierra Firme.[90] As in the case of Pánuco and Guzmán, some Indian caciques,
or other principal Indians, found a way to profit from the indigenous slave
trade, declaring free Indians as slaves and selling them to unscrupulous Spanish traders. While indigenous leaders at first sold their enemies into slavery,
gaining political and economic benefits, as the supply of slaves captured in
war dwindled, caciques began selling relatives or neighbors to maintain their
alliances with the Spanish.[91] The drive to find and supply Indian slaves created a new enterprise along the northern coast of South America, mirroring
what occurred in Central America after the fall of Tenochtitlan. For a list of
documented slaving expeditions from 1527 to 1528 see Table 5.

The key to gaining access to the slaving business in Tierra Firme was a
royal license giving permission to a colonist to organize a voyage to trade for
or capture slaves. Elite Spanish officials issued the licenses as favors, payments,

Table 5. Slaving Expeditions in 1527–1528

Slaver/sponsor	Taken from	Transported to	Estimate of number of Indians taken
Pedro de Barrionuevo	Gulf of Cariaco	Santo Domingo	60
Gonzalo Hernández and Gonzalo Martel	Cupira	Santo Domingo	8
Fernando Riberos and Andrés de Villacorta	Piritu and Maracapana	Santo Domingo	Unknown
The Crown	Paria	Santo Domingo	180
Pedro de Rios and Diego Lopez	Nicaragua	Panama	200
			Total known: 448

or ways to deal with specific conflicts or rebellions. Licenses differed slightly depending on the location it gave access to, what types of slaves could be taken with it, and how often it could be renewed. For instance, royal judges of Nueva Cádiz issued one license to Pedro de Herrera, the mayor of the town, in 1528. The license permitted him to organize an armada of rescate. With the profit from this mission, Herrera was to improve the conditions of his "house, land, and wife."[92] Even religious officials turned to slaving licenses as their salary, including the priest Francisco de Villacorta, who accepted his payment in the form of several licenses of rescate in 1532.[93] Often, multiple officials combined their licenses to be able to maximize the impact of a given slaving mission. Some included as many as one hundred Spaniards traveling in anything from canoes to larger brigantines and caravels. In 1527 the governor of Cubagua issued an islandwide slaving license to all residents for the region of Maracapana.[94] Even when a colonist could not or did not want to use his license, he could still profit from it by selling the document. Some licenses sold for as much as ninety pesos.[95] Some larger more flexible licenses were especially valuable. It makes sense then that many officials, as high as the Crown, considered slaving licenses as forms of payment in place of currency or gold. By using slaving licenses as compensation for services rendered, the Crown acknowledged and participated in the industry of harvesting Indians.

After their capture, Indian slaves were taken first to Cubagua. There the alcalde mayor, vicar, royal treasurer, and general inspector (essentially the elite officials of a given colony) examined and questioned the captives. They also interviewed the slavers, checking licenses and inquiring where, how, and why they had captured the slaves. If an Indian were found to be a legal slave, he or she was branded on the face or arm, solidifying the enslaved status.[96] At least this was how things were supposed to work. Because slavers eagerly wanted all their Indian captives declared as legally obtained slaves, bribery was common during the process of examination. The scribe recording an Indian's status received one tomín of gold for finding them to be a slave. Then the wielder of the royal brand collected another tomín to brand the slave.[97] The business of Indian slavery touched nearly all levels of colonial society.

After their examination slaves were either sold in Nueva Cádiz or loaded on boats destined for Española, Cuba, or Puerto Rico. Slaves with diving or swimming skills were kept to labor in the Pearl Islands. Most women and children were sent to the Greater Antilles to work in domestic service. Men who could not dive or were of smaller stature would work on cattle ranches, in gold mines, or at sugar ingenios.[98] At the end of the 1520s Spaniards were removing more and more slaves from the Pearl Islands. The change resulted from twin transformations in the Spanish Caribbean. First, sugar plantations and cattle ranches of the Greater Antilles were becoming more successful and desperately needed laborers due to the precipitous death rate of Taíno populations. Second, by 1528 Cubagua's oyster and pearl beds were being depleted, leaving merchants with little or no ready income source.[99] With less profit in pearls, Spaniards turned increasingly to the slave trade. Already in 1528, the indigenous slave trade was the second best way to profit from Tierra Firme, just behind the pearl fisheries.[100] By the 1530s the Spanish slavers moved beyond the coastline of Tierra Firme, into the interior of South America, searching for and finding larger sources of indigenous slaves. At the same time the pearl industry was slowly exhausted, leaving many without the need to own hundreds of Indian slaves in Cubagua or Margarita proper. The Pearl Islands transformed from a destination for Indian slaves to one where slaves were harvested and processed.

As the business of slaving grew, competition between slavers increased, resulting in an explosion of violence and legal disputes between the locals of the Pearl Islands and slavers from Española or Cuba. At the heart of most of these cases was the question of jurisdiction, or more specifically who had the right to legally take Indians from different parts of Tierra Firme. While all the cases or complaints were supported by moral or humanitarian reasons, the real source of quarrels was competition for valuable resources, in this case Indian slaves. Underneath the language of justice, one finds pragmatic or economic reasons behind legislation.[101] Regardless of the actual motivations of the plaintiffs, the cases open a window into the circum-Caribbean slave trade of the 1530s.

Disputes over the control of indigenous slaves were not limited to those between colonies. The Crown also fought to regulate the industry, and at times limit the trade, in colonial courtrooms. For example, a royal provision, passed in August 1530, abolished *all* legal forms of indigenous enslavement in the islands and coast of Tierra Firme, including during "just war."[102] The new legislation ended earlier policies from 1503 forward that provoked massive slave raiding in the late 1520s. Though the change in policy could have been prompted by altruistic impulses, it is more likely that widespread tax evasion was the real impetus behind the alteration of laws. Reports abounded across Tierra Firme of colonists failing to pay the quinto de esclavos on all slave sales just before the change in legislation. One instance was recorded in June 1530 when Antonio de Alfinger, governor of Venezuela, captured and sold 107 Indians in Española without paying the quinto.[103] To explain his misstep, Alfinger described the poverty of Venezuela, whose only resource was indigenous slaves. He then promised to send the royal fifth at the first chance he got in the form of either slaves or gold.[104] Later, in December 1530, Luis González de Leiva was caught failing to pay the quinto on 222 Indians that he captured and (illegally) branded in Maracaibo. He argued that he should be exempt from paying the fifth on the slaves, which he sold in Santo Domingo, because they were enslaved in new territories that the Spaniards were still trying to pacify. To defend his actions, he cited conquistadors in Venezuela, like Alfinger, who did not pay the quinto on slaves they caught while waging war on bellicose Indians.[105]

Regardless of the reasons behind the new law outlawing Indian slavery, whether to protect the Indians or to control the profit made from slave raiding, residents and leaders throughout the Caribbean immediately protested the new law and solicited its abolishment. One official, López de Archuleta, a judge in Nueva Cádiz, went so far as to refuse to even publish the legislation.[106] And Archuleta was not the only official to ignore the new policy. Many of Cubagua's elite continued to grant licenses for rescate and to engage in war against rebellious Indians throughout Tierra Firme. In early 1531 Pedro Ortiz de Matienzo, alcalde mayor of Cubagua, issued a license permitting Andrés de Villacorta and Fernando Riberos to pacify rebel Indians of Cumaná. According to the license, the conquistadors were to receive payment for their work in addition to what they would make selling enslaved Indians.[107] During Villacorta's expedition, at least five hundred Indians were captured and branded as slaves, with three hundred later sold in Española and Puerto Rico.[108]

While many of the illegal slaving voyages went unpunished, or even unquestioned by Caribbean authorities, some of the most prolific slave traders, like Nuño de Gúzman in Pánuco, did face legal repercussions. In 1530, just after the change in Crown legislation that outlawed nearly all forms of indigenous enslavement, the royal court in Española filed a lawsuit against the inspector general of Cubagua, Juan López de Archuleta (the same official who had refused to publish the new law). They accused Archuleta of illegally enslaving peaceful Indians during multiple raids in the province of Cariaco from the end of 1529 through the beginning of 1530. He later sold the questionably begotten slaves to several Cubaguan pearl fisheries.[109] During the trial, which took place in Nueva Cádiz under the leadership of judge Antonio Clavijo, Archuleta was accused not only of organizing illegal armadas to Cariaco, but also of leaving the region in a state of upheaval as a result of the raids.[110] In addition to the expeditions that he participated in, Archuleta also distributed several illicit licenses to residents of Cubagua, giving them permission to conduct rescate and capture Indians in Cariaco. Many of the

Indians captured during these unlawful expeditions were branded as slaves and sold in full public view in Nueva Cádiz without being examined to determine the legality of their enslavement.[111] From their sale, Archuleta claimed half of the profits.[112]

The insufficient examinations resulted in the branding of an important allied cacique named Chatima and his wife. Shortly after, Pedro de Herrera purchased the cacique to work in a pearl fishery located near Nueva Cádiz.[113] Prior to his enslavement, cacique Chatima was a well-known friend of the Spanish, even participating in military engagements against the Caribs of Cumaná. Testimony presented at the trial determined that Chatima had been enslaved illegally, and so the judge declared that he be returned to his territory. Chatima was removed from Herrera and placed in the protective custody of Antón de Jaén.[114] Here is the last detailed documentation of Chatima, though some claim he remained with Antón de Jaén as a naboría and was never actually freed.[115] Many other Indians enslaved with Chatima were transported to Santo Domingo and sold there with the help of Pedro de Alegría.[116] Archuleta's slaving operations effectively destroyed once-friendly relationships between the Spaniards and Indians of Cariaco, leaving the territory in a state of war. Religious officials also blamed Archuleta's slave raids for preventing the regions' indigenous populations' conversion to Christianity.[117]

Chatima was neither the first nor the last friendly indigenous leader to be unlawfully enslaved by unscrupulous traders along the coast and islands of Tierra Firme.[118] Only one year after the disputed enslavement of Chatima, conquistador Diego de Ordás took well-known allied cacique Turipiari of Paria during an illicit entrada. Instead of laying the groundwork for a new settlement at the mouth of the River Marano, as his contract stated he would be doing, Ordás continued upriver into the province of Paria where he seized an unknown number of Indian slaves. One of these was the cacique Turipiari, an ally of the colonists of Cubagua. The inhabitants of Cubagua engaged in frequent trade with Turipiari, stating that the cacique journeyed to their island multiple times a year.[119] The capture of this important cacique, and possibly others alluded to in the letter, not only ended the commercial relationship between the Cubaguans and Turipiari but also endangered their affiliation with Indians in all of Paria. The bishop and other leaders worried about the province's future stability if slave raids continued, especially if the Spanish persisted in the capture of powerful caciques. Cubaguans feared that the loss of allied native leaders, who had served as intermediaries for years, would lead to the loss of obedience of larger indigenous populations. In addition, the Spanish feared that even if the Indians did not rebel, they would flee to the mountains or the interior, leaving coastal areas depopulated and the Spaniards without a ready labor force or trading partners.

To highlight the potential danger of the slave raids, the bishop of Santo Domingo, Sebastián Ramírez de Fuenleal, reminded the king of the recent destruction of the port city Santa Marta, which daily suffered robberies and attacks by formerly friendly Indians.[120] Here, as in other places across the Americas, indigenous populations rose up against the Spanish after decades of unfettered slaving. The capture of slaves from present-day Colombia grew exponentially with the founding of Santa Marta by Rodrigo de Bastidas in 1525. From then forward, the city served as a base for exploratory ventures into the interior. In nearly all the entradas, indigenous slaves were taken, both to serve as guides and to sell as consolation prizes after returning to Santa Marta. The slaving produced conflict, leading to rebellion and the destruction of Santa Marta. The violence then only increased the taking of slaves, this time in "just war." By the late 1530s Santa Marta was infamous as a slave market where one could legally purchase men, women, and children, regardless of the questionable origins of their enslavement.[121] After purchasing the captives, slavers usually took their cargo first to the markets of Cubagua, followed by Santo Domingo and finally Havana. Many of the enslaved children were still destined for Spain in the 1540s. Iberians preferred female and child slaves, especially those sent to Europe or to work as household servants, because they were perceived to be more docile than their male counterparts.[122] With the fate of Santa Marta in mind, the bishop asked the king to prohibit any traders or conquistadors from slaving in Paria.[123] Specifically he cited delays in building a new cathedral in Tierra Firme following the destruction of Santa Marta's church.[124] His letter also focused on how the actions of Ordás and other conquistadors impeded regular trade and economic development of the region.

Regardless of the consequences of slave raiding, financial or social, and in direct contradiction of the 1530 law, the Crown issued a new decree in 1532 that made it legal for residents of Cubagua *only* to attack and enslave rebellious Indians on the coast of Tierra Firme. These Indians would then be allowed to toil *only* in the pearl fisheries of Cubagua, Coche, and Margarita. It was illegal to sell the slaves elsewhere. Perhaps the Crown was trying to resuscitate the pearl fisheries at this juncture, so that is why the slaves had to remain in the Pearl Islands. Just as the legislation specified where the slaves could be sold, it also stipulated where the indigenous slaves were to be captured: from the interior of the Paria province.[125] A recent rebellion in the province opened the region to enslavement. It is likely that the newly defiant Indians were the same populations devastated by recent slave-raiding expeditions, like that of

Ordás. Nor did the new Crown legislation help the situation. Despite the new and very specific provisions, ship after ship, piloted by residents of Cubagua and filled with indigenous slaves from Tierra Firme, began arriving in the ports of Española, Cuba, Puerto Rico, and Panama. Most of the Indians were transported to Panama and sold to Spaniards heading across the isthmus to recently discovered Peru.[126] The Cubaguans were using their ability to conduct slaving raids to supply themselves with more than a renewed labor force for the pearl fisheries; they were also using the licenses to sell Indian slaves as a separate and profitable business.

By June 1532 Puerto Rican officials wrote the king, confused about what to do with the Indian slaves from Tierra Firme. As far as the administrators of Puerto Rico knew, the slaving of Indians *anywhere* along the coast of Tierra Firme or in the Pearl Islands was still illegal. Yet they were faced with the delivery of hundreds of indigenous slaves. Things grew more convoluted when Cubaguan slavers claimed that they had royal licenses to conduct the slave raids. This presented the Puerto Rican officials with a legal quandary. Did everyone in the Spanish Caribbean have license to engage in rescate or enslave rebellious Indians in Tierra Firme, or were the residents of Cubagua trying to sell illegal slaves?[127] The case for deceit from the Cubaguans appeared more likely, especially since the slavers refused to show Puerto Rican officials the licenses permitting them to enslave rebel Indians, probably because these licenses allowed for local enslavement only.

Even without receiving answers to their queries about the Cubaguan slaves, Puerto Rican officials purchased the slaves. They then excused their actions by describing how few native Indians the island had left, making the indigenous slaves especially necessary to keep the Spaniards' farms producing and to continue to serve the king.[128] Puerto Rican officials then requested that they too be allowed to send armadas to Tierra Firme to enslave rebellious Indians, or more specifically Caribs. Puerto Ricans argued for the right based upon frequent attacks that the island suffered from Caribs of the Lesser Antilles and the coast of Tierra Firme. Puerto Rico was especially vulnerable due to the island's proximity to the Carib islands, with only a short canoe ride separating the populations. Going beyond the excuse that they should be allowed to enslave Indians who attacked their island, the inhabitants of Puerto Rico also employed the tried-and-true accusation of cannibalism to support their request: "Your majesty will be served if the Caribs are made slaves and they deserve to be enslaved because of their bad custom of eating human flesh as they commonly do."[129] Here is another example of colonies competing over both the right to and profits from Indian slaves. Through their letters and correspondence, it is evident that residents of Puerto Rico were not satisfied with simply purchasing already-enslaved Indians from Cubaguans. Instead they sought their own licenses to personally profit from the trade in Indian slaves, not only their labor.

While the Crown did not provide the residents of Puerto Rico and Española with slaving licenses for Tierra Firme, the residents did receive permission to conduct slave raids to Guadalupe, Trinidad, Dominica, and Tabaco in September 1533. Those islands were conveniently inhabited by Carib Indians.[130] One such beneficiary of this decree was Antonio Sedeño, who received a license to enslave Caribs residing in Trinidad in 1533, a territory he attempted to conquer in both 1530 and 1532.[131] Because conquering the island proved a very difficult task and the indigenous population of Trinidad was very difficult to subdue, he focused on slave raids both in Trinidad and on the nearby coast of Tierra Firme to make a profit out of his unsuccessful ventures.[132] He too, like fellow unsuccessful conquistadors, dealt in selling "consolation prizes." Sedeño's slave raids into Tierra Firme from Trinidad proved so lucrative that he organized a much larger slaving expedition to Paria a few years later. Throughout the 1530s men like Sedeño, Ordás, and others launched raid after raid to the Lesser Antilles and Tierra Firme, capturing Carib Indians to sell in the markets of Española, Cuba, Puerto Rico, and Central America.

As the "industry" of Indian captives grew, involving more and more Europeans as well as indigenous groups, what little control the Crown had over the practice steadily decreased. While some Indians were legally enslaved, many more were taken illegally. Quite a few of these captives were former allies of the Spanish, particularly of those in Cubagua. In February 1533 Judge Francisco de Prado of Cubagua complained that as a result of the illegal capture of friendly Indians the pearl fisheries were shorthanded, lacking about three hundred Indian laborers normally sent by allied caciques.[133] As economic ventures across the Spanish Empire grew, from New Spain to Peru, so did the demand for Indian slaves. Then at the end of the 1530s the Spaniards discovered new, untouched pearl fisheries at Cabo de la Vela. This created another new market for Indian slaves in Coro and Margarita, pushing the hunt for captives to new heights.[134]

With the rise in slaving expeditions, more conflicts developed across the Caribbean. Competing colonies and merchants fought over the right to capture and sell Indians. Meanwhile, the Crown endeavored to control the trade and to make both religious officials and colonists happy. It was nearly an impossible project, and by the late 1530s disputes over the trade and accusations of Indian abuse were filling colonial courts. The cases included clashes between various conquistadors searching for El Dorado, as well as complaints about collecting and selling slaves as "consolation prizes." Cases also involved the entradas of Alfinger, Nicolás Féderman, Jorge de Espira, and Gonzalo Jiménez de Quesada. Other entradas were more directly linked to the circum-Caribbean indigenous slave trade. In particular, from 1535 to 1537 a group of Cubaguan officials (including treasurer Francisco de Castellanos and inspector general Francisco de Lerma) waged a legal battle against conquistador Gerónimo Ortal. At the center of the dispute was the taking and enslaving of hundreds of Indians in the province and Gulf of Paria.[135] Central to the debate was the question of who could profit from either the labor or sale of the Indians in question.

Alonso Diaz de Gibraleón of Nueva Cádiz first brought Ortal's actions to the Crown's attention in February 1536.[136] In his letter he reminded the king about the royal ordinances forbidding any unauthorized person from taking Indians from the Pearl Islands or the adjacent coastline without express permission and license from a judge in Nueva Cádiz. These laws ensured that residents and leaders of Cubagua, at this point a deteriorating colony after the decline of its pearl fisheries, controlled the trade in Tierra Firme's Indians. Any legal license, again only legal when granted by a Cubaguan judge, also limited a slaver to capture only rebel (Carib) Indians. If the licensed individual enslaved any unsanctioned or allied Indians, they would be banned from Cubagua for two months and have to pay a fine to the royal court at Nueva Cádiz of ten thousand maravedíes.[137] Among the Indians who were *not* considered to be rebels, and therefore *not* legal slaves, were those inhabiting the coast of Tierra Firme from Maracapana to Enmanagoia. Avoiding the involvement of these Indians in the slave trade was especially important to the Cubaguans because these indigenous groups helped them in wars against neighboring Carib Indians, coincidentally the Indians whom they could enslave.[138]

Unfortunately for Ortal, it was from the interior of this very territory (between Maracapana to Enmanagoia) that he engaged in slave raiding, meaning that the slaves he captured were legally free according to current laws. Per the officials of Nueva Cádiz, Ortal and his men entered the province of Cumanagoto via Paria for the express purpose of taking and capturing indigenous slaves. This province was within the government of Cubagua's jurisdiction; thus, for Ortal to legally capture slaves in these territories, he needed a license from the judges of Nueva Cádiz—something he most definitely did not possess in 1535.[139] Therefore, when Ortal's ship anchored in Nueva Cádiz's port, its officials took control of all the Indians onboard, which Ortal had already illegally branded prior to inspection. Whether he gained access to a royal brand or if he forged his own was unspecified. The officials of Cubagua then began a lengthy process to determine whether any of the Indians on Ortal's ship had been legally enslaved. If they were slaves, then Cubagua's officials would oversee their sale and take one half of Ortal's profit. However, if the Indians were free, then they would be returned to their lands.[140] Until a decision was reached the Indians remained in the custody of Francisco de Reina, a resident of Nueva Cádiz. In addition to the judgment regarding the future of the Indians, if found guilty of illegal slaving, Ortal would have to pay two hundred gold pesos to Nueva Cádiz.[141]

As the trial progressed, it became clear that Ortal never possessed the legal right to capture slaves from Paria and Cumanagoto.[142] Regardless, he captured and shipped about one hundred Indians (mainly women and children) to Cubagua. In addition to the Indian slaves delivered to Cubagua, Ortal had already sold an unknown number in Trinidad. Adding to the crime of operating beyond his jurisdiction, Ortal was also accused of grave atrocities while capturing the Indians in question. According to multiple testimonies, he gained the slaves through extreme violence, burning and destroying entire towns and robbing the surviving Indians of all clothing and corn.[143] This left the region in complete upheaval. Beyond his own escapades, Ortal also ordered one of his captains, Alonso de Herrera, to continue deeper into the interior of Tierra Firme to engage in even more slave raids. Herrera, following Ortal's instructions, traveled to the nearby province of Rio Huyaporia where he attacked several peaceful indigenous groups and captured up to 150 Indians. Again the majority of Herrera's victims were women and children.[144] These Indians were later sold on the islands of Margarita and Trinidad.[145] As a result of Herrera's attacks, former allies of Cubagua rose against the colonists, murdering several Spaniards, including and perhaps fittingly Herrera, in retaliation for the slave raids.[146]

Ortal's testimony also revealed that he and Herrera were not the only Spaniards slaving in Paria and nearby territories. Ortal's men faced competition from the entrada of Antonio Sedeño, the governor of Trinidad.[147] Sedeño's expedition was much larger than Ortal's, with around six hundred men (both foot soldiers and some cavalry).[148] In addition, Sedeño also received financial and legal backing from the court in Santo Domingo, which provided him with a license to explore and engage in rescate in the province of Cumanagoto.[149] The amount of funding that Sedeño received, along with the size of his forces, reveals the profitability of slave raids like this. Likely due to his much larger force, Sedeño succeeded in capturing close to four hundred slaves in the provinces of Cumanagoto and Neveri, near the Mara-capana River. Sedeño then took the slaves to Puerto Rico where he sold them publicly without the slaves being branded or examined. The presence of both armies unsettled the formerly peaceful province and left it barren and largely depopulated, at least according to the Cubaguans.[150] The competing slavers caused even more damage in the region by fighting one another for control of the provinces and their native populations. Officials of Cubagua claimed that Sedeño and Ortal burned entire villages to the ground and turned the province into a war zone.[151]

Despite atrocities committed by Ortal (and Sedeño, though his entrada was at least nominally legal), the court of Nueva Cádiz decided that the Indian captives confiscated from Ortal were legal slaves. The ruling directly contra-dicted all testimonies presented that described the Indians of Cumanagoto, Paria, and the River Huyaporia as allies of the Spanish, even detailing their part in fighting the Caribs. The ruling again proved that despite discourse censoring the capture of peaceful Indians, especially allies of the Spanish, the allure of profit superseded moral impulses. Only adding to the profit from the sale of the slaves, the court of Nueva Cádiz also benefited from fines lev-ied on the original sellers and purchasers.[152] For example, Francisco de Lerma had to pay two hundred pesos, half to the judges of Cubagua and half to the Crown, for buying slaves without a license. In another instance, Francisco de Mellan had to pay forty pesos and Alonso Diaz owed ninety pesos for his indiscretion.[153]

Upon deciding that the Indians could be sold, the surviving thirty-four Indian captives were sold in public on November 14, 1536.[154] The Indians sold for anywhere from five to twelve pesos each, depending on their sex and age. Francisco de Reina bought or kept eight of the Indians that were placed in his care, while the other twenty-six were sold to various residents of Cubagua. The males sold for more than the females did, and the older slaves (that is, not boys or *muchachos*) went for a higher price. Also telling is that in the document at least half of the Indian slaves were referred to as "piezas," even as half pieces, demonstrating their continued commodification.[155] For example, Juan de Ribas (the scribe of Nueva Cádiz) purchased "dos piezas," as did Alonso de Burgos (in the name of the town's alcalde mayor). In this case, and many others like it, profit superseded morality in the business of Indian slavery. Tables 6 and 7 show many of the documented slaving expeditions that assaulted the coast and interior of Tierra Firme from 1530 to 1537.

In late 1538 multiple officials reported to the king that there were no Indi-ans in all of Venezuela.[156] According to Bishop Bastidas, the government of

Table 6. Documented Slaving Expeditions and Armadas, 1530–1536

Slaver	Year	Captured in	Taken to	Estimate of number of Indians taken
López de Archuleta	1530	Cariaco	Pearl Islands	unknown
Cristóbal Alvarez and Pedro de Paz	1531	Santa Marta	Santo Domingo	unknown
Adrés de Villacorta and Fernando Riberos	1531	Cumana	San Juan and Santo Domingo	300–500
Luis Guerra	1533	Tierra Firme	Santo Domingo	252
Gerónimo Ortal	1535	Paria	Nueva Cádiz	unknown
Alonso de Herrera	1535	Meta	Margarita	150
Antonio Sedeño	1536	Neveri	Puerto Rico	400
				Total known: At least 1,102

Table 7. Indian slaves captured during entradas into Nueva Granada and Venezuela, 1530–1537

Slaver	Year	Captured in	Taken to	Estimate of Number
Antonio Sedeño	1530	Paria	Puerto Rico	Unknown
Nicolás Féderman	1530	Paraguana	Unknown	Unknown
Antonio de Alfinger	1530	Venezuela	Santo Domingo	107
Antonio de Alfinger and Luis González de Leiva	1531	Maracaibo	Santo Domingo	222
Diego de Ordás	1531	Paria	Cubagua	Unknown
Antonio Sedeño	1532	Trinidad and Paria	Puerto Rico	Unknown
Luis González de Leiva	1533	Venezuela	Jamaica	65
Nicolás Féderman	1535	Venezuela	Santo Domingo	174
Gonzalo Jiménez de Quesada	1537	Nueva Granada	Unknown	300
				Total known: 868

the Welsers reported selling 1,005 indigenous slaves obtained through "just war" since 1529, for which they garnered 1,499 pesos, 1 tomín, and 11.5 grams of gold. In the two years, 1536–1538, that the Welser Company reported slaves obtained through rescate, the total sale of 539 indigenous persons was 3,713 pesos.[157] These numbers reflect only the recorded sales that were considered legal and therefore taxable. Many more remain hidden, especially those where indios amigos were sold into slavery or where slave traders avoided paying the quinto. One example is the entrada of Agustín Delgado into Neveri, which purportedly was only to gather trade goods and food. Instead he emerged with five hundred slaves that he sold in Santo Domingo, Margarita, and Puerto Rico in 1538. Concurrent with Delgado's expedition was one by Pedro de Limpias to Lake Maracaibo where he took another five hundred Indian slaves. This mission, though illegal, was supported surreptitiously by Bastidas.[158]

Once again, we see the limits of royal control in the Americas. This was especially true by the late 1530s, when pearl fisheries of Nueva Cádiz stopped producing. In 1537 the king received a report claiming that no pearls had been harvested for a year and a half. This pushed residents of Cubagua to look to other industries, namely the Indian slave trade. With the majority of pearls coming from Cabo de la Vela or Panama, the coast and interior of Venezuela became a prime place to harvest Indian slaves for residents of Española, Cuba, Peru, and other more productive colonies.[159] Indians were one of the only products available for these colonists to profit from for most of the 1530s.

*   *   *

From New Spain southward to Nicaragua, the coast of Venezuela, and into the interior of Colombia, the hunt for Indian slaves consumed hundreds of Spanish colonists throughout the late 1520s and 1530s. These men were doing much more than searching for new sources of labor or attempting to pacify new territories for settlement. Their focus was the gathering of Indian slaves. In so doing they created a new business in the colonies. In many areas of present-day Central and South America, the removal and sale of indigenous peoples was the quickest and easiest way to make a profit. As a result, the laws regarding who could be enslaved, how and when they could be branded, and, most importantly to the Spaniards themselves, who could profit from the sale of these slaves were ignored or stretched.

While it is impossible to know how many slaves were taken from various regions of the circum-Caribbean, the sheer number of documented cases gives us an idea of the enormity of the slave trade. For each case we know of, there could be as many as three or four more raids that went unaccounted. Of the documented slaving expeditions, thousands of Indian captives were ripped from their homelands and shipped across the Caribbean within a single decade. Undoubtedly there were many more who went unrecorded. Many did not survive the journeys, silencing their stories. Regardless of the actual number of Indians captured and transported throughout the Caribbean, by the 1530s the commerce in Indian slaves was one of the largest businesses in the Spanish Empire. It also caused untold suffering, chaos, violence, and the depopulation of huge swaths of territory. It was the magnitude of the Indian slave trade, enveloping so much of the Spanish Americas in the late 1530s, that finally forced the Crown to take firm action against the slave raiders in the form of the New Laws of 1542.

CHAPTER 6

_____

Crossroads of Slavery

The African Slave Trade Meets the Indian Slave Trade

While Europeans transported hundreds of thousands of Indian captives across the greater Caribbean, another form of slavery was on the rise in the Americas. Africans, both slave and free, had been present in the New World since the first voyages across the Atlantic. But it was not until the third decade of colonization that the transatlantic African slave trade grew substantially. The increase in the importation of African slaves was due to several factors. First was the shortage of labor, which also propelled the Indian slave trade, as the indigenous population of the Americas continued to decline. Second was the push from reformers like the Jeronymite friars and Bartolomé de las Casas, who believed that African slaves were more suited to toil in the tropical climate of the Spanish colonies. There were also fewer arguments against the enslavement of Africans, a group that Europeans had enslaved in varying numbers since the Greek Golden Age.[1] With waning profits and calls to protect the Americas' indigenous populations, the Crown endeavored to expand the availability of African slaves. From 1518 forward, European ships and merchants transported more African slaves to the Spanish colonies.

Today, many view the two slave trades as completely separate. However, sixteenth-century Spanish colonists and officials understood the enslavement of both Africans and Indians as slavery, as part of the same system governed by the same laws. Both Indian and African slaves did similar work, were referred to with the same inhumane term (piezas), lived under the same legal code, were branded upon enslavement, and were sold in the same markets. Of course, there were differences between the two types of slaves, namely in price. However, the important point here is that the rise of the African slave trade did not bring an end to Indian slavery in the Caribbean or the wider and growing Spanish Empire. Instead the two trades coexisted for several decades, influencing one another. And on the ground, African and Indian slaves lived and worked together. At times the two groups even rebelled together, fulfilling the Spanish elite's worst fears. These slaveries were intertwined; this chapter shows the connections and linkages between the two, examining Indian and African slavery together. In particular, the chapter investigates the impact of African slavery on indigenous populations across the Caribbean, both enslaved and free, and how slavery, both African and Indian, more broadly influenced the development of the early Spanish Caribbean.

The Rise of the African Transatlantic Slave Trade

Africans were present in the Americas at the beginning of the sixteenth century. While it is possible that there were African passengers on Columbus's second voyage, the first documented reference to Africans in the Americas is in 1502.[2] Soon thereafter Juan Garrido, one of the earliest and most famous free Africans, crossed the Atlantic.[3] As a free man and servant to Pedro Garrido, Juan Garrido participated in the conquests of Puerto Rico, Florida, Cuba, and New Spain. It is nearly certain, however, that African slaves were in the Americas before Garrido's arrival; for example, "Diego el Negro" appears on the passenger list for Columbus's fourth voyage, which set sail in May 1502.[4]

By the early 1500s, Europeans sought to purchase African slaves, believing they were the answer to increasing profits from the faltering Caribbean gold mines. Spaniards hoped to exploit both Africans' knowledge of gold mining and their ability to endure arduous labor in tropical climates; then the Spaniards needed to use their Indian slaves only to execute the supporting tasks of mining.[5] According to Spanish officials, one African slave could do the equivalent work of 140 Indians.[6] In 1505 King Ferdinand sent one hundred African slaves to Española to work in the royal gold mines. Then in 1510 he sent fifty more slaves to replenish the ranks of those who had perished toiling in the mines or who had run away.[7] Other African slaves were destined to serve as domestic servants, auxiliaries, soldiers, and commercial assistants as they were often more trusted than indigenous slaves.[8] Even while the availability of indigenous slaves was high, the African trade grew both to fulfill royal demands and to answer the colonists' pleas.

The limited transatlantic slave trade was an extension of the trade in slaves between the Portuguese and various African groups dating from the 1450s.[9] Up to one thousand African slaves entered Lisbon annually by the mid-fifteenth century, growing to two thousand by the time Columbus crossed the Atlantic. In the early sixteenth century there were as many as four thousand African or mulatto slaves residing in Sevilla alone.[10] Many of these ladino Africans were the first to journey to the Americas. This pattern changed in 1510 when the Crown authorized the introduction of slaves directly from Africa, Guinea in particular, to the Greater Antilles. In 1513, the Crown continued to formalize the trade by organizing a system of licenses for anyone bringing Africans to the Americas whether to sell or own themselves.[11]

With more African slaves being transported to Española, runaways became an issue. Already in 1503, both Governor Ovando and settler Juan de Ayala reported African runaways.[12] In his correspondence to the king, Ovando wrote that ladino slaves were fleeing the mines, running to live with Indians on distant mountains where they taught the indigenous peoples "bad customs."[13] However, Ovando had a solution to the problem. Instead of bringing more ladino slaves, he requested that the king send bozal slaves to Española, as he believed that bozales would be easier to control.[14] Ovando's assumption proved faulty as Judge Zuazo still complained about runaway African slaves in 1518. Zuazo's solution was more violent at this point: to cut off the ears of any recovered slaves as an example.[15] From 1508 forward, the colonists of Española persisted in requesting African slaves, resulting in the Crown issuing several licenses for the transportation of slaves to the Americas in 1513.[16] One such royal order procured 250 slaves, 100 of which were to be purchased directly from Lisbon. Still, the number of Africans, at least those legally enslaved and transported, who arrived in the Caribbean was small and bought by and for specific colonists.[17]

From 1510 to 1518 the majority of slaves who disembarked in the Caribbean belonged to particular colonists, most of whom owned only one or two African slaves.[18] In addition, many of the African slaves who made it to the Caribbean were quickly taken to other, more promising territories. The lack of African slaves left most colonists in Cuba or Española to rely on the Indian slave trade for much of the first half of the sixteenth century. As we have seen, the reliance on indigenous slavery took an enormous toll on Indians across the Caribbean as thousands were displaced, perished, or rebelled against their oppressors. All this led to calls for reform, including the end of Indian slavery and its replacement with African slavery.[19]

As covered in Chapter 3, the Crown charged the Jeronymite government with reforming the empire in 1517, leading it to briefly outlaw Indian slavery and advocate for an expansion of the African trade. Responding to pressure, the Crown issued the first large licenses for African (bozal) slaves in 1518.

From this initial license, granted to Genoese Laurent de Gouvenot, the governor of Bresa, four thousand slaves were shipped directly from Africa to the Caribbean. To facilitate the transport of these slaves, the Jeronymites asked whether ships could sail directly from Española to the Cape Verde Islands to purchase slaves without having to wait for the Genoese merchants to deliver the merchandise.[20] Zuazo and other officials echoed the Jeronymites' request, even asking if Portuguese merchants could bring slaves directly from Cape Verde or Guinea.[21] Zuazo elaborated that the preferred slaves would be bozales between the ages of fifteen and twenty, with equal numbers of male and female slaves who could be married to prevent revolts. His other suggested method to curtail rebellious or runaway slaves was to whip them or clip their ears.[22] Though the requested licenses were not granted, documents do suggest that merchants from Sevilla first stopped in the Cape Verde Islands on their way to the Caribbean throughout the 1520s. One such ship delivered 139 "piezas" from San Tomé to Puerto Rico in 1522.[23] Others undoubtedly followed the same pattern, purchasing slaves from the Portuguese without proper licenses for Caribbean markets.[24]

More African slaves, both those through royal licenses and those via contraband, *slowly* journeyed to the Caribbean. The total number from Gouvenot's license did not arrive in Española until 1528, with the first individuals disembarking between 1520 and 1522.[25] The government soon issued other licenses allowing for the transport of several hundred African slaves. In 1523 Juan de Polanco Maluenda, a merchant, acquired a license to deliver two hundred Africans to San Juan and Cuba.[26] Then in 1528 German merchants Heinrich Ehinger and Hieronymus Seiler were granted a license to transport another four thousand African slaves to the Americas.[27] But these numbers were not enough to solve the labor issue, especially as the Spanish Empire grew. Cuban authorities felt the problem more acutely as they received fewer slaves than those in Española did. Of the four thousand slaves transported by the Welsers, only three hundred were allotted for Cuba, in large part because Cuba did not offer an attractive market, as few colonists could purchase slaves priced above forty-five pesos.[28] As a result, no more than 1,500 legal African slaves entered Cuba before 1590, preventing African slavery from replacing Indian slavery for decades, or completely for centuries.[29] Nevertheless, by the 1530s the numbers of African slaves shipped to the Americas grew to nearly three thousand annually, many of which embarked directly from the African coast.[30]

As the number of African slaves grew, so did the diversity of their employment. They served as agricultural laborers, ranch hands, sailors, cooks, carpenters, masons, and guards, to name a few. The majority were young and approximately 60 percent were male, with women destined for domestic labor.[31] Due to their high prices African slaves, regardless of sex, were more likely to conduct domestic, agricultural, or specialized labor while indigenous slaves worked in mines extracting or cleaning gold, which was more dangerous work.[32] African slaves supported all aspects of Spanish colonization and exploration, as did Indian slaves and naborías.[33] Already by 1534, officials in Puerto Rico described African slaves as a "necessary evil" because of the high death rate of indigenous populations and the reluctance of Spanish colonists to engage in hard labor.[34] In Puerto Rico's 1530 census there were nearly double the number of African slaves as Indian slaves, despite the high cost of African slaves.[35] And colonists continued to purchase and request more African slaves despite their high price.

African slaves were initially four to five times more expensive than indigenous slaves and by the 1530s, the price for an African slave grew exponentially from around fifty gold pesos to two hundred pesos.[36] The prices of slaves included reimbursement for the merchant's slave license, life insurance (so the merchant could recoup what he paid if a slave died prior to their sale), and taxes among other costs.[37] In the second half of the sixteenth century the price for an African slave went as high as 350 pesos, causing renewed efforts to reopen the then-closed indigenous circum-Caribbean slave trade.[38] The high price of African slaves also led to a secondary slave trade from Española to Peru and other colonies with more economic opportunities in the 1540s and 1550s. By this point, many bozal African slaves had served on Española and other islands for several years, receiving "instruction" and seasoning. After a few years the trained slaves sold for even higher prices to other parts of the empire and the mainland.[39] Slaves who remained in the Caribbean islands after "seasoning" usually worked in domestic service and served as status symbols for their owners, many of whom were newly wealthy or titled as a result of rewards from conquest.[40]

The prohibitive prices of African slaves caused residents of Cuba to petition the Crown for loans to purchase enslaved Africans five times between 1523 and 1550.[41] Residents of Española also requested help from the Crown, asking that merchants not be allowed to charge eighty or ninety pesos for a slave that they had bought in Cape Verde for only forty-five pesos. The petition requested that a maximum price of sixty-five pesos be set on any slave in order to prevent *desorden* and *daño* (disorder and harm) to the colony. In particular Judge Melchor de Torres feared that residents would abandon Española if they could not afford to buy African slaves.[42] While the Crown agreed to impose the limit, a year later colonists continued to report merchants charging much higher fees.[43] Thus, it is not surprising that the majority of Caribbean colonists continued to turn to indigenous slaves over African for much of the sixteenth century.[44]

Seeing the ineffectiveness of the Crown's orders, others turned to the church for help. In Puerto Rico in April 1533, a Dominican friar gave a fiery sermon condemning slave traffickers and merchants of usury and excessive prices. He further explained that innocent colonists simply needed access to African slaves, or they would be unable to mine gold and pay their royal taxes. Some colonists were in so much debt from purchasing African slaves that they were in danger of losing their property. The price of one slave was nearly equivalent to an entire year's earnings for most Spanish colonists. Recent hurricanes, which flooded estates and destroyed sugar crops, and attacks from "Caribs" only made things worse for many. A few colonists fled the cities to hide in the mountains because they could not pay their debts. Others gave up on the Caribbean all together, heading to new territories like Peru or Mexico.[45]

Because of the value of their African slaves, colonists also paid more for their return than for their indigenous slaves. Though officials reported runaway slaves as early as 1503, the post of *recogedor* (slave catcher) was not requested in Española until 1518, when the royal treasurer Gil Gonzaléz Dávila wrote to the Crown asking for such an official.[46] While the reward for the return of a slave was not specified in this particular correspondence, other cases shed light on prices paid for the capture of African versus indigenous slaves. For example, the recogedor of Mexico City was reimbursed all costs incurred while finding slaves plus five gold pesos for each African slave, one half peso for each Indian slave, and one gold peso for each returned piece of livestock.[47] Note here that not only were African slaves valued higher than Indian, but that an indigenous slave was worth less than an animal. This can also be seen in the prices paid for livestock versus indigenous slaves in the markets of New Spain. In 1525, thirty Indian slaves cost 140 gold pesos while one African female slave cost 200 pesos and one horse was purchased for 400 gold pesos.[48] While African and Indian slaves often worked and lived together in the Caribbean, the Spanish colonists viewed them distinctly.

From the start of their tenure in Spanish America, Indian and African slaves' lives overlapped, from the marketplace on. At a public auction in Santo Domingo in 1520, ingenio owner Francisco Tostado purchased a variety of slaves, including "*una india y dos niñas esclavas.*"[49] Another encomendero, Diego Caballero, bought both Indian and African slaves at the same auction.[50] While Indian and African slaves were sold in the same markets and worked in the same industries, their positions within mining or plantation enterprises were different. One of the reasons that African slaves sold for much higher prices than their indigenous counterparts was due to their technical skills for blacksmithing and sugar production. Many African slaves became "sugar masters," supervising their fellow African and indigenous slaves through the complicated process of heating and crystallizing sugar.[51] The stratification of labor is visible in Hernando Gorjón's sugar ingenio Santiago de la Paz, located near Azua, Española. In 1547, at Gorjón's death, the Crown conducted an extensive census of his properties, revealing much about the ethnic composition and daily life of slaves on a sixteenth-century Caribbean sugar plantation.[52] The census lists the occupations and positions of many of the slaves. All of the elite positions on Gorjón's ingenio were filled by African slaves; these positions included shepherd, *mandador* (who was in charge of the sugar fields), *estanciero* (who regulated the harvesting of crops beyond sugar), *purdagor* (who ordered supplies and maintained inventory records), sugar master, brickmaker, cartwright, and blacksmith. These positions gave the African slaves a great deal of mobility and required high skill levels, even literacy.[53]

Censuses from the 1530s taken across Española and Puerto Rico underscore the diversity of slaves. While the number of African slaves was on the rise, Indian slaves and free Indians were still present in equal if not higher numbers. Francisco Manuel de Lando, the governor of Puerto Rico, reported the island's slave population in December 1530. In the city of San Juan alone, there were 1,486 male African slaves, 360 female African slaves, 774 Indian slaves (of both sexes) from various islands, including a few native to Puerto Rico, and 332 free, indigenous peoples. In the second largest town on Puerto Rico, San Germán, there resided 170 male African slaves, 61 female African slaves, 226 enslaved Indians, and 175 free, native peoples. All the wealthiest and most powerful proprietors of the island owned both African and Indian slaves. A treasurer, Bals de Villasante, held seventy African slaves and fifty-one Indians. Francisco Manuel de Lando claimed sixty Africans and eight Indians. Even the bishop held many slaves: forty-three Africans and seven Indians.[54] The clergy owned so many slaves that some colonists claimed that priests and friars were hoarding slaves. The letter, sent to the Crown by judges Espinosa and Zuazo, asserted that some clergy owned as many as one hundred African slaves, with the majority owning between twenty and thirty (both indigenous and African).[55] Sixty-two percent of slaveholders in San Juan owned both African and Indian slaves while 58 percent in San Germán held both enslaved Indians and Africans.[56] These documents show both the diversity of slaves present on a small island and the disparity between the number of slaves available to colonists living in larger cities versus rural areas. Of even more interest is that many of the Indian slaves were from the Yucatán; they might have been taken during the Montejo family's recent attempts to conquer the peninsula.[57]

In 1533 Santo Domingo's archbishop ordered a census of the island's plantations and ingenios to determine how many clergymen the island required. Archbishop Avila surveyed twenty-three ingenios while conducting the census, during which he found enslaved Indians and Africans in every ingenio. In total he found 1,880 Africans and 200 Indians. He also counted 1,525 persons of unspecified ethnicity. It is possible that these individuals were indigenous slaves from other regions or were of mixed-race origin. The ambiguity of the 1,525 persons helps to explain the rapid rise in Indians in the same region in the very next census conducted in 1539, which found 1,212 Indians. And the number of Indian slaves continued to rise. By 1545's census there were 5,125 Indian slaves, and of the twenty-nine ingenios included, only nine counted more African slaves than Indian.[58] While some of those labeled as Indians could have been mestizos or mulattos, there is no doubt that even as African slaves became more readily available, Indian slaves were still widely employed and sought after. So it is likely that the ambiguous group contained a combination of questionably begotten Indian slaves and mixed-race slaves.

As in the Greater Antilles, both African and Indian slaves worked side by side throughout the early years of Cubagua's and Margarita's pearl fisheries. Indian slaves in these markets drew some of the highest prices across the Caribbean. While most Indian slaves sold for no more than ten or twelve gold pesos, residents of the Pearl Islands were willing to pay between 50 and 150 pesos for a Lucayan Indian because the Spanish recognized the Lucayans' ability to dive for pearls.[59] This skill set led to a preference for indigenous slaves over their African counterparts in the Pearl Islands, and that perhaps explains why these slaves operated under quite a bit of autonomy. The historian Gonzalo Fernández de Oviedo described unsupervised Indian crews who located oyster beds, gathered oysters, and delivered the bivalves to their masters. Nonetheless at night, Spanish owners locked both their African and Indian slaves into their island huts. Pearls were locked into a separate guarded building. There were also laws prohibiting any "black, Indian slave, or Lucayo" from exiting their huts or master's residence after dark.[60] The Spanish feared that their slaves would take advantage of the proximity of Tierra Firme, and the plethora of canoes in the fisheries, to escape.[61] Because these slaves were so highly prized for their skill set, they were watched more carefully than other indigenous and African slaves across the burgeoning Spanish Empire.

African and indigenous slaves across the Caribbean worked and lived together for the first decades of Spanish colonization and conquest. Some even married each other. In Puerto Rico's 1543 census, several witnesses testified that some Indians (both men and women) had married African slaves.[62] No doubt this trend likely appeared throughout the rest of the Caribbean. While censuses and records of sale provide a glimpse into relationships between African and Indian slaves, we can gain a more complete picture by investigating the earliest slave revolts and maroon communities in the Caribbean. Most of these uprisings, especially in the first half of the sixteenth century, were multiethnic. These coalitions show that the experiences and opportunities of African and Indian slaves were similar in the Americas, leading to interethnic alliances and communities: the worst nightmare for the Spanish officials.

The Rebellion of Cacique Enrique

Conditions for the native peoples of Española deteriorated dramatically in the third decade of colonization alongside the growing trades in foreign Indians and Africans, even for once-protected caciques. In this environment, cacique Enrique, a literate and ladino chief, challenged Spanish dominance. In 1519 he fled his encomienda in San Juan de la Maguana, taking with him his wife and several of his followers.[63] Enrique's flight began the first slave revolt in the Americas.[64] After his escape, Enrique returned to his cacicazgo within the caves of the Bahoruco Mountains, near his childhood home of Verapaz.[65]

Runaway African and Indian slaves, known as *cimarrones* (maroons), soon augmented Enrique's small group.[66] Together Indians and Africans challenged the Spanish government and control of the island for fourteen years, with the indigenous contingent ultimately triumphing by securing their rights and liberty. Enrique's rebellion helped direct the development of Spanish colonial society from inspiring legal mandates to influencing the debate on Indian slavery.

Just as Enrique and his actions were felt across the circum-Caribbean, his choice to rebel must be understood within the context of larger political and social policies.[67] Enrique responded to a series of laws and policies that left him and the rest of Española's indigenous population in upheaval. Nor was Enrique alone. Dozens of other slaves rose against the Spanish in the first half of the sixteenth century.

By the third decade of colonization, very few vestiges of caciques' pre-contact power remained. Through a series of reducciones, caciques were

ripped from their ancestral lands and watched as Spaniards divided their cacicazgos. Meanwhile the trades in both Africans and Indians grew, bringing
more and more foreign slaves to the island. The majority of the newcomers
did not share the same culture, nor did they have any allegiance to Taíno
caciques. The 1518 smallpox outbreak only made the situation worse as surviving Taínos watched their compatriots die, while also enduring the arrival
of even more foreign slaves. Experiencing spiritual, political, and physical
displacement, Taínos of Española suffered their own small-scale diaspora.
Enrique serves as a concrete example of how both Indian and African slave
trades negatively impacted Taíno caciques.

Moreover, the Laws of Burgos in 1512 failed to ameliorate rampant abuse
of Indians, while the debacle of the Jeronymite intervention illustrates the
contradictory nature of Spanish policies. While some Indians found themselves nominally free in pueblos tutelados, others remained in encomiendas
as still more Indian slaves arrived, despite the Jeronymite decrees to end the
Indian slave trade in 1517. The various competitions and tensions between
secular and religious officials further disrupted indigenous life in the Caribbean. All of these conflicts, abuses, tensions, and changes resulted in the first
large-scale indigenous, and soon after African, revolt in the Spanish Empire:
the rebellion of Enrique.

Enrique's rebellion stemmed from an accumulation of grievances. After
the Repartimiento of 1514, Enrique suffered physical and spiritual displacement from his homeland. He left his ancestors, less portable cemíes (like
paleoglyphs and pictographs), and other sacred spaces behind. The distance
from these important elements decreased his political and spiritual power,
perhaps in both his eyes and those of his subject Indians. In addition to the
loss of indigenous symbols of power, Enrique was also separated from the
Franciscan clergy, monastery, and school where he had spent much of his
childhood, learned Spanish, and married his wife. The loss of these Spanish and Catholic connections might have diminished his commitment to
Spanish culture and society.[68] Lastly the Repartimiento divided him and
his wife, Mencia, by placing them in separate encomiendas, though in the
same settlement of San Juan de la Maguana. Despite all these difficulties,
Enrique remained in his encomienda for several years, until the death of his
encomendero Francisco Valenzuela in 1517 when Francisco's son inherited
the property and, by extension, Enrique.

It is unclear what exactly transpired between Enrique and his new
encomendero, but it did help lead Enrique to forsake the Spanish legal and
political system that he once trusted.[69] Perhaps his disillusionment was the

result of larger changes in the social and political hierarchy of the island. In the wake of the massive Taíno population loss and an increasing influx of foreign slaves, both Indian and African, Spaniards' respect for Taíno caciques waned. With fewer Indians in their power, Taíno leaders could contribute less tribute or laborers, making their cooperation less valuable. Meanwhile more slaves, owned outright by the Spaniards, replaced Taíno laborers. The rise in foreign slaves was especially visible in settlements near Crown gold mines, like San Juan de la Maguana, where most slaves were sent.

Enrique experienced the impact of both the influx of foreign slaves beholden directly to his encomendero and the deaths of many of his subject Indians. In 1514 he governed 109 Indians, but by the time of his escape in 1519 only a few dozen Indians accompanied him.[70] Many of Enrique's subject Indians likely perished in the smallpox epidemic of 1518. It is also possible that some chose not to flee San Juan de Maguana. Regardless, the loss of subject Indians diminished Enrique's influence in Valenzuela's eyes, especially because along with Enrique's cacicazgo, he received unaffiliated Indians from the dissolution of other encomiendas.[71] Enrique likely realized that Taíno caciques could not wield the influence that they had once enjoyed.[72] The lack of respect for the indigenous elite is revealed in Enrique's separation from his wife.[73] The fact that the Spaniards would separate a legally married couple underscores how they viewed the Taínos at this point. Despite his noble blood and faith, the Spaniards treated Enrique little better than a slave during the Repartimiento and thereafter.[74]

The change in treatment and loss of status propelled Enrique to forsake his alliance with the Spanish. In early 1519, Enrique fled San Juan de la Maguana and headed to the refuge of the Bahoruco Mountains and his ancestral territory, where he garnered his power and solace.[75]

While Enrique became the most famous Indian maroon of Española, he was certainly not the first. From the first days of the encomienda system, Spaniards complained of their Indians running to the Bahoruco Mountains. Many Indians recently assigned to pueblos indios or pueblos tutelados also escaped to the unpopulated region. Rodrigo de Figueroa testified that when the Jeronymites left the island, most of the few remaining pueblos tutelados disbanded, leaving the Indians without supervision. Though still nominally free, many Spanish colonists tried to take advantage of the now-unprotected Indians, attempting to enslave them. Many Indians then sought refuge in the Bahoruco Mountains. At least one of the pueblos tutelados was located near Verapaz, so it is likely that Enrique knew some of the freed Indians, particularly those from the pueblo of Santa Maria del Puerto or Verapaz.[76] So

Enrique might have been able to join other maroon Indians in the caves of the Bahoruco.

After Enrique's flight was discovered, Andrés de Valenzuela responded by sending eleven Spaniards in pursuit of the cacique, his wife, and followers. When Valenzuela was unable to stop Enrique, the government of Santo Domingo became involved, gathering together seventy or eighty Spanish soldiers to capture the runaways.[77] At this point, Enrique committed his first violent act, killing four unnamed Spaniards and one of the soldiers sent to capture him.[78] Enrique and his followers also robbed many farms around Verapaz, taking chickens, yucca, and other foodstuffs.[79] Worse of all for the Spanish government were the dozens of Indians, both commended and enslaved, who escaped from their masters to follow Enrique. Las Casas estimated that between one hundred and three hundred Indians joined Enrique's community within a few months of his flight. To stem the rebellion, Judge Figueroa provided the residents of Verapaz with a license to enslave Enrique and his followers.[80] By going against the Spanish government, Enrique lost all protection that his status as cacique once afforded him.

Indians and Africans: The Development of a Multiethnic Alliance

On Christmas Day of 1521, twenty African slaves rebelled on and fled from Diego Colón's ingenio.[81] Escaping into Española's countryside, the slaves soon gained another twenty followers with whom they attacked and destroyed Melchor de Castro's cattle ranch. In the process they killed several Spaniards and liberated at least a dozen slaves, including twelve Indians and one African. They also stole provisions from the ranch, burning all that they were unable to carry.[82] Next, the group set course for licenciado Alonso de Zuazo's ingenio, located only eight leagues from Santo Domingo. At this point the Spanish government rallied, sending a small group of foot soldiers and cavalry to stop the rebels before they reached Santo Domingo or Zuazo's ingenio. The governor's forces confronted the rebels (numbering up to 120, according to Oviedo) at the mouth of the Nizao River where they killed six slaves before most of the rebels escaped to the Bahoruco Mountains.[83]

Safely within the mountains, the African rebels likely joined with Enrique's growing group of indigenous fugitives, all of whom were soon identified as *indios negros* (black Indians). The Audiencia of Santo Domingo first referred to the maroon community as indios negros in a letter to the king in

1530, describing the tenuous position of the island's residents who were still combating the rebels.[84] From 1521 until 1534 the two groups melded together, fighting the same enemy and terrorizing the countryside surrounding Santo Domingo. In Enrique's rebellion, Española witnessed the realization of one of their worst fears: the creation of a maroon community of both runaway Indians and African slaves.[85]

While there is no evidence that Colón's slaves were aware of Enrique's revolt and his community in the Bahoruco Mountains, their actions point to at least some knowledge of the Indian maroons and possibly to a preexisting relationship between the island's African and indigenous populations. The fact that African rebels freed both African and Indian slaves from Melchor de Castro's cattle ranch supports the existence of prior connections. In addition, as discussed, by this point Indian and African slaves had worked and lived together for many years. This proximity made it likely that Indians and Africans developed relationships that eventually facilitated the formation of mixed maroon communities in the Bahoruco Mountains.

While the African slaves who rebelled in 1521 were recent arrivals to the island, the result of the slave license issued to Gouvenot in the wake of the Jeronymites' calls for reform in 1518, they may have been uniquely equipped to ascertain the opportunities for maroonage on the island. The slaves were Wolofs, from Senegambia, which formed part of a declining African empire that dealt with the Portuguese regularly, providing them with at least some knowledge of their European counterparts. Some Wolofs even worked as traders and merchants prior to being enslaved.[86] Thus, the newly arrived slaves were prepared to deal with diverse groups of people in new, strange situations. Finally, the Wolof people were known to be skilled warriors, who often acted as slave catchers in Africa.[87] The rebellion in 1521 only added to the Wolofs' fearsome reputation within the Spanish Empire.

Whether the Wolofs knew of Enrique's community or not, it likely influenced them to seek refuge in the Bahoruco Mountains, an area familiar to the Taínos but not to the recently arrived Africans. Although this is speculation, recent archaeological finds prove that the two groups did in fact reside in the same caves of El Limona. El Limona, a group of caves deep in the Bahoruco Mountains, corresponded to geographic descriptions of Spanish accounts from the rebellion. Here archaeologists have uncovered twelve skeletons and various ceramic pieces. While the skeletons show diverse stages of fossilization, the archaeologists identified three as contemporaneous with Enrique's rebellion, two of which were adult African males and one whose ethnicity could not be determined. Alongside these remains were Taíno ceramics and swine bones dating from the early colonial period, leading archaeologists to conclude that the caves more than likely were inhabited by both Africans and Indians during the early 1500s.[88]

In addition to the archaeological evidence, numerous contemporary Spanish accounts unite the two rebellious groups by 1523. The governor of Española declared official war against *both* Indians and Africans on October 19, 1523.[89] For the next decade residents of Española constantly begged the Crown for the manpower, supplies, and funds necessary to combat the uprising in the Bahoruco Mountains, which expanded daily as slaves continued to desert to the rebels. As they grew more powerful, the rebels began executing raids on Spanish ingenios, farms, and towns, stealing what provisions they needed and killing any Spaniards that they encountered.

By the mid-1520s Española's residents were confined to the capital city of Santo Domingo or its immediate environs, with the rest of the island dominated by African and Indian rebels led or inspired by Enrique. The united forces (reportedly a group of at least four hundred Indians and Africans) even attacked Enrique's former residence, San Juan de la Maguana, where they both robbed and killed many residents before retreating to the mountains.[90] The rebels succeeded in gaining the advantage not only because of their numbers, but also because of the natives' knowledge of the island's geography. The Spaniards mentioned repeatedly the difficulties they had when attacking the rebels in the Bahoruco Mountains, where the landscape posed as many if not more obstacles than the maroons themselves.[91] Although the mountains were quite high and rocky, even described by one Spanish official as bigger than those of Granada, the greatest difficulty for the Spanish soldiers, and their African and Indian porters, was the distance of the mountains from Spanish settlements. By the time the soldiers reached the caves and valleys from which Enrique organized his assaults, they had already traveled up to forty leagues (over 150 miles), carrying all their provisions with them. Once in the mountains, food was hard to locate as the region is incredibly dry and barren, making even fresh water a trial to obtain. Taking advantage of the situation, the cimarrones often climbed to the highest peaks where Spaniards with all their artillery and baggage could not reach. The Indians also set up spies throughout the mountains to report on the Spanish army's progress so that Enrique and his troops were always prepared.[92] The last advantage possessed by the Indian and African rebels was their knowledge of Spanish weaponry and tactics of war. These were ladino Indians who spoke Spanish and had lived alongside the Spaniards for years, some since birth like Enrique.[93] Zuazo also reported that the rebels possessed and used Spanish swords and lances in the later years of the war.[94]

Trying to overcome these obstacles, the Spanish sent out three squadrons from San Juan de la Maguana, a city closer to Bahoruco than Santo Domingo, in 1528. Each group had at least eighty Spanish soldiers accompanied by an unknown number of African and Indian slaves. The use of Indian and African slaves turned out to be a mistake because many escaped the squadrons to join the cimarrones instead of fighting them.[95] At the end of the year all three squadrons failed to capture more than a few rebels and spent 25,000 gold pesos during the conflict.[96] By 1532 officials of Santo Domingo estimated that 40,000 ducados (a type of gold coin, with each ducado being worth approximately three quarters of a gold peso) had been spent on the war against the cimarrones of Bahoruco.[97] Officials even organized slave raids to fund the conflict. In 1526 Jácome de Castellón (the governor of Nueva Cádiz) and Pedro de Talavera organized a slaving armada to Cumaná to capture indigenous slaves in "just war." These slaves were then sold, and the profits were used to fund squadrons sent against Enrique.[98]

Only making matters worse for the Spanish were new attacks from other caciques across the island in the late 1520s and early 1530s. The caciques included Ciguayo, Murcia, Hernandillo el Tuerto, and Tamayo. As had Enrique, other leaders suffered from the continual arrival of foreign Indians, clearly marked by their C (for Carib) tattoos, and African slaves both of whose presence diminished Taíno caciques' status and power. Perhaps this explains why in the late 1520s, years into Enrique's revolt, other Taíno caciques began rebelling against the Spaniards. The caciques also may have responded to Enrique's success, having witnessed the Spaniards' inability to capture Enrique for nearly ten years. Maybe the other caciques viewed the Spanish as weak at this point. One final possibility is that the caciques joined with Enrique due to intimate connections they had with the cacique. At least one of the caciques, Tamayo, attended the school at Verapaz with Enrique. The others might have attended similar institutions in Concepción de la Vega or Santiago.

In 1528 cacique Ciguayo assaulted Spanish mining towns in the Cibao.[99] Ciguayo started by attacking small groups of Spaniards working in mines or on farms of the central valley. During all of the attacks, Ciguayo and his companions killed any Spaniard they encountered.[100] After several of these assaults, Ciguayo gathered together a larger group, of up to eighty Indians, to attack central mining towns, including Concepción de la Vega, burning Spanish haciendas and killing at least five men.[101] The group of Indians also kidnapped several women and children. The documents shed little light on the fate of these captives, but it is possible that Ciguayo expected to gain a ransom for their return, or that they were taken to replace recently deceased members of his chiefdom. Regardless of the captives' fate, or the intentions of Ciguayo and his men, seventy Spaniards pursued the group but were able to capture only one Indian. While Ciguayo and his men escaped this encounter largely intact, by July 1529 captains Alonso Silvestre and Bartolomé Cataño reported that they killed the cacique. For his death the men received five gold pesos each.[102]

Then in 1532 cacique Tamayo joined the fray, attacking the northern port city of Puerto Real.[103] Like Enrique, Tamayo suffered displacement and loss of stature in the wake of the Repartimiento of Albuquerque. Prior to the Repartimiento, Tamayo attended the school at Verapaz and was originally commended to Bartolomé Colón. Following the Repartimiento, Tamayo suffered the breakup of his cacicazgo and his own relocation. He, with 102 Indians of service, twelve aged Indians, and sixteen children, moved to Concepción de la Vega to work under Juan de Fonseca.[104] Presumably these Indians were destined to work in the Crown's gold mines. Another portion of Tamayo's subject Indians, twenty-six, was commended to the Franciscan monastery of Santo Domingo.[105]

In 1519, nearly concurrent with Enrique's original flight, Tamayo and his subjects organized a small rebellion near Puerto Real.[106] While the Spaniards succeeded in quickly quelling this revolt, Tamayo and his followers did not give up. Documents suggest that Tamayo might have spent time living with Enrique in his maroon community, along with his nephew, at various points during his maroonage.[107] Perhaps he learned new tactics while in the Bahoruco Mountains, tactics that he implemented in his 1532 attack, again on Puerto Real.[108] During this encounter the rebels killed a Spanish woman and two children, prompting the colonial government to renew their offensive against Tamayo with two squadrons.[109] In the same attack they killed fourteen Indian slaves.[110]

The killing of these slaves causes one to wonder about their ethnicity or Tamayo's grievances. Enrique's squadrons consistently freed both Indian and African slaves during assaults, but Tamayo killed these Indians. Perhaps they defended their Spanish masters, or maybe they were Indian slaves from places like Florida, with whom Tamayo and the other Taínos had little connection. At this point both Puerto Real and Puerto Plata were centers for the Indian slave trade, especially for armadas heading north toward southeastern North America or the Lucayos Islands.[111] Tamayo possibly saw the foreign

Indian slaves as interlopers diminishing his power. Or Tamayo did not share the same respect for Spanish government and institutions that Enrique possessed. Throughout his revolt, Enrique tried to minimize bloodshed, and when his followers did escalate the level of violence, he apologized for their actions. So it is likely that Enrique did not sanction Tamayo's use of gratuitous violence, demonstrating a lack of coordination between the groups. It could even point to a lack of connections between Enrique and Tamayo by 1532. In any case, the Spanish government admitted their failure to militarily subdue Enrique, his followers, and his allies by 1533. They then turned to a new strategy: diplomacy and negotiation through religious officials to finally end the conflict.

The End of Enrique's Rebellion

Paradoxically or not, while Enrique and his compatriots warred against Spanish officials, civilians, and military of the island, they also maintained friendly relationships with the clergy. Nor were Enrique's bonds with the clergy unique. In a letter to the Crown dating from February 1532, Doctor Infante complained about clergy hiding and defending maroon African slaves, even those who had "committed grave crimes."[112] It was well known that maroons, indigenous or African, could find refuge with the Catholic clergy within their monasteries. Enrique and Spanish officials used the clergy to facilitate peace talks. Priest Fray Remigio de Mejía, one of Enrique's former teachers at the monastery and school in Verapaz, was central to the negotiations that ended Enrique's revolt. After Remigio's tenure in Verapaz, he spent time in Spain, France, Cuba, and New Spain, before returning to Española in 1526.[113] As soon as he heard of Enrique's revolt, Remigio wrote to the Crown in defense of the cacique.[114] Then in 1527, Remigio tried to meet with Enrique in the Bahoruco Mountains. This meeting, however, was a disaster.

Upon reaching the Bahoruco Mountains, Enrique did not meet the friar but instead sent some of his supporters, who mistrusted the intentions of the priest or his indigenous companion (a cacique named Rodrigo). The meeting quickly fell apart, ending with the maroons attacking Remigio and Rodrigo, stripping them of their clothing. They then drowned Rodrigo, perhaps for being a traitor to the larger indigenous cause.[115] Why they spared Remigio is unclear. What is visible within the episode is that Enrique's personal bonds with the friar, or perhaps the larger Catholic Church, were not shared by all his followers.

Despite this setback Remigio returned to the Bahoruco Mountains, at least twice more, to speak with Enrique. During the second visit, in 1528, the cacique apologized to the priest for his followers' actions the previous year.[116] During this meeting Remigio delivered Enrique's first letter of pardon from the governor of Española, asking the cacique to desist from all attacks on the Spanish. In exchange he and his followers would become free Spanish subjects. Additionally, the letter promised that the government would deliver sheep, cows, and other provisions to the community.[117] Despite the letter of pardon, delivered by his former priest and teacher, Enrique questioned the offer, partially because it came from the governor and not the king. This shows the cacique's in-depth knowledge of Spanish hierarchy. A military force (led by Captain Hernando de San Miguel) also accompanied Remigio. Enrique was wary of the military officials, whose presence made him fear that the negotiations were a ruse. As a result, the arbitration fell through.[118]

On the agreed-upon day for Enrique's surrender to Hernando de San Miguel and Remigio, he did not appear. Instead of Enrique, the Spanish found 1,500 pesos that Enrique hoped would help defray at least some of the costs of the cimarron assaults.[119] The offering may have also been an attempt to hide the true intentions of the rebels. Only days after the failed peace treaty, Enrique's forces launched an attack on a nearby ranch belonging to none other than Captain Hernando de San Miguel. During the attack they took Indians and horses, burned many dwellings, and drowned one three-year-old Spanish child.[120] The renewed violence prompted the Spanish government to launch several more military campaigns against the cacique. Note that the breakdown of negotiations with Enrique occurred at the same time as Ciguayo's attacks against the mines of the Cibao, including those of Concepción de la Vega. Perhaps the two events were not connected, but it is also possible that Enrique saw Ciguayo's involvement as an opportunity to prolong his own maroonage.

After several more failed efforts to pacify Enrique and his followers, the Crown sent two hundred professional soldiers, led by the new governor of Tierra Firme, Francisco de Barrionuevo, to the island in 1533.[121] Barrionuevo then recruited another thirty-five of the best, most experienced local colonists who had served in *cuadrillas* (quasi-militias) over the years.[122] While Barrionuevo possessed the military capacity needed to pacify Enrique, he did not want to win via fighting. Instead, he sought to end the conflict through diplomacy. Queen Juana sent Barrionuevo with a complete pardon for Enrique, directly from the Crown.[123] Additionally, Barrionuevo took two female relatives of Enrique, a mestizo translator, indigenous guides, and

Figure 3. Statue of Enrique outside of the Museo del Hombre Dominicano in Santo Domingo. Photo by author.

ENRIQUILLO

Remigio with him.[124] First, Barrionuevo arranged a meeting with Enrique, with the help of one of Enrique's female relatives, along a lake in the Bahoruco Mountains.[125]

Enrique brought eighty armed Indian and African followers to the meeting, but after he saw the letter with the royal seal and spoke for nearly two hours to Barrionuevo, he verbally agreed to surrender and promised his allegiance to the Spanish Crown.[126] During the meeting Enrique professed his sincere wishes for peace and apologized for all acts of violence that he and his followers executed throughout the lengthy conflict.[127] A statue of Enrique stands at the edge of Lago Enriquillo (also named after the cacique) memorializing Enrique's legacy. Another statue of the revered cacique stands outside of the Museo del Hombre Dominicano in the capital city of Santo Domingo. See Figure 3 for an image of the statue.

A few weeks later Barrionuevo sent another delegation, led by Pedro Romero, equipped with wine, clothes, and religious ornaments for Enrique's church. Romero's goal was to obtain a written declaration of peace from the cacique.[128] Barrionuevo chose Romero as his envoy because Romero and Enrique knew one another, possibly even from Enrique's childhood as Romero possessed an encomienda in Enrique's ancestral land of Jaragua and was married to a Taíno woman.[129] During his stay in the maroon community, Romero observed that every bohio in Enrique's town possessed a cross on the door.[130] Whether or not the placement of crosses was a sign of true belief and conversion to the Catholic Church is impossible to know, but the crosses without a doubt made a positive impression on the Spanish. Romero also noted the size of the community, with as many as four hundred inhabitants spread through a series of caves nearly invisible to the naked eye. Enrique reacted positively to the eight-day visit, demonstrating his commitment to peace by turning over six African maroons to Romero.[131] Central to the Spanish Crown's offer of pardon was Enrique's future help in capturing runaway African and indigenous slaves. For each African slave turned over to the Spanish, Enrique would receive four wool shirts.[132] While Enrique opposed this clause at first, by Romero's visit he acquiesced to the Spaniard's conditions.[133]

Even after his meetings with both Barrionuevo and Romero, and a visit by one of his indigenous aides named Martin Alonso to Santo Domingo, Enrique still felt the need to ensure that the offer of peace and forgiveness was valid.[134] To do so, he traveled to Azua, the city closest to the future location of the promised free Indian town, accompanied by fifty armed Indians.[135] All of Azua's residents verified the armistice and future town. While in Azua, Enrique also met with Bartolomé de las Casas. A few months after the encounter, Las Casas described his monthlong visit with cacique Enrique and his family in a letter to the Crown. During their time together, the friar gave confession to Enrique, his wife (Mencia), and all the cacique's captains, while also soothing their fears regarding their upcoming surrender.[136] According to the letter, Las Casas even accompanied the cacique and his people to their new residence seven leagues outside of Azua, a free town given to them in exchange for their peaceful surrender. In the new settlement the friar, along with Spanish residents of Azua, helped the new arrivals to procure bread and other necessary provisions.[137]

After the visit to Azua, Enrique ended his revolt in October 1533. Again showing his reliance on religious officials and distrust of military leaders,

Enrique requested several Franciscan friars come to his maroon community to baptize all the children living there before he journeyed to Santo Domingo to formalize the peace agreement.[138] This might have been to ensure that the children could be not declared slaves after surrender. After Pedro Romero, and the requested Franciscan friars, spent time with Enrique in his maroon community, the cacique finally journeyed to Santo Domingo. Enrique, along with twenty of his soldiers, spent two months in the capital, during which time he recorded his surrender to the Crown in a letter that is now the only existing document written by a Taíno Indian.[139] The document is quite formulaic, following and using established language, demonstrating Enrique's extensive knowledge of Spanish culture. On the other hand, he may have received help while writing the document, or a scribe could have written it, with Enrique simply signing the finished letter. An excerpt follows: "For the mercies provided by your Majesty, I kiss your imperial feet and hands to show the eternal obedience that I owe you as your lowly vassal who will obey everything that you mandate, as will all of my Indians of my land. We will also now come to the Spanish towns after having captured some maroons that were moving about the island."[140]

In exchange for his surrender, the cacique received the title "don" (becoming Don Enrique), acquired amnesty for all of his followers, collected numerous presents (including clothing and furniture), and secured his own family's freedom in a free Indian town called Sabana Buey, seven leagues from Azua.[141] And despite the entreating tone adopted by Enrique in the letter, he described his surrender as a "consultation" with the officials of the royal court. This implies that he saw himself as an equal to the colonists and as a subject only to the Crown of Spain.

Enrique died only a year later, in 1535, leaving behind a testament (still undiscovered) declaring that his surviving wife, Doña Mencia, and nephew should govern the town as caciques in his place.[142] He was buried, after receiving the sacraments, in Azua's church.[143] Prior to his death, Enrique fulfilled his allegiance to the Spanish as he did help to capture numerous runaway slaves. In particular, he helped the Spanish locate African maroon communities not affiliated with his own group, though Oviedo claimed that he also turned in Africans once affiliated with his community.[144] He even volunteered to help capture the indigenous rebel Tamayo who was still wreaking havoc along the northern coast of the island.[145] This calls into question whether or not he and Tamayo were ever working together, or if their alliance had recently fallen apart. In either case, the Spaniards successfully destroyed the alliance, uniting multiple Indian caciques and African slaves, a situation they tried their hardest to avoid in future colonies.

Beyond attempting to keep Indian and African slaves separate (an effort that had little effect for decades), the Spaniards also hardened their slave codes following the series of rebellions in the early 1520s. These codes are the Ordenanzas of 1522, written only thirteen days after the initial rebellion of Wolof slaves in Colón's ingenio. These new laws made running away a crime punishable by mutilation, even if the slave voluntarily returned to their owner, and made rebellion a capital crime. Additionally, the ordinances made it illegal for slaves to carry weapons, except for a small knife, and also restricted the movement of slaves unaccompanied by their masters.[146] In 1528 the Audiencia of Santo Domingo promulgated an additional set of laws governing slaves.[147] This set included one entry that sheds some light on the prevalence of runaway slaves, both Indian and African. Number sixty-nine states that residents of Santo Domingo needed to secure any canoes they owned so that "Indians, slaves and other delinquents" could not steal and use them in their flight.

These laws along with Enrique's surrender did bring a degree of peace to Española, but colonial officials still faced pockets of rebellion across the island for decades, even centuries.[148] The archbishop of Santo Domingo counted as many as two or three thousand runaway slaves across the island, with most in Punta de Samaná on the north coast and Cabo de Higuey in the southeastern quadrant of the island.[149] In 1543, Melchor de Castro wrote to the Crown, trying to explain the decline in gold sent from Española to Spain. In the correspondence he blamed the decline in productivity on the huge number of "rebel Negroes" who controlled much of the island subsisting on wild pigs, cows, and other foodstuffs.[150] Some of the most violent of these rebels found refuge in Enrique's former caves and community in the Bahoruco Mountains.[151] In 1545, Castro reported that the African rebels were so brave as to rob and attack Spaniards located only three leagues from Santo Domingo. In this message he requested that the king send five thousand or more soldiers to help quell the maroons and gain control of the island.[152]

Nor did the African rebels attack only Spanish towns. Perhaps in retaliation for Enrique turning over the six African slaves to Romero, along with the others he volunteered to capture in his surrender to the Crown, a group of African maroons attacked and destroyed Sabana Buey (the free Indian town awarded to Enrique in 1534) at some point in the 1540s.[153] Only eight or ten of Enrique's Indians survived the attack and went on to serve as spies for the Spanish, hunting for African runaways and maroon communities.[154] Enrique's successors maintained their allegiance with the Spanish, perhaps seeing their link to the colonists as their only avenue of survival. Meanwhile, these episodes point to tension and conflict developing between Indian and African slaves as a result of the terms of Enrique's surrender.

While the story of Enrique is extraordinary, at least partially because of how the rebellion ended, it is only one of many uprisings that wreaked havoc across the early Spanish Caribbean. There were reports of indigenous and African maroon communities and rebellions throughout the greater Caribbean in the 1520s, 1530s, and 1540s. Many of these groups were likely responding to the same pressures and changes that pushed Enrique to flight and violence. In 1526 the procurador of San Germán complained of attacks from "negros e indios que hay alzados."[155] And the problem grew over the years. By 1531, a much larger conflict with Indian and African maroons enveloped Puerto Rico. Many of the maroons were described as "Jelofes" or Wolofs, an already stigmatized group after the 1521 rebellion in Española. The injury of the maroons and fear of further revolts caused Puerto Rican officials to attempt to prohibit the sale or importation of any more Wolofs. Some Puerto Rican officials even suggested the cessation of the African slave trade in its entirety in 1534.[156]

Cuba began reporting larger numbers of runaway slaves two years later, in 1536. In Cuba, the maroons were able to quickly disrupt island life, attacking Spanish colonists' farms and assaulting residents along the roads.[157] One of the reasons they were able to so quickly unsettle life on the island was that they joined with escaped indigenous slaves and commended Indians. In 1526, governor Gonzalo de Guzmán first reported the problem of escaping Indians, many of whom were also committing frequent assaults, robberies, and murders across the island. When these rebels were caught, they were usually punished with enslavement or death.[158] The problem for Guzmán was that many believed his actions were much too limited. Some accused him of using Crown funds meant to combat maroons for his own personal benefit. Nor did he expend any of his own funds on the effort. As a result, numerous towns in Cuba, including Puerto Principe and Trinidad, suffered losses at the hands of numerous indigenous assaults. Indians burned all of Puerto Principe, killing many Spaniards and causing grave injury to allied Indians along the northern coast of Cuba. When Guzmán did gather a force large enough to combat the rebellious Indians and maroons, most of those captured were then enslaved to address the labor shortage. However, maroon leaders were executed.[159]

The next governor of Cuba, Manuel de Rojas, looked to extreme punishment to discourage further maroonage or rebellion. In 1533, Captain Diego Bonela defeated rebel cacique Guama and his followers (it is unclear how many escaped slaves made up his forces), killing most and also enslaving seventeen women and children.[160] Two years later, upon the capture of four African maroons, Rojas not only ordered their execution, but also had their corpses cut up and their heads removed and placed on stakes. The pikes were then displayed publicly in the town of Bayamo.[161]

In ensuing years administrators attempted to address the issue of runaways and rebellion by using diplomacy. One such effort occurred in 1537 when Gonzalo de Guzmán conducted a *visita* (an inquiry) of the island's properties. As with any census, Guzmán wanted to know who owned each property and the identity of its diverse inhabitants. But this was not an ordinary census. Guzmán was also trying to ascertain whether the island's encomenderos were following Crown policy, from how slaves were clothed and fed to whether encomenderos were teaching their commended Indians and slaves the ways of the Catholic faith. To ascertain this, Guzmán did not simply count slaves or interview owners. He questioned each slave, asking about their diet, workload, if they were Christians, and if they could recite the Ave Maria. In nearly every property listed, Guzmán found both Indian and African slaves, the majority of whom could not recite the Ave Maria. He also found cases of grievous abuse. The visita reveals much about the state of the "spiritual conquest," the extent of Crown control in the Caribbean, and intimate details of the lives of indigenous and African slaves in Cuba, lives that were closely connected.

As Guzmán, along with parish priest Santo Selo, traveled across the island, he also questioned the slaves about how their masters treated them. Then, depending on their answers, the slaves were baptized and their masters were admonished and fined, as it was their duty to both care for and educate and convert both their indigenous and African slaves.[162] The normal fine for each slave was two or three gold pesos.[163] One owner, Andrés Rano, was fined ten pesos not only for failing to teach his slaves Catholicism, but more importantly for having an affair with his indigenous slave named Elvira with whom he had two children. Andres not only had to pay the fine, but had to stop the affair and relocate Elvira, sending her to a convent in Havana.[164]

During his survey, for which he visited twenty-one residences or plantations located close to Santiago, Guzmán counted 215 African slaves, 55 Indian slaves (many of whom were from the Guanaxas Islands), and 92 Indians from Cuba (presumably Taíno Indians who might have been commended, free, or enslaved, as the report did not make their legal status clear). Except for two properties, all housed *both* Indian and African workers, the majority enslaved, but with quite a few listed as native to the island. Here we see the diversity of laborers on the island, with most being foreign slaves, whether indigenous or African. In this particular survey there were nearly quadruple the number of African slaves to Indian slaves, though this does not include the more ambiguous ninety-two natives of the island whose status was murky. This seems to contrast with many other contemporary censuses and reports in both Cuba and other Caribbean islands. Perhaps the numbers can be explained by the focus of the inquiry. The census was not of the entire island, but only the properties within walking distance to Santiago. These residents likely had more capital to invest in more expensive African slaves. In fact, many of the encomenderos included in the report were Crown officials.

But the visita was not simply concerned with numbers. Guzmán also sought information on the care of Cuba's slaves. Per the slaves' responses, most owners fed their commended Indians and slaves well, giving them both meat and bread. Only one owner was reported as abusive, often beating African slaves with sticks. Additionally, many African slaves and native Indians were baptized, though very few could accurately recite the Lord's Prayer and Ave Maria or had regularly attended church on Sundays. The group least likely to have received the sacrament of baptism were foreign Indian slaves. As one might expect, the owners who did not provide their slaves with adequate food, limiting them to cazabe with little to no meat or bread, were also those who did not follow Crown laws regarding religious instruction. Overall those who worked in mines received less food and religious training than those who worked in households or agricultural enterprises. While the origins of most indigenous slaves were not listed, in six of the twenty-one properties Indian slaves from the Guanaxas Islands were specifically identified.[165] This makes sense as Cuba was the launching point for expeditions of slaving and exploration to the Yucatán coast from 1517 onward. What is not clear is why the report specifically singled out those from the Guanaxas, not giving the origin or ethnicity of other Indian slaves who could have hailed from locales as disparate as Florida, Venezuela, Brazil, or the Lesser Antilles. While the visita answers some questions, it inspires many more. Nor did it stop the rebellions as the island still battled both Indian and African maroons in 1539 and 1540. In these years, officials requested more funds, troops, and supplies to help them defeat both the maroons and encroaching French pirates.[166]

Nor were Caribbean islands the only sites of rebellion. By 1535 Panama was also witnessing widespread slave revolts and the creation of small maroon communities, which robbed and assaulted Spanish settlements.[167] In 1538, the Crown addressed the problem of runaway slaves, both Indian and African, in Cubagua, as Rojas had in Cuba, by increasing punishments for any slave who fled the pearl fisheries. They could suffer up to one hundred lashes, the amputation of a foot or both ears, or death. The harsher penalties applied to slaves who not only fled but also took pearls with them. The legislation also prescribed punishment for anyone caught harboring an escaped slave. The problem of runaway slaves was so great that a communal fund was created in 1550 to pay slave catchers or to compensate owners for executed slaves.[168]

*   *   *

The problem of runaway and rebellious slaves continued to plague the greater Caribbean throughout the sixteenth, seventeenth, and eighteenth centuries. In many ways the rebellions, violence, and unrest pushed the Crown to finally act definitively against the indigenous slave trade and the larger abuse of both free and enslaved Indians. Indian enslavement and the violence it entailed put indigenous cooperation in jeopardy. Rebellions such as Enrique's in Española taught the Spaniards a hard lesson. Rebellions impeded economic growth across the Caribbean, and so the Crown sought to prevent uprisings by reforming the relationship between the indigenous peoples of the Americas and the Spanish colonists. The reform came in the shape of the New Laws in November 1542.[169] The laws attacked the class of powerful encomenderos, especially those in Peru, and, most importantly for our purposes, outlawed most forms of Indian slavery.[170]

At this point, African slaves began to outnumber and, in many colonies, replace Indian slaves. Access to African slaves increased exponentially, following the unification of Spain and Portugal, allowing Spanish colonies to benefit from Portuguese control of the African slave trade. Between 1590 and 1640 nearly five hundred thousand African slaves were shipped to the Americas.[171] As the availability of African slaves increased, the risks involved in the indigenous slave trade proved to be too high. Not only was the trade now illegal, but the Spaniards also had learned that indigenous cooperation was crucial for the economic prosperity of their American colonies. It still took decades, and in some locations centuries, for the indigenous slave trade to end completely, but 1542 marked the beginning of the end.

The Slow Decline of the Indian Slave Trade

By the late 1530s a trade in indigenous slaves had engulfed the Spanish Caribbean. Merchants and officials captured, displaced, and shipped hundreds of thousands of indigenous peoples across the Caribbean to toil in mines, at plantations, and on ranches far from their homes. The search for enslaved laborers inspired exploration, drove conquest (both military and spiritual), and kept early Spanish colonies afloat, but it also caused severe problems and wrought havoc among an increasingly wide swath of indigenous peoples in the Americas. Legislation passed from the Laws of Burgos in 1512 onward failed to reform or limit the slave trade in meaningful ways. Instead both legal and illegal methods of attaining Indian slaves abounded. Spanish traders and indigenous leaders continued to enslave free Indians, selling them to eager colonists for low prices.[1] From the coasts of Venezuela and Colombia to Española and New Spain, these practices devastated native populations and sparked indigenous uprisings that disrupted colonization, conversion, and trade. By the 1540s most colonists and officials accepted that the indigenous slave trade was not the answer to procuring a sustainable labor force in the Caribbean.

With the consequences of the indigenous slave trade increasingly apparent, and following years of debate and pressure from religious leaders like Bartolomé de las Casas and Pope Paul III, in November 1542 King Charles I passed legislation known as the "New Laws," which outlawed Indian slavery.[2] The legislation specifically forbade the taking of Indians in warfare or via rescate as well as the removal of Indians from any island or Tierra Firme. The New Laws even prohibited Spaniards from purchasing previously enslaved Indians.[3] Though it took decades, even in some isolated areas along the frontiers of the empire centuries, the New Laws marked the end of the widespread, legal Indian slave trade in the Spanish Americas. By the early seventeenth century, Indian slavery was no longer a viable industry for Spanish and Portuguese merchants within the circum-Caribbean, even in areas such as Brazil and the Guianas, where it persisted into the final decades of the sixteenth century.[4] African slavery truly began to replace Indian slavery at this point.

By 1542 the Indian slave trade had changed hundreds of thousands of indigenous lives. At its height, it scattered diverse ethnic groups and cultures across the Americas. Indigenous slaves from Mexico, Colombia, Florida, Venezuela, and Brazil all found themselves transported to Española and other Caribbean islands like Cuba, Puerto Rico, and the Pearl Islands. Some were shipped as commodities to various islands, or as far away as Spain, to be sold for immediate profit. Others became military auxiliaries, guides, miners, pearl divers, servants, or, in the case of women, unwilling sexual partners. While some slaves were taken from one location and sold in another, many other slaves were displaced numerous times, moving in multiple directions. A few traveled through the entire Atlantic World. The multidirectional movement of slaves underscores that removal of Indians was a key component to the early colonial project. Indigenous populations did not simply collapse from disease or warfare; a significant number were first removed through the Indian slave trade.

The slave trade took many forms, both legal and illegal, documented and undocumented. Involving captives taken in "just war" as well as Caribs and Indians living on "useless" islands, the slave trade engulfed much of the Americas. Within this trade Indians themselves played a central role in shaping the *early* Indian slave trade. Indigenous politics, connections, and knowledge in many ways dictated who was enslaved in the first two decades post-conquest. But, by the 1520s, this changed. Due to population loss, cultural change, and an influx of Spaniards, the Indians of the Caribbean began to lose control of the slave trade and the larger colonial project. As native leaders' status diminished, Spanish colonists began to act with greater impunity. It was this attitude that led the Indian slave trade to reach new heights in the 1520s and 1530s, during which the Caribbean became a "shatter zone" ripped apart by violence, warfare, and slavery.

Within the chaos and pain is evidence of survival and incorporation, especially when considering precolonial relationships between and across islands. Indians themselves contributed greatly to the trade, both voluntarily and through coercion. Indians resisted Spanish incursions, at times forcing the Spanish to alter their practices and policies of colonization. At this very early stage of colonization, Indians, even some enslaved, were able to influence and inhibit the Spanish conquest of their lands. In many cases it was the Indians who determined both where the Spanish settled and which locations were successful.

Even as new Crown legislation attempted to end the legal circum-Caribbean slave trade, Indian slavery continued along Spanish frontiers and borderlands, in some cases for hundreds of years. And even at the core of the empire, Spanish colonists and merchants fought to maintain Indian slavery.[5] It was difficult for colonists to abandon a practice that had been so necessary, widespread, and at times lucrative for the previous five decades. Nor were all or most enslaved Indians freed following the change in policy. In one example, in 1545 Española's government recorded five thousand legal Indian slaves from various parts of the Caribbean still working on the island.[6] Officials judged them to be legal slaves because they had been captured in "just war" or were labeled as Caribs.[7] The actual number of Indian slaves was likely higher, with most being of questionable origin and legality. In 1547 a priest at Concepción de la Vega relayed to the Crown that most Indians on the island were slaves or in some state of unfreedom despite the passage of the New Laws.[8] And colonists still sought new Indian slaves.

Well into the 1570s, letters continued to reach the Crown pleading for the reinstatement of the indigenous slave trade. Concurrently, an illegal Indian slave trade thrived at the edges of the empire. Letters from Caracas in the 1550s relate numerous armadas hailing from Española and Puerto Rico that raided the Venezuelan coast. They assaulted the salt mines near Caracas.[9] Many more slaves came from Portuguese Brazil. Brazilian indigenous slaves, who were particularly sought after, began arriving in the Spanish Caribbean in the 1530s. Officials of Santo Domingo were even willing to pay a 7.5 percent tax on each slave, the same amount as for an African slave. This willingness suggests that Indians from Brazil had a higher perceived value, perhaps because they lived longer or were already accustomed to growing sugar cane, the strongest industry in the Caribbean by the 1530s.[10] However, indigenous slavery in Brazil did not increase significantly until the 1540s and 1550s *after* the passage of the New Laws.[11] The basis of the trade were Tupiniquins selling captive Tupinambás and Carijos, their enemies, to the Portuguese, their allies.[12] And the number of captives was not insignificant. According to a German visitor to Brazil in 1553, the Tupiniquins gathered and delivered as many as five thousand indigenous captives in a single day.[13] While the Portuguese enslaved many of these Indians in situ, largely to cut and process Brazil wood, they sent many more to the Spanish Caribbean. By the late 1550s, the Portuguese no longer relied on their indigenous allies to procure slaves. Mem de Sá, the governor of Brazil from 1557 to 1572, with the support of Jesuits like Manoel de Nóbrega, sought to conquer and pacify the still largely independent Tupinambá villages that surrounded Salvador. Violent campaigns from

1558 to 1560 resulted in the capture of hundreds of Tupi Indians.[14] And the number of slaves only increased in the 1580s as relations between the Portuguese's former ally, the Tupiniquin, deteriorated, inspiring European expeditions into the interior of Brazil.[15]

Well after the passage of the New Laws, Brazilian indigenous slaves continued to arrive in Santo Domingo. In an attempt to receive permission to buy these slaves, officials of Santo Domingo created a compromise that they argued would benefit the Indians, since they were already enslaved, removed from their native lands, and likely Caribs.[16] The essence of the compromise was first proposed by Doctor Mexia in October 1568 in response to the arrival of eight Brazilian Indian slaves. He suggested that the colonists of Española be allowed to buy the slaves, who were sold for the very moderate price of twelve gold pesos, but be permitted to retain them for only seven to eight years, during which time they would also be tutored in the Catholic faith.[17] After eight years, the enslaved Indians would be free and have the benefit of this education. On the other hand, Mexia reasoned, if the Indians remained with the Portuguese, they would be destined for servitude in the Madeira Islands or Portugal and remain slaves for the duration of their lives.

Mexia soon gained the support of several other officials in Santo Domingo, specifically the judges Caceres, Peralta, and Santiago de Vera, and they collectively wrote to the king in June and August 1569 asking for licenses to purchase Brazilian slaves. In both letters they reiterated the benefits of the plan for both Brazilian Indian slaves and the residents of Española, the majority of whom could not afford more expensive African slaves. At the same time, they increased the number of years that the Indians would serve to twelve.[18] By 1569 even the archbishop of Santo Domingo, Friar Andrés de Carvajal, wrote to the king championing Mexia's plan for Brazilian slaves, adding the traditional argument that they were in fact Caribs who consumed human flesh. According to Carvajal, serving as a slave or working in the gold mines or sugar ingenios of Española would dissuade them from their immoral practices and make them more easily converted to the Catholic faith.[19] Despite all the letters, from both secular and ecclesiastical officials, the king refused to grant the residents of Española permission to buy Brazilian slaves, though they persisted with their petitions as late as 1573.[20] Notwithstanding the king's refusal, it is likely that his ruling was often ignored and that Brazilian slaves were purchased regularly via illicit channels.

Indian slaves hailing from Brazil were not the only indigenous captives that Spanish colonists sought to purchase as the sixteenth century came to a close. After several years of attempting to peacefully negotiate with the native peoples of Florida, the territory's governor and conqueror, Pedro Menéndez de Avilés, wanted to force the Indians into submission. Whereas he had once praised Florida's indigenous peoples for their physical strength, prowess in battle, and generous nature, by the 1570s Menéndez and his men commonly referred to their former allies as savages, brutal devil worshippers, and liars who could not be trusted.[21] Menéndez even went so far as to advocate for the extermination of Florida's natives, or at the very least their enslavement and removal from the province. According to Menéndez's proposal, these Indian slaves could be sold in Cuba, Santo Domingo, and Puerto Rico, benefiting all the colonies involved.[22] As with the Brazilian Indian slaves, the king failed to respond to Menéndez's proposal, and the colonists of Florida were left to fight rebellious Indians for decades to come.

These examples illustrate the reticence of both the residents and leaders of Spanish colonies to give up the Indian slave trade. Nor, for that matter, did most Iberians stop viewing Indians as perpetual servants following the passage of the New Laws. Few masters willingly freed their Indian slaves, and the majority of colonial officials found it difficult to force residents to give up their slaves.[23] By 1545 Santo Domingo's royal court had only liberated one hundred Indian slaves, the majority of whom were surrendered and freed due to their age and poor health. To make matters worse, new Indian slaves from Tierra Firme continued to arrive in Española. In April 1545 two ships from Margarita and Cubagua docked in Santo Domingo with 250 branded indigenous slaves. The merchants claimed they were captured before the passage of the New Laws. While the adult male slaves were sold, the slaves under the age of fourteen and all the women were freed.[24]

Even in the courtrooms of Castile, where King Charles I tried to implement the new legislation to the fullest, Indian slaves had to battle their masters in lengthy trials. Though approximately one hundred Indian slaves did gain their freedom through these procedures, the majority hailed from New Spain.[25] Many others who attempted to sue for their freedom were sold, beaten, or branded by their masters before they could attain liberty. Slaveholders utilized illegal means because most did not hold legal documents stating how or where their indigenous slaves were captured. According to the New Laws, slaveholders could retain their slaves only if it could be proven that they were taken in "just war" or were Caribs from Portuguese territories.[26] Increasingly slaveholders used physical traits to distinguish their Indian slaves, bringing race and appearance into the discussion of indigenous slavery for the first time. By the 1550s many Indian slaves were identified as *loro* (or black) to defend their status as slaves.[27] The fact that these cases continued to be presented in American and Iberian courts well into the early seventeenth century is testimony to the longevity of the indigenous slave trade, even if in a more limited form. It is also likely that the growing African slave trade, and its legal justifications, contributed to the increasingly racialized discourse of the Indian slave trade.

Despite the Indian slave trade's persistence, the practice did eventually subside, at least at the core of the Iberian Empire, including the circum-Caribbean. The decline was due to both the rise in African slaves and the concurrent drop in Indian populations across the Americas. Additionally, as time passed, the Crown was able to gain more control over the governance of the Americas. Royal control curtailed illegal and rogue activity. The Crown also provided laws authorizing other forms of indigenous labor and servitude within which indigenous people could be and were legally exploited in the more profitable centers of the empire (for example, the mines of Mexico, Peru, and Bolivia).[28] Indian slaves were no longer exported from areas with mineral resources. At the edges of empire, however, Indian slavery persisted for decades, especially in northern New Spain and southern Chile and Argentina. For example, the Chichimec wars of northern Mexico (Zacatecas, Guanajuato, Durango, and Mazapil) provided thousands of slaves during the 1560s and 1570s, all captured in "just war."[29] Indian slaves still served as one of the few marketable commodities in underpopulated and violent frontier zones.

The Spanish also justified the enslavement of Indians on the Venezuelan coast and in the Pearl Islands (as the fisheries diminished in profitability) through "just war." An investigation from 1552 until 1554 in Coro showed that numerous Indians, even women and children, were captured and transported from Margarita and Cubagua to other areas of the empire. Often these slaves were exchanged for livestock, with one witness specifically mentioning sheep. The inhabitants of the Pearl Islands and Venezuela defended their actions by claiming that the Indians in question had attacked Spanish settlements and were Caribs.[30] Nor were Venezuelan colonists alone. The residents of both Puerto Rico and Española requested and received permission to enslave Caribs of Dominica, Martinique, Grenada, Guadeloupe, Paria, and the Orinoco River in 1547 and 1554 in the wake of rebellions and attacks. Spaniards accused Carib Indians of attacking Puerto Rico, Margarita, and other islands during which they took Indians, Africans, and Spaniards hostage. As a result of these conflicts, Puerto Rico and other islands continued to receive licenses that allowed for the capture of Caribs throughout the 1550s and 1560s in the Lesser Antilles.[31] Despite the New Laws, indigenous slavery was not over.

The Indians of the Americas were not the only targets for Spanish and Portuguese enslavers. By the end of the sixteenth century the Spanish Empire reached the Pacific, adding the Philippines to its claims. The territory gave Spain access to a new slave trade with Muslims captured during conflicts in the East Indies. These "chinos" served the same function as African slaves, replacing the diminishing indigenous population of the Americas, specifically in Mexico.[32] But just as with enslaving Caribs or Indians during "just war" in the circum-Caribbean, the number of illegally enslaved indigenous peoples of the Portuguese East Indies dwarfed the number of legally enslaved Muslims. Though officials immediately questioned the legality and origins of the slaves arriving from Manila, it took nearly one hundred years for the Crown to end that trade.[33]

Not only did the Spanish and Portuguese depend on Indian slavery for decades, but all other colonial powers followed the path of Spanish slavers, continuing to enslave indigenous peoples. Even as the number of enslaved Africans increased, and Spanish enslavement of Indians waned, indigenous slavery in the Americas did not disappear. Other emergent colonial powers picked up where the Spaniards left off. By the early seventeenth century, English and Dutch explorers, merchants, and colonists were all embroiled in the circum-Caribbean indigenous slave trade centered on Indians from the Guyanas and Brazil. These territories were the same as those exploited by German and Spanish raiders and conquistadors, such as Diego Ordás, in the 1530s and 1540s.[34] Moreover, as a result of both their pre-contact slaving traditions and recent experiences with Spanish merchants, the Indians of the region engaged in an active slave trade, selling "cannibals" into slavery. During his travels through Guyana, Sir Walter Raleigh witnessed one such slave market near the intersection of the Orinoco and Meta rivers where Arawak Indians sold Caribs to the Spanish of Nueva Granada for three to four pesos each.[35] Here is more evidence of an illegal indigenous slave trade persisting decades after the passage of the New Laws, especially on the edges of the empire.

Even though Raleigh criticized the Spanish for enslaving Indians along the Orinoco, the English and Dutch soon began purchasing captives in the very same slave markets. Pirates, merchants, explorers, and soldiers all engaged in the Indian slave trade, with or without sanction and license from their governments. Indian slaves were important for the larger contraband system in the circum-Caribbean.[36] War between European powers especially accelerated the slave trade. Throughout the Anglo-Dutch wars of the 1660s and 1670s, both sides captured and enslaved their enemy's indigenous allies. For example, English captain Peter Wroth took several Indians captive when attacking the Dutch at Approwaco in 1666, selling them soon after in Barbados. Conversely, the Dutch commander Cornelis Evertsen sold 206 Indian slaves, all declared Carib allies of the English, in Curaçao in 1673.[37]

An Indian slave trade also prospered in the territories that became the continental United States. There, English, Scottish, Welsh, French, and Spanish colonists perpetrated a large-scale Indian slave trade, often defined by pre-contact indigenous politics and customs. An Indian slave trade engulfed, and in many ways connected, the southeastern colonies of the Carolinas, the Chesapeake, Florida, and the lower Mississippi for much of the seventeenth and early eighteenth centuries.[38] Indian slavery in New France, from the Caribbean to the Pays d'en Haut, endured well into the colonies' last century. Indian slavery in the Pays d'en Haut linked the various territories of the French Empire and provided a space for Indian leaders and groups to harness power and manipulate colonization.[39] The Indian slave trade in the Illinois Country created opportunities for indigenous women, who played a central role in the formation of French and indigenous alliances and in the indigenous slave trade.[40] These examples, among many others, show the reach and significance of Indian slavery throughout the Americas.

The trade also inspired a variety of responses in indigenous populations across the Atlantic World. While one common consequence of indigenous enslavement was rebellion, in other cases new indigenous cultures and identities arose out of the trade. These new groups changed the landscape and influenced the paths to colonization of future European powers in the Caribbean. Indians themselves influenced colonization and conquest. They resisted Spanish incursions, at times forcing the Spanish to alter their practices and policies of colonization. At this very early stage of colonization, Indians, both enslaved and free, were still able to influence and inhibit the Spanish conquest of their lands. In many cases it was the Indians who determined where the Spanish settled and which locations were successful. One example is the Taíno Indian who shared his knowledge of the Spanish with the Calusa, resulting in Juan Ponce de Léon's first failed attempt to establish a colony in Florida. Another is the alliance created between the Taínos of Puerto Rico and the "Caribs" of the Lesser Antilles against the Spanish from 1512 until at least 1514. Pre-contact networks and connections gave indigenous peoples the tools to influence the nature of Spanish colonization.

As Indians from distant parts of the Americas came together on the islands of the Caribbean, they formed new cultures. These indigenous cultures then melded together with Iberian and African traditions, ultimately creating Creole societies. Within the blended cultures one finds vestiges of

Taíno culture, including language, culinary practices, and elements of cosmology. Before the arrival of the Europeans, inhabitants of Grenada, one of the southernmost of the Lesser Antilles, had few if any cemíes. However, by the seventeenth century Dutch colonizers discovered a religion centered on cemíes. The Indians of Grenada buried three-pointed cemíes in fields of recently planted crops.[41] Ethnographers reported this tradition in the first writings about the Taino in the 1490s. How exactly this sharing occurred is difficult to ascertain, but it is possible that runaway Taínos, fleeing Spanish enslavers and colonizers, brought the cult of cemíes to Grenada. Another possibility is that enslaved Caribs adopted the practice in the Greater Antilles and were able to bring it back to their homelands after running away or simply being moved by their owners. The Taíno language also spread throughout the Caribbean, and even into the mainland, largely as a result of the Spanish conquest and indigenous slave trade and diaspora. One example of the survival and even spread of the Taíno or Arawak language is the word "cacique." Spaniards continually referred to indigenous leaders as "caciques" across the Americas, despite the term's inaccuracy in most territories. "Barbecue," "maize," "potato," "canoe," "hurricane," and "hammock" are some of the other Taíno words still in use today.[42]

In Cuba both written and archaeological records suggest a high rate of assimilation of Yucatec Maya into Taíno culture and society. By the middle of the sixteenth century Governor Gonzalo Pérez de Angulo found it difficult to differentiate between the native Taínos and the "indios de Campeche," or Yucatec Maya. It was a challenge due to the rate of intermarriage between the two groups.[43] Nor were these short-lived alliances. In the twentieth century, searches for surviving Taínos in Cuba led to the discovery of a largely indigenous town, Hanabana Quemada, in western Cuba. However, its residents were not just descendants of native Taínos as expected. In fact, the original cacique's relative was married to none other than a woman of Yucatec Maya heritage. Even more striking was a group of Yucatec Maya living near Havana in the 1970s, still practicing classic *milpa* agriculture and speaking the Yucatec language.[44] This all suggests that despite the precipitous decline in population during the first decades of colonization, at least some Taíno (and Maya) peoples and customs survived across the greater Caribbean. But Taíno culture was not left untouched. Instead Taínos were influenced by the diverse indigenous populations they encountered, largely as a result of the indigenous slave trade and diaspora.

Archaeological evidence also points to the creation of new cultures across the Caribbean. For example, unidentifiable indigenous pottery was found at Nueva Cádiz on the island of Cubagua. Here the Spaniards employed Guaquerí Indians of Margarita, Lucayan Indians of the Bahamas, and Taínos from the Greater Antilles in the pearl fisheries. The presence of the diverse indigenous groups could explain the mysterious pottery. This foreign ceramic style might have been brought by Indian slaves from the northern Caribbean in the early 1520s. Or the various Indians may have created the new fusion style in situ. The pottery was found alongside typical ceramics of Venezuelan Indians, highlighting the distinction.[45] While this example suggests cultural mixing and the creation of new societies out of the destruction or displacement of others, the best support for cultural formation out of an indigenous diaspora is the creation of the Kalinago identity in the Lesser Antilles.

Through ethnographic accounts written by French missionaries, we know that the inhabitants of the Lesser Antilles referred to themselves as Kalinago by the middle of the seventeenth century.[46] And today indigenous peoples of the Caribbean, of Dominica in particular, identify themselves as Kalinago, rejecting the Spanish-imposed title of "Carib."[47] By the 1600s a new ethnic identity had formed in the Lesser Antilles, one that developed from the cohesion of Caribs with other indigenous (and perhaps African) groups of the Caribbean. Archaeologists have been unable to identify a unique Carib or Kalinago ceramic style or signature. Instead at sites in Dominica, Guadeloupe, and St. Vincent they found a conglomeration of Taíno, European, African, and Cayo (a style from Guyana) material culture.[48] The language spoken by the Kalinago in the seventeenth century was also a mixture of Arawakan and borrowed words from mainland Caribs.[49] Both the archaeological record and linguistic evidence then point to a mixing of cultures and peoples throughout the first century after European arrival to the Caribbean. This culture was influenced by fleeing Indians from across the Caribbean, escaped African slaves, and briefly resident European pirates, to name a few.

Other indigenous groups, particularly those along the northern coast of South America, embraced the Spanish-imposed moniker of the Carib. In fact, some records point to indigenous peoples, both in the Lesser Antilles and along the coast of mainland South America, using the idea and label of the "Carib" to scare their enemies, taking advantage of the Carib's feared reputation for ferocity and cannibalism.[50] The idea of the Carib was central to the creation of new military alliances and political realignments in present-day Venezuela and Guyana.[51] By the seventeenth century, Jesuit missionaries reported that many Arawakan groups in the interior of the Orinoco basin were "becoming Caribs" as a result of political and military alliances with the Karina peoples, or Caribs along the coast.[52] Indigenous peoples did not simply fall victim to European conquest and colonization. They reacted and responded in ways that helped them to survive and rebuild whenever possible.

Though begun by the Spanish, the indigenous slave trade impacted more than the Iberian colonial experiment, effecting the social and cultural formation of English, Dutch, and French colonies. Wherever Europeans faced labor shortages or encountered challenges of taming a new land, Indian slavery was found. The Indian slave trade was not a short-lived or unsuccessful practice quickly replaced by African slavery. Instead Indian slaves were continually relied upon and sought after, first by Iberian conquerors and colonists and in later decades and centuries by newly arriving northern Europeans. Throughout the creation of American colonies, the constant search for and enslavement of Indians helped to shape the circum-Caribbean and Atlantic World.

NOTES

Introduction

1. The historian Toby Green discusses the link between the American genocide of indigenous peoples, the Taíno in particular, and the rise of the transatlantic slave trade in his monograph. He points out that, without the massive death rate of indigenous laborers, the transatlantic slave trade would have looked very different, especially in the sixteenth century. See Green, *The Rise of the Trans-Atlantic Slave Trade in Western Africa, 1300–1589* (Cambridge: Cambridge University Press, 2012), 186–187.

2. Not only did the Spanish and Portuguese depend on Indian slavery for decades, but all other colonial powers continued to enslave indigenous peoples, pushing the numbers of enslaved Indians into the millions by the early nineteenth century. Brett Rushforth, *Bonds of Alliance: Indigenous and Atlantic Slaveries in New France* (Williamsburg, VA / Chapel Hill: Omohundro Institute / University of North Carolina Press, 2012), 9.

3. "Real cédula de Fernando V, creando una Audiencia en Santo Domingo," printed and transcribed in *Colección de documentos inéditos para la historia de Ibero-America/Hispano-America*, 15 vols., various comps. (Madrid: Compañía Iberoamericana de Publicaciones, 1925–1937), 2:285–293.

4. For more on indigenous slaves taken to Spain (Sevilla in particular) and those who managed to petition for their freedom, see Nancy E. van Deusen, *Global Indios: The Indigenous Struggle for Justice in Sixteenth-Century Spain* (Durham, NC: Duke University Press, 2015). While van Deusen examines some examples of the early indigenous slave trade, her focus is not on the institution of slavery, but on what it tells us of identity formation in the early Spanish Atlantic.

5. Some examples of more focused works on slavery and the early Spanish colonial economy include Carlos Esteban Deive, *La Española y la esclavitud del indio* (Santo Domingo: Fundación García Arévalo, 1995); Morella A. Jiménez, *La esclavitud indígena en Venezuela, siglo XVI* (Caracas: Fuentes para la Historia Colonial de Venezuela, 1986); and Molly Warsh, *American Baroque: Pearls and the Nature of Empire 1492–1700* (Williamsburg, VA / Chapel Hill: Omohundro Institute / University of North Carolina Press, 2018).

6. An excellent example of some of this new scholarship can be found in Arne Bialuschewski and Linford Fisher's special issue of *Ethnohistory*, published in January 2017, that focused on Native American slavery in the seventeenth century. A few of the articles include Arne Bialuschewski, "Slaves of the Buccaneers: Mayas in Captivity in the Second Half of the Seventeenth Century"; Carolyn Arena, "Indian Slaves from Guiana in Seventeenth-Century Barbados"; and Linford Fisher, "Why Shall Wee Have Peace to Bee Made Slaves: Indian Surrenderers During and After King Phillip's War." Rushforth's *Bonds of Alliance* serves as one of

the best monographs on indigenous slavery. It not only examines how Indian slavery shaped French Canada but also compares Indian slavery in Canada to African slavery in the French Caribbean.

7. Some of the most significant of these studies include Daniel H. Usner Jr., *Indians, Settlers, and Slaves in a Frontier Exchange Economy: The Lower Mississippi Valley Before 1783* (Williamsburg, VA / Chapel Hill: Omohundro Institute / University of North Carolina Press, 1992); Alan Gallay, *The Indian Slave Trade: The Rise of the English Empire in the American South, 1670–1717* (New Haven, CT: Yale University Press, 2002); James F. Brooks, *Captives and Cousins: Slavery, Kinship, and Community in the Southwest Borderlands* (Williamsburg, VA / Chapel Hill: Omohundro Institute / University of North Carolina Press, 2002); Christina Snyder, *Slavery in Indian Country: The Changing Face of Captivity in Early America* (Cambridge, MA: Harvard University Press, 2012); and Alan Gallay, ed., *Indian Slavery in Colonial America* (Lincoln: University of Nebraska Press, 2015). For a recent historiographical summary of scholarship on Indian slavery in the Americas, see Rebecca Goetz, "Indian Slavery: An Atlantic and Hemispheric Problem," *History Compass* 14, no. 2 (2016).

8. Andrés Reséndez, *The Other Slavery: The Uncovered Story of Indian Enslavement in America* (New York: Houghton Mifflin, 2016).

9. Jalil Sued-Badillo, "Facing Up to Caribbean History," *American Antiquity* 57, no. 4 (October 1992): 601; Ida Altman, "The Revolt of Enriquillo and the Historiography of Early Spanish America," *Americas* 63, no. 4 (April 2007): 16; and James Lockhart and Stuart Schwartz, eds., *Early Latin America: A History of Colonial Spanish America and Brazil* (Cambridge: Cambridge University Press, 1982). Lockhart gestures toward the importance of the Caribbean in the formation of larger Latin American colonial structures in the volume's third chapter, where he states that the Caribbean experience left "such an imprint on all that followed that treatment of it is an indispensable introduction to discussion of the European occupation of the central areas" (60). Among the historians who bypassed the Caribbean were Charles Gibson in *The Aztecs Under Spanish Rule: A History of the Indians of the Valley of Mexico, 1519–1810* (Stanford, CA: Stanford University Press, 1964) and John Hemming in *The Conquest of the Incas* (New York: Mariner Books/Houghton Mifflin Harcourt, 1970).

10. A new edited volume, *The Spanish Caribbean and the Atlantic World in the Long Sixteenth Century*, ed. Ida Altman and David Wheat (Lincoln: University of Nebraska Press, 2019), both addresses the dearth of scholarship on the early Spanish Caribbean and showcases new scholarship on the region. The book argues that the Caribbean was the most diverse and international part of the sixteenth-century Spanish Empire, that it was a "microcosm of the Atlantic world; arguably it was also the first full-fledged incarnation of that world" (xii).

11. Nor were Indians of the Americas the only enslaved indigenous peoples. After the conquest of the Philippines, the Spanish engaged in a vibrant trade in Asian slaves well into the seventeenth century. In many ways this trade mirrored the early trade in Indians in the greater Caribbean. For more, see Tatiana Seijas's excellent work *Asian Slaves in Colonial Mexico: From Chinos to Indios* (Cambridge: Cambridge University Press, 2006).

12. Green, *Rise of the Trans-Atlantic Slave Trade*, 187.

13. According to the Siete Partidas law code, justifiable war included when one was under attack or fighting in defense of one's own sovereignty or the safety of an ally. Usually Christians were exempt from bondage. The Spanish already used this law code to justify the enslavement of both the "infidel" Moors in Iberia and Guinea as well as the inhabitants of the Canary Islands. Van Deusen, *Global Indios*, 3–4; Rushforth, *Bonds of Alliance*, 92.

14. Carl Ortwin Sauer, *The Early Spanish Main* (Berkeley: University of California Press, 1966), 85.

15. Van Deusen, *Global Indios*, 5.

16. Robbie Ethridge and Sheri M. Shuck-Hall, eds., *Mapping the Mississippian Shatter Zone: The Colonial Indian Slave Trade and Regional Instability in the American South* (Lincoln: University of Nebraska Press, 2009). In the introduction, Ethridge defines the Mississippian shatter zone as "a large region of instability in eastern North America that existed from the late sixteenth through the early seventeenth centuries and was created by the combined conditions of the structural instability of the Mississippian world and the inability of Native polities to withstand the full force of colonialism; the introduction of Old World pathogens and the subsequent serial disease episodes and loss of life; the inauguration of a nascent capitalist economic system by Europeans through commercial trade in animal skins and especially in Indian slaves, whom other Indians procured and sold to European buyers; and the intensification and spread of violence and warfare through the Indian slave trade and particularly through the emergence of militaristic Native slaving societies who held control of the European trade" (2). In this text I argue that the idea of the "shatter zone" applies well to the Spanish circum-Caribbean by the 1530s and 1540s.

17. In 1518 two leading Spanish judges, Rodrigo de Figueroa and Alonso Zuazo, claimed that at least fifteen thousand Indian slaves (largely Caribs from the mainland, which was also called Tierra Firme) arrived in Santo Domingo. Neil Whitehead, *Of Cannibals and Kings: Primal Anthropology in the Americas* (University Park: Pennsylvania State University Press, 2011), 9.

18. My estimates match those of Nancy E. van Deusen who argues that the number of enslaved and relocated indigenous peoples over the entire sixteenth century was *at least* 650,000. Van Deusen, *Global Indios*, 2.

19. For more on the types of records available to historians of the African slave trade, see Marc Eagle, "The Early Slave Trade to Spanish America: Caribbean Pathways, 1530–1580," in Altman and Wheat, *Spanish Caribbean*, 139–142.

20. Daniel J. Rogers and Samuel M. Wilson, *Ethnohistory and Archeology: Approaches to Postcontact Change in the Americas* (New York: Plenum Press, 1993), 8.

21. Some of the best and most recent works on Caribbean archaeology include Kathleen Deagan and José María Cruxent, *Archeology at La Isabela: America's First European Town* (New Haven, CT: Yale University Press, 2002); Scott M. Fitzpatrick and Ann H. Ross, eds., *Island Shores, Distant Pasts: Archaeological and Biological Approaches to the Pre-Columbian Settlement of the Caribbean* (Gainesville: University Press of Florida, 2010); and José R. Oliver, *Caciques and Cemí Idols: The Web Spun by Taíno Rulers Between Hispaniola and Puerto Rico* (Tuscaloosa: University of Alabama Press, 2009).

22. Neil L. Whitehead, "The Historical Anthropology of Text: The Interpretation of Ralegh's *Discoverie of Guiana*," *Current Anthropology* 36, no. 1 (February 1995): 53, 58. Whitehead points out that Ralegh's text likely refers to an Orinoco tribe's tradition of wearing their defeated enemies' heads around their necks to display their fierceness. Whitehead, "Historical Anthropology of Text," 58.

23. Marshall Sahlins, *Islands of History* (Chicago: University of Chicago Press, 1985), xiv.

24. In my work I use William H. Sewell Jr.'s definition of "agency," as something that is derived directly from societal structures and the ability of the individual to manipulate and act within them. Structures are dualistic, meaning they are both virtual, including schemas, and real resources. William H. Sewell Jr., "Historical Events as Transformations of Structures:

Inventing Revolution at the Bastille," in *Logics of History: Social Theory and Social Transformation* (Chicago: University of Chicago Press, 2005), 143–144.

25. Much literature on slave agency focuses on the simple act of survival as resistance, for example, James Scott's *Domination and the Arts of Resistance: Hidden Transcripts* (New Haven, CT: Yale University Press, 1992), where he finds evidence of "everyday forms of resistance" in "hidden transcripts" as the "discourse that takes place 'offstage,' beyond direct observation of powerholders," and he contradicts this with the "public transcripts," which are the "open interactions between subordinates and those who dominate" (2–4).

Chapter 1

1. For more on Christopher Columbus, his writings, and his voyages, see Felipe Fernández-Arnesto, *Columbus on Himself* (Indianapolis: Hackett Publishing Company, 2010); and William D. Phillips Jr. and Carla Rahn Phillips, *The Worlds of Christopher Columbus* (Cambridge: Cambridge University Press, 1992). For a more heroic telling of Columbus, see the writings of his son in *The History of the Life and Deeds of the Admiral Don Christopher Columbus Attributed to His Son Fernando Colón*, ed. Caraci Luzzana, trans. Geoffrey Symcox and Blair Sullivan, Repertorium Columbianum, vol. 13 (Turnhout, Belgium: Brepols Publishers, 2004).

2. The Taínos of Española referred to their southern neighbors as "Caribe" while the Lucayan Indians called these same people "Caniba." It is unknown how those in the Lesser Antilles identified themselves in 1492. However, by the early seventeenth century they referred to themselves as "Kalinago." Fernando Santos-Granero, *Vital Enemies: Slavery, Predation, and the Amerindian Political Economy of Life* (Austin: University of Texas Press, 2009), 18. It is very likely that this identity developed as a result of European colonization. Because of this, throughout the book I use the term "Carib," despite its controversial meaning today in many of the Lesser Antilles. For more, see Erin Stone, "Chasing 'Caribs': Defining Zones of Legal Indigenous Enslavement in the Circum-Caribbean, 1493–1542," in *Slaving Zones: Cultural Identities, Ideologies, and Institutions in the Evolution of Global Slavery*, ed. Jeff Fynn-Paul and Damian Alan Pargas (Leiden: Brill Publishers, 2017).

3. Peter Hulme, *Colonial Encounters: Europe and the Native Caribbean, 1492–1797* (London: Methuen, 1986), 46–47. In addition to Hulme, other historians and anthropologists like Neil Whitehead, Jalil Sued Badillo, and José R. Oliver support this assertion.

4. The Taíno language belongs to the larger Arawakan family, but there were considerable differences between the languages spoken by the Taíno of the Greater Antilles and the Arawaks of the Orinoco River. Additionally, there were several variations of the language spoken within the Greater Antilles and even on the island of Española. This accounts for the Ciboney (of Cuba), Lucayans (of the Bahamas), and Macorix-Ciguayo (of Española) from whom the Taíno distinguished themselves. William Keegan, *The People Who Discovered Columbus: The Prehistory of the Bahamas* (Gainesville: University Press of Florida, 1992), 11.

5. Whether or not this is how the Taínos referred to themselves prior to 1492 is difficult to ascertain. The first European to record the term "Taíno" was Dr. Diego Álvarez Chanca in a letter to the court of Sevilla in 1493. Antonio M. Stevens-Arroyo, *Cave of the Jagua: The Mythological World of the Taínos* (Albuquerque: University of New Mexico Press, 1988), x; Ángel Rodríguez Álvarez, ed., *Mitología Taína o Eyeri, Ramón Pané y la relación sobre las antiguedades de los indios: El primer tratado etnográfico hecho en América* (San Juan: Editorial Nuevo Mundo, 2009), 3; and Keegan, *People Who Discovered Columbus*, 11.

6. Samuel M. Wilson, *Hispaniola: Caribbean Chiefdoms in the Age of Columbus* (Tuscaloosa: University of Alabama Press, 1990), 4. For more on the global development and evolution

of chiefdoms, see Timothy Earle, ed., *Chiefdoms: Power, Economy, and Ideology* (Cambridge: Cambridge University Press, 1991).

7. Irving Rouse, *The Taínos: Rise and Decline of the People Who Greeted Columbus* (New Haven, CT: Yale University Press, 1992), 9.

8. However, indigenous inhabitants of the mainland in South, Central, and North America were much more familiar with a more European practice of slavery. Some studies of indigenous slavery elsewhere include J. A. Saco, *Historia de la esclavitud de los indios en el nuevo mundo*, 2 vols. (Havana: Librería Cervantes, 1932), 1:3–55; Julio Valdivia Carrasco, *El imperio esclavista de los Inkas* (Lima: Grabado de Guamán Poma de Ayala, 1988); and Rushforth, *Bonds of Alliance*, 12.

9. For more on distinctions between captivity and slavery, especially regarding female captives and their use as social and political capital (not economic), see Juliana Barr, "From Captives to Slaves: Commodifying Indian Women in the Borderlands," *Journal of American History* 92, no. 1 (June 2005).

10. Santos-Granero, *Vital Enemies*, 107–109. These captives were also deprived of their names and identities for the first years after their capture. Nevertheless, if they survived several years with the "Caribs," they were often assimilated into larger society.

11. Santos-Granero, *Vital Enemies*, 129–131

12. For more on the difference between indigenous captivity/servitude/slavery and European slavery, see Santos-Granero, *Vital Enemies*, 3–5.

13. Lynn Guitar, "Cultural Genesis: Relationships Among Indians, Africans and Spaniards in Española, First Half of the Sixteenth Century" (PhD diss., Vanderbilt University, 1998), 11.

14. Stevens-Arroyo, *Cave of the Jagua*, 56.

15. Fray Bartolomé de las Casas, *Apologética historia Sumaria, capitulo CXX*, in Álvarez, *Mitología Taína o Eyeri*, 185.

16. Oliver, *Caciques and Cemí Idols*, 62.

17. Oliver, *Caciques and Cemí Idols*, 59–61.

18. Oliver, *Caciques and Cemí Idols*, 59–61. The most powerful or senior of all the cemíes was Yocahu Vagua Maorocoti, who, according to Pané, was the "señor de los cielos" and was immortal. Roberto Cassá, *Los Taínos de la Española* (Santo Domingo: Editora Búho, 1990), 157.

19. Oliver, *Caciques and Cemí Idols*, 103–149.

20. Wilson, *Hispaniola*, 22.

21. Oliver, *Caciques and Cemí Idols*, 83–85; Roberto Valcárcel Rojas, César A. Rodríguez Arce, and Marcos Labada Ochoa, "Trabajos arqueológicos en la cueva Cerro de los Muertos I, Banes, Holguín, Cuba," *El Caribe arqueológico* 7 (2003): 33–49.

22. There is limited but provocative ceramic evidence that occasional trade occurred between the inhabitants of the Florida Keys and Cuba. However, this passing contact (perhaps between fishermen) did not take place until very late in the pre-contact era, between 1200 and 1400 AD. John H. Hann, *Indians of Central and South Florida, 1513–1763* (Gainesville: University Press of Florida, 2003), 43. However, Florida's Indians did maintain complex trade networks with other groups throughout much of eastern North America. For example, whelk shells from the coast of Florida were found in present-day Oklahoma and North Dakota, while galena (a lead ore) produced in southeast Missouri and dating from 1200 was discovered at a Calusa site called the Pineland complex in Florida. Darcie A. MacMahon and William H. Marquardt, *The Calusa and Their Legacy: South Florida People and Their Environment* (Gainesville: University Press of Florida, 2004), 80–82. They also traded with the peoples of the Lucayos Islands. John H. Hann, *A History of the Timucua Indians and Missions* (Gainesville: University Press of Florida,

1996), 1; Carl Ortwin Sauer, *The Early Spanish Main* (Berkeley: University of California Press, 1966), 189.

23. Bartolomé de las Casas was initially a conquistador, but he later felt a change of heart and became a Dominican friar and one of the most prolific and vocal defenders of the Indians. He discusses canoes in his work *Historia de las Indias*, 3 vols., ed. Lewis Hanke and Agustín Millares Carlo (Mexico City, Mexico: Fondo de Cultura Economica, 1951), 1:206. Dr. Chanca, or Diego Álvarez Chanca, was a doctor from Sevilla who accompanied Columbus on his 1493 voyage to the Americas. His letter is one of the best accounts of the Antilles. For more on the canoes, see Sebastián Robiou Lamarche, "La navegación indígena Antillana," *Boletín del Museo de Hombre Dominicano*, no. 25 (Santo Domingo, 1992).

24. Lamarche, "Navegación indígena," 77.

25. Lamarche, "Navegación indígena," 75.

26. Lamarche, "Navegación indígena," 75–76. While currents in some parts of the Caribbean were dangerous during certain seasons, navigation was possible, especially if one stayed close to land. Nor were distances far between ports and islands. For example, it would have taken only six days to paddle from Cuba to southeastern Florida. Scott M. Fitzpatrick, "Seafaring Capabilities in the Pre-Columbian Caribbean," *Journal of Maritime Archaeology* 46, no. 4 (June 2013): 119–120.

27. Lamarche, "Navegación indígena," 78.

28. Sebastián Robiou Lamarche, *Taínos y Caribes: Las culturas de aborígenes antillanas* (San Juan: Editorial Punto y Coma, 2003), 36–37.

29. William F. Keegan, "Islands of Chaos," in *Late Ceramic Age Societies in the Eastern Caribbean*, ed. A. Delpuech and C. L. Hofman, BAR International Series (Oxford: Archaeopress, 2004), 33–44.

30. Louis Allaire, "The Lesser Antilles Before Columbus," in *The Indigenous People of the Caribbean*, ed. Samuel Wilson (Gainesville: University Press of Florida, 1997), 25–26.

31. Arie Boomert, "Island Carib Archaeology," in *Wolves from the Sea: Readings in the Anthropology of the Native Caribbean*, ed. Neil Whitehead (Leiden: KITLV Press, 1995), 27–32.

32. Louis Allaire, "On the Historicity of Carib Migrations in the Lesser Antilles," *American Antiquity* 45, no. 2 (April 1980): 238–241.

33. Boomert, "Island Carib Archaeology," 28.

34. Taínos believed that at night the dead transformed into bats, allowing them to leave the underworld and exist among the living and to eat the fruit of the guava tree. Ramón Pané, quoted in Álvarez, *Mitología Taína o Eyeri*, 28.

35. Corinne L. Hofman and Menno L. P. Hoogland, "Unraveling the Multi-Scale Networks of Mobility and Exchange in the Pre-Columbusial Circum-Caribbean," in *Communities in Contact: Essays in Archaeology, Ethnohistory, and Ethnography of the Amerindian Circum-Caribbean*, ed. Corinne L. Hofman and Anne van Duijvenbode (Leiden: Sidestone Press, 2011), 22.

36. There is evidence that marriages linked not only the Greater to the Lesser Antilles but also the various islands of the Lesser Antilles to one another. At Anse à la Gourde on the island of Guadeloupe, many deceased women were of nonlocal origin, suggesting intercommunity mobility for purposes of marriage. Many of these women were also buried with objects made from nonlocal materials (a bead belt of foreign origins, artifacts made from St. Martin greenstone, and one made of Antigua flint). Menno L. Hoogland, Corinne L. Hofman, and Raphael G. A. M. Panhuysen, "Interisland Dynamics: Evidence for Human Mobility at the Site of Anse à la Gourde, Guadeloupe," in Fitzpatrick and Ross, *Island Shores, Distant Pasts*.

37. Jalil Sued Badillo, "Guadalupe: ¿Caribe o Taina? La isla de Guadalupe y su cuestionable identidad caribe en la época pre-Colombina: Una revisión etnohistórica y arqueológica preliminar," *Caribbean Studies* 35, no. 1 (2007): 39–40. It is also possible that this effort at extending alliances and power could have caused recent tensions between the peoples of the Greater and Lesser Antilles, thus explaining the negative depiction of the Caribs by the Taínos of Española.

38. David R. Watters, "Maritime Trade in the Prehistoric Eastern Caribbean," in Wilson, *Indigenous People of the Caribbean*, 88.

39. The presence of dual ceramics also helps to explain the Spanish assertion that Trinidad was inhabited by both Caribs and Arawaks at the time of conquest. However, the number of Caribs could have been exaggerated by the Spanish so they could legally enslave more of the indigenous population. Many even claimed that the island was populated only by Arawaks. Linda A. Newson, *Aboriginal and Spanish Colonial Trinidad: A Study in Culture Contact* (London: Academic Press, 1976), 17–19.

40. Even though jade, quartz, and turquoise are found naturally *only* in South America, beads made from the materials were found on various islands in both the Greater and Lesser Antilles. Watters, "Maritime Trade," 94–98.

41. M. John Roobol and James W. Lee, "Petrography and Source of Some Arawak Rock Artefacts from Jamaica," in *The Earliest Inhabitants: The Dynamics of the Jamaican Taíno*, ed. Lesley-Gail Atkinson (Kingston: University of West Indies Press, 2006), 140.

42. Watters, "Maritime Trade," 89–91.

43. Bernardo Vega, *Santos, shamanes, y zemíes* (Santo Domingo: Fundación Cultural Dominicana, 1987), 44.

44. Reniel Rodriguez Ramos, *Rethinking Puerto Rican Pre-Columbian History* (Tuscaloosa: University of Alabama Press, 2010), 156–157.

45. Angus A. A. Mol, *Costly Giving, Giving Guaízas: Towards an Organic Model of the Exchange of Social Valuables in the Late Ceramic Age Caribbean* (Leiden: Sidestone Press, 2007), 65.

46. Colin Renfrew, "Alternative Models for Exchange and Spatial Distribution," in *Exchange Systems in Prehistory*, ed. Timothy K. Earle and Jonathan E. Ericson (New York: Academic Press, 1977).

47. Oliver, *Caciques and Cemí Idols*, 104–105.

48. Oliver, *Caciques and Cemí Idols*, 107.

49. Nineteen guaízas have been located in Cuba to date. Mol, *Costly Giving, Giving Guaízas*, 110.

50. Ten guaízas have been unearthed in total on the Leeward Islands, while five were found on the Windward Islands. Mol, *Costly Giving, Giving Guaízas*, 110, 114.

51. John G. Crock and James B. Petersen, "Inter-Island Exchange, Settlement Hierarchy and Taíno-Related Chiefdom on the Anguilla Bank, Northern Lesser Antilles," in Delpuech and Hofman, *Late Ceramic Age Societies in the Eastern Caribbean*; Oliver, *Caciques and Cemí Idols*, 163–165.

52. Oliver, *Caciques and Cemí Idols*, 159.

53. Hofman and Hoogland, "Unraveling the Multi-Scale Networks," 27.

54. Johnsson Marquet, "Contextual Analysis of the Lesser Antillean Windward Islands Petroglyphs: Methods and Results," in *Rock Art of the Caribbean*, ed. Michael A. Cinquino, Lesley-Gail Atkinson, and Michele H. Hayward (Tuscaloosa: University of Alabama Press, 2008), 156–157.

55. Marquet, "Contextual Analysis," 158.

56. Neil Whitehead, "Ethnic Plurality and Cultural Continuity in the Native Caribbean: Remarks and Uncertainties as to Data and Theory," in Whitehead, *Wolves from the Sea*, 96–97. Whitehead also argues that the persistent association of Caribs with the mainland was largely a post-conquest development and that the island Caribs actively participated in Arawak or Taíno political and social realms both before and after Spanish colonization.

57. Dave D. Davis and R. Christopher Goodwin, "Island Carib Origins: Evidence and Non-evidence," *American Antiquity* 55, no. 1 (January 1990): 37. Davis and Goodwin also dismantle the very ethnic term "Carib," demonstrating its origins in the Taíno word for the inhabitants of the Lesser Antilles, as well as the later political use of the identification by the Spanish, showing that the term had little to do with a self-ascribed identity and much more to do with both inter-island and colonial political realities.

58. Taíno vomiting sticks, usually made from manatee bones, have also been located in Guadeloupe and Dominica. Mol, *Costly Giving, Giving Guaízas*, 65–66.

59. Dicey Taylor, "El juego de pelota Taíno y su relación con las culturas continentales," *Museo del Hombre Dominicano* 34 (Santo Domingo: Museo del Hombre Dominicano, 2003), 63.

60. Archaeologists are using craniometrics and modern geometric morphometric evaluation of dental samples to test possible dispersal theories of Caribbean populations. Ann H. Ross and Douglas H. Ubelaker, "A Morphometric Approach to Taíno Biological Distance in the Caribbean," in Fitzpatrick and Ross, *Island Shores, Distant Pasts*; Alfredo Coppa et al., "New Evidence of Two Different Migratory Waves in the Circum-Caribbean Area During the Pre-Columbian Period from the Analysis of Dental Morphological Traits," in *Crossing the Borders: New Methods and Techniques in the Study of Archaeological Materials in the Caribbean*, ed. Corrine Hofman, M. L. P. Hoogland, and A. L. van Gijn (Tuscaloosa: University of Alabama Press, 2008), 199.

61. Fitzpatrick, "Seafaring Capabilities," 120.

62. Taylor, "Juego de pelota," 51–71.

63. Jacques Soustelle, *Daily Life of the Aztecs on the Eve of the Spanish Conquest* (Stanford, CA: Stanford University Press, 1955), 73–78. In many ways this resembled the Iberian law code, Siete Partidas, wherein slaves were property but were still viewed as persons with the same natural rights as every other member in society.

64. Richard F. Townsend, *The Aztecs* (London: Thames and Hudson, 2000), 181–182. For more on southern pre-European Meso-American slavery, see Eugenia Ibarra Rojas, *Pueblos que capturan: Esclavitud indígena al sur de América Central del siglo XVI al XIX* (San José: Universidad de Costa Rica, 2012).

65. Felipe Fernández-Armesto, *Before Columbus: Exploration and Colonization from the Mediterranean to the Atlantic, 1229–1492* (Philadelphia: University of Pennsylvania Press, 1987), 155.

66. Eduardo Aznar Vallejo, "The Conquests of the Canary Islands," in *Implicit Understandings: Observing, Reporting, and Reflecting on the Encounters Between Europeans and Other Peoples in the Early Modern Era*, ed. Stuart Schwartz (Cambridge: Cambridge University Press, 1994), 139–141.

67. David Abulafia, *The Discovery of Mankind: Atlantic Encounters in the Age of Columbus* (New Haven, CT: Yale University Press, 2008), 67.

68. Vallejo, "Conquests of the Canary Islands," 139–145.

69. Fernández-Armesto, *Before Columbus*, 172.

70. Abulafia, *Discovery of Mankind*, 74–75.

71. The Spanish needed a new entrée into Africa after they lost any claim to gold-rich Africa to the Portuguese in the Treaty of Alçacovas. Fernández-Armesto, *Before Columbus*, 175–205.

72. Vallejo, "Conquests of the Canary Islands," 135–136.

73. Vallejo, "Conquests of the Canary Islands," 143–145.

74. Vallejo, "Conquests of the Canary Islands," 138; Miguel Angel Ladero Quesada, "Spain, Circa 1492: Social Values and Structures," in Schwartz, *Implicit Understandings*, 99–100. Treatment of pagans contrasted with how the Spanish viewed both Jews and Muslims, who were infidels but still people of the book who were often allowed to live under their own religious and judicial system, at least until 1492.

75. Title XXI, "Concerning Slaves," of the Siete Partidas states that "there are three kinds of slaves, the first is those taken captive in war who are enemies of the faith; the second, those born of female slaves; the third when a person is free and allows himself to be sold. Five things are necessary in the case of the third. First, the party must voluntarily consent to be sold; second, he must receive a part of the price; third, he must know that he is free; fourth the party who purchases him must believe that he is a slave; fifth, he who permits himself to be sold must be more than twenty years of age." Title XXI, "Concerning Slaves," Law 1, "What Servitude Is, Whence It Derived Its Name, and How Many Kinds There Are." Transcribed and translated in *Las Siete Partidas: Family, Commerce, and the Sea: The Worlds of Women and Merchants*, vol. 4, trans. Samuel Parsons Scott, ed. Robert I. Burns, S.J. (Philadelphia: University of Pennsylvania Press, 2001), 977. The law code also discusses the rights of slaves and masters, who can hold slaves, and how slaves can be emancipated.

76. Rushforth, *Bonds of Alliance*, 92.

77. Emily Berquist Soule, "From Africa to the Ocean Sea: Atlantic Slavery in the Origins of the Spanish Empire," *Atlantic Studies* 15, no. 1 (2017): 4. However, in 1403, in the wake of failed attempts at Catholic conversion by missionaries from Mallorca and Iberia, the pope did elevate the Canarian conflict to a religious crusade, making all defiant Canary Islanders infidels. Soule, "From Africa to the Ocean Sea," 6.

78. Soule, "From Africa to the Ocean Sea," 8–9.

79. Antonio Rumeu de Armas, *La conquista de Tenerife, 1494–1496* (Madrid: Aula de Cultura de Tenerife, 1975), 104.

80. The Guanches' reaction to this threat explains why the conquest of the island was so difficult for the Spanish. Already by the early fifteenth century, the Guanches had moved most of their settlements from the coastline to the rocky and mountainous interior of the island to escape the slave raiders. While this topography provided refuge for the Guanches, it was challenging for Spanish conquistadors and their horses, prolonging the conquest of the island. De Armas, *Conquista de Tenerife*, 107.

81. De Armas, *Conquista de Tenerife*, 108.

82. "Petición de Alvaro de Piñán," February 22, 1490, Archivo General de Simancas (archive located in Simancas, Spain; hereafter AGS), Real Chancillería de los Reyes de Castilla, Registro del Sello del Corte, file 149002, doc. 338, 1.

83. De Armas, *Conquista de Tenerife*, 231–232.

84. In his account Munzer seemed fascinated by the Guanches, as he described them as barbarous, yet not black with more brown skin tones, and well formed, especially the women. He had never seen any people like them before. He also noted that within a few days fourteen

of the captives had already perished due to the new climate. De Armas, *Conquista de Tenerife*, 202–203.

85. De Armas, *Conquista de Tenerife*, 283.

86. Soule, "From Africa to the Ocean Sea," 9.

87. De Armas, *Conquista de Tenerife*, 351–354.

88. "Orden real de liberación de guanches de las paces cautivados contra todo derecho por el capitán conquistador Alonso de Lugo," March 29, 1498. Transcribed and printed in De Armas, *Conquista de Tenerife*, 461–462.

89. De Armas, *Conquista de Tenerife*, 404–406.

90. "Carta ejecutoria a favor de Juana, la Canaria," February 21, 1491, AGS, Real Chancillería de los Reyes de Castilla, Registro del Sello del Corte, file 149102, doc. 96.

91. Rushforth, *Bonds of Alliance*, 98.

92. For more on African slaves in Spain and Portugal in the fifteenth and sixteenth centuries, see James Sweet, *Recreating Africa: Culture, Kinship, and Religion in the African-Portuguese World, 1441–1770* (Chapel Hill: University of North Carolina Press, 2006); and A. C. Saunders, *A Social History of Black Slaves and Freedmen in Portugal, 1441–1555* (Cambridge: Cambridge University Press, 1982).

93. Alfonso Franco Silva, *La esclavitud en Andalucía, 1450–1550* (Granada: University of Granada, 1992), 80–83.

94. Abulafia, *Discovery of Mankind*, 101. The majority of enslaved Canary Islanders in Sevilla were from Gran Canaria and Tenerife, with only a few from Hierro and Gomera. The smallest number came from La Palma and Lanzarote. Silva, *Esclavitud en Andalucía*, 41.

95. De Armas, *Conquista de Tenerife*, 396.

96. Whether or not that was the case, Riberol was caught and fined 200,000 maravedíes, and he spent a short amount of time in prison. De Armas, *Conquista de Tenerife*, 392–393.

97. Mervyn Ratekin, "The Early Sugar Industry in Española," *Hispanic American Historical Review* 34, no. 1 (1954): 2; Carmen Ortíz García, "Islas de ida y vuelta: Canarias y el Caribe en contexto colonial," *Revista de dialectologia y tradiciones populares* 2, no. 1 (2004): 201–202. The sugar masters and mill technicians of Gonzalo de Vellosa's sugar ingenio (located on the southern coast of Española) were also imported from the Canary Islands in 1515. Ratekin, "Early Sugar Industry," 6.

98. "Carta de Lope de Sosa gobernador sobre Canarias," July 1514, Archivo General de Indias (archive located in Seville, Spain; hereafter AGI) Panama 233, legajo 1, fol. 60v: "canarios que sean los mas sueltos y mejores nadadores que se hallen."

99. Carlos Esteban Deive, "Las ordenanzas sobre esclavos cimarrones de 1522," *Boletín Museo del Hombre Dominicano* 19, no. 25 (1992): 136.

100. Other slaves considered "white" in Iberia during the fifteenth century included Circassians, Russians, Tartars, and even Greek Orthodox Christians. Soule, "From Africa to the Ocean Sea," 3.

Chapter 2

1. Phillips and Phillips, *Worlds of Christopher Columbus*, 145–155. Debate continues regarding which island Columbus and his men first touched. Geographers, historians, and archaeologists have identified at least ten different islands they believe to be Guanahaní and more than thirty different routes through the Bahamas Islands to the Greater Antilles. For more on the dispute, see Keegan, *People Who Discovered Columbus*, 183–187.

2. While accounts provided by Columbus and later chroniclers describe interactions between the Spaniards and the Indians of the Caribbean as straightforward, they were likely filled with misunderstandings. Their conversations depended heavily on gestures and interpretations. Conclusions made by the explorers could have been wrong or misunderstood, but regardless they have been accepted as fact for centuries. "Diario del primer viaje," October 1492, transcribed in *Cristóbal Colón: Textos y documentos completos*, ed. Consuelo Varela (Madrid: Alianza Editorial, 1992), 110–111; and Peter Hulme, "Tales of Distinction: European Ethnography and the Caribbean," in Schwartz, *Implicit Understandings*, 157–197. For more on issues of translation, the benefits of using indigenous-language documents and sources, and the school of New Philology, see James Lockhart, *The Nahuas After the Conquest: A Social and Cultural History of the Indians of Central Mexico, Sixteenth Through Eighteenth Centuries* (Stanford, CA: Stanford University Press, 1992).

3. For more on the importance of indigenous intermediaries, allies, and go-betweens from the initial conquest to the creation of colonial societies, see Laura E. Matthew and Michel R. Oudijk, eds., *Indian Conquistadors: Indigenous Allies in the Conquest of Mesoamerica* (Norman: University of Oklahoma Press, 2007); Alida C. Metcalf, *Go-Betweens and the Colonization of Brazil, 1500–1600* (Austin: University of Texas Press, 2005); and Yanna Yannakakis, *The Art of Being In-Between: Native Intermediaries, Indian Identity and Local Rule in Colonial Oaxaca* (Durham, NC: Duke University Press, 2008).

4. Phillips and Phillips, *Worlds of Christopher Columbus*, 161–162.

5. "Diario del primer viaje," 111.

6. Nicolás Wey Gómez, *The Tropics of Empire: Why Columbus Sailed South to the Indies* (Cambridge, MA: MIT Press, 2008), xiv.

7. Lamarche, "Navegación indígena," 75.

8. Phillips and Phillips, *Worlds of Christopher Columbus*, 186.

9. Lamarche, "Navegacion indigena," 75–76.

10. Gonzalo Fernández de Oviedo y Valdés, *Historia general y natural de las Indias*, vol. 1 (Madrid: Ediciones Atlas, 1959), 31. One of the Indians singled out in the record was the "faithful" interpreter taken from Columbus's first port in the Lucayos, a man baptized as Diego Colón after the admiral's firstborn son, who continued to travel with Columbus serving as his guide and translator for many years. It seems that Diego Colón's service was rewarded as he is listed in Española's 1514 census and the Repartimiento as a holder of an encomienda. Phillips and Phillips, *Worlds of Christopher Columbus*, 190.

11. For this voyage, which was much better funded than his first, Columbus sailed with seventeen ships that held between 1,200 and 1,500 men. Deagan and Cruxent, *Archaeology at La Isabela*, 4.

12. Though speakers of the Arawakan language, the inhabitants of the Lesser Antilles appear to have been culturally and politically distinct from the Taíno of the Greater Antilles. Whether or not they identified themselves as Caribs or whether the Taino called other different cultures Carib is unknown. Hulme, *Colonial Encounters*, 63.

13. "Letter of Dr. Chanca, written to the City of Seville," 1493, transcribed and translated in *The Four Voyages of Columbus: A History in Eight Documents Including Five by Christopher Columbus, in the Original Spanish with English Translations*, ed. and trans. Cecil Jane (New York: Dover Publications, 1988), 26. In fact, it is from the term "Cariba" or "Carib" that the very word "cannibal" as well as the name "Caribbean" was derived. Abulafia, *Discovery of Mankind*, 125.

14. While it is possible that the inhabitants of the Lesser Antilles did consume human flesh, especially given their cultural and geographical proximity to the Indians of Brazil, it is unlikely that they did so as part of their regular diet or to the extent that the Spanish reported. As the French, Dutch, and Italians soon discovered during the colonization of Brazil, the custom of cannibalism was much more complicated and had very specific political and ritual significance. This was especially true for the leaders of a tribe who sought to capture and then consume their enemies to avenge the deaths (and probable consumption) of their own loved ones. Additionally, the leader who successfully captured a man during war, and then ate him, would receive a new and more prestigious name, thereby elevating his status within the group. Some of the most detailed accounts of Brazil's native peoples come from the narratives of Jean de Léry, *History of a Voyage to the Land of Brazil*, trans. Janet Whatley (Berkeley: University of California Press, 1990); Hans Staden, *The True History of His Captivity*, trans. Malcolm Letts (London: George Routledge and Sons, 1928); Amerigo Vespucci, *Letters of the Four Voyages to the New World*, trans. Bernard Quaritch (Hamburg: Wayasbah, 1992); and Gabriel Soares de Sousa, *Tratado descriptivo do Brasil em 1587* (São Paulo: Companhia Editora Nacional, 1938).

15. William F. Keegan and Lisabeth A. Carlson, eds., *Talking Taíno: Essays on Caribbean Natural History from a Native Perspective* (Tuscaloosa: University of Alabama Press, 2008), 106.

16. Robert L. Paquette and Stanley L. Engerman, eds., *The Lesser Antilles in the Age of European Expansion* (Gainesville: University Press of Florida, 1996), 18, 29.

17. "Carta de Colón," 1493, in Jane, *Four Voyages of Columbus*, 14–15.

18. "Letter of Dr. Chanca," in Jane, *Four Voyages of Columbus*, 32.

19. Elsa M. Redmond, "Meeting with Resistance: Early Spanish Encounters in the Americas, 1492–1524," *Ethnohistory* 63, no. 4 (October 2016): 676–677.

20. "Relación del segundo viaje," in Varela, *Cristóbal Colón*, 237.

21. "Carta de Michael Cuneo," 1495, transcribed in *Primeras cartas sobre América (1493–1503)* by Francisco Morales Padrón (Sevilla: Universidad de Sevilla, 1990), 143.

22. Neil Whitehead hypothesizes that the Caribs used the captive women to produce and weave cotton cloaks, a valuable trade item in the Caribbean. Neil Whitehead, *Of Cannibals and Kings: Primal Anthropology in the Americas* (University Park: Pennsylvania State University Press, 2011), 36.

23. "Letter of Dr. Chanca," in Jane, *Four Voyages of Columbus*, 38.

24. "Carta de Michael Cuneo," in Jane, *Four Voyages of Columbus*, 143.

25. Columbus gave one woman to his friend Cuneo as a concubine. In his letter Cuneo describes how he subdued the woman who fought his every sexual advance with her teeth and nails. He was eventually able to overpower her by beating her, something he seemed quite proud of in his letter. Cuneo even claimed that once he succeeded in raping her, the woman seemed pleased. "Carta de Michael Cuneo," in Jane, *Four Voyages of Columbus*, 144.

26. Silvio A. Zavala, *Las instituciones jurídicas de la conquista de America* (Madrid: Centro de Estudios Historicos, 1935), 183.

27. "Memorial que para los reyes Católicos dio el almirante Don Cristóbal Colón en la ciudad de Isabela," January 30, 1494, transcribed in Varela, *Cristóbal Colón*, 259–261.

28. "Real carta de la reina," May 16, 1495, AGI Patronato 9, ramo 1, fols. 85v–86r; Soule, "From Africa to the Ocean Sea," 16.

29. "Real orden mandando se entregasen a Juan de Lezcano cincuenta indios para distribuirlos en las galeras de su mando," January 13, 1496, transcribed and printed in *Colección*

de documentos para la historia de la formación social de Hispanoamérica, 1493–1810, vol. 1, ed. Richard Konetzke (Madrid: Consejo Superior de Investigaciones Científicas, 1953), 3; Esteban Mira Caballos, "Isabel la Católica y el indio americano," in *La Española: Epicentro del Caribe en el siglo XVI* (Santo Domingo: Academia Dominicana de la Historia, 2010), 44.

30. Deive, *Española y la esclavitud del indio*, 68.

31. "Real cédula que los indios que se trajeron de las islas y se vendieron por mandado del almirante, se pongan en libertad y se restituyan a los países de su naturaleza," June 20, 1500, in Konetzke, *Colección de documentos*, 1:4; Mira Caballos, "Isabel la Católica," 47–48.

32. Deive, *Española y la esclavitud del indio*, 70.

33. "Instrucción para el gobernador de las Indias acerca de la población y regimiento de ellas, de la contratación, de la hacienda, y otras cosas," March 20, 1501, transcribed and printed in *Santo Domingo en los manuscritos de Juan Bautista Muñoz*, comp. Roberto Marte (Santo Domingo: Ediciones Fundación García Arévalo, 1981), 45. The Marte work is a collection of documents discovered and then transcribed by the Crown historian Juan Bautista Munoz in 1793 and later reprinted by Roberto Marte.

34. "Instrucción al comendador Frey Nicolás de Ovando, gobernador de las islas y tierra firme del mar océano," September 16, 1501, in Konetzke, *Colección de documentos*, 1:4–5.

35. Sauer, *Early Spanish Main*, 113.

36. "Orden de informe de los indios traído por Cristóbal Guerra," 1501, AGI Indiferente General 418, file 1, fol. 70r.

37. "Orden del rey y la reina sobre los indios que trajo Cristóbal Guerra," December 2, 1501, in Enrique Otte, *Cedulas reales relativas a Venezuela (1500–1550)* (Caracas: Edición de la Fundación John Boulton y la Fundación Eugenio Mendoza, 1963), 11–12.

38. Deive, *Española y la esclavitud del indio*, 72. At the same time she did revoke the earlier clause that had given license to enslave any Indians already held as slaves by their peoples.

39. Abulafia, *Discovery of Mankind*, 126. Isabela also reiterated the prohibition to take any slaves to Spain; however, Caribs could be captured and sold throughout the Caribbean.

40. "Cédula real," 1503, AGI Indiferente General 418, legajo 1, fol. 116r–v.

41. Jalil Sued Badillo, "The Island Caribs: New Approaches to the Question of Ethnicity in the Early Colonial Caribbean," in Whitehead, *Wolves from the Sea*, 69.

42. Deive, *Española y la esclavitud del indio*, 76. Some (including Las Casas) argued that had Isabela not died in 1504, she would have attempted to curtail the abuse of Caribs across the Americas and the extensive slave raiding that followed in its wake. Mira Caballos, "Isabel la Católica," 56–57.

43. Deive, *Española y la esclavitud del indio*, 77.

44. Saco, *Historia de la esclavitud de los indios*, 1:135. He sold the Indian slaves to Luis Guerra, who in turn sent them to Spain.

45. "Capitulación con Diego de Nicuesa y Alonso de Hojeda para ir a la tierra de Viaba y Veragua," 1508, AGI Indiferente General 415, legajo 1, fols. 6v–7v.

46. Karen F. Anderson-Córdova, *Surviving Spanish Conquest: Indian Fight, Flight, and Cultural Transformation in Hispaniola and Puerto Rico* (Tuscaloosa: University of Alabama Press, 2017), 173; Guitar, "Cultural Genesis," 127; Enrique Otte, *Las perlas del Caribe: Nueva Cádiz de Cubagua* (Caracas: Fundación John Boulton, 1977), 103.

47. "Licencia para hacer guerra a los caribes," December 24, 1511, AGI Indiferente General 418, legajo 3, fol. 91r.

48. "El rey al almirante," July 25, 1511, in Marte, *Santo Domingo en los manuscritos*, 96–97.

49. Saco, *Historia de la esclavitud de los indios*, 1:155–156; "Licencia para hacer guerra a los caribes"; "Introducción de indios de otras islas en Santo Domingo," June 21, 1511, AGI Patronato 275, ramo 1, no folio; Anderson-Córdova, *Surviving Spanish Conquest*, 174.

50. When Ponce de León first landed on Puerto Rico, he met and allied with Agueybana I. Agueybana even accompanied León to Santo Domingo in May 1509, possibly to visit relatives, including a cacique, in the cacicazgo of Higuey. Oliver, *Caciques and Cemí Idols*, 202; Badillo, "Island Caribs," 77. However, by 1510 his brother, Agueybana II, had become supreme cacique of the territory after Agueybana I and his mother perished from an unknown illness. Karen F. Anderson-Córdova, "The Aftermath of Conquest: The Indians of Puerto Rico During the Early Sixteenth Century," in *Ancient Borinquen: Archaeology and Ethnohistory of Native Puerto Rico*, ed. Peter Siegel (Tuscaloosa: University of Alabama Press, 2005), 344.

51. Jalil Sued Badillo, *Agueybana el bravo: La recuperación de un simboló* (San Juan: Ediciones Puerto, 2008), 70–72.

52. "Real cédula al virrey D. Diego Colon y a los oficiales reales en la isla Espanola," July 25, 1511, in *Colección de documentos inéditos de ultramar* (hereafter, *CDI*), vol. 1: Isla de Cuba (Madrid: Real Academia de la Historia, 1885), 20–21; Eugenio Fernández Méndez, *Las encomiendas y esclavitud de los indios de Puerto Rico, 1508–1550* (Puerto Rico: Editorial Universitaria, 1976), 32–33.

53. "Carta de Don Fernando al prelados," December 23, 1511, in Marte, *Santo Domingo en los manuscritos*, 101; Whitehead, *Wolves from the Sea*, 70.

54. Anderson-Córdova, *Surviving Spanish Conquest*, 346; Badillo, "Guadalupe," 48.

55. "Informaciones: Juan González Ponce de León," 1532, AGI Mexico 203, no. 19, fols. 19v–20r. This document details Juan González's lengthy career in Santo Domingo, Puerto Rico, and Mexico. González acted as a soldier, interpreter, and spy in the various conquests. This particular information was given by witness Francisco Rodríguez.

56. Méndez, *Encomiendas y esclavitud*, 31.

57. Cacey Farnsworth, "The Revolt of Agueybana II: Puerto Rico's Interisland Connections," in Altman and Wheat, *Spanish Caribbean*, 33–34.

58. "Informaciones: Juan González Ponce de Leon," 1532, AGI Mexico 203, no. 19, fols. 28r–29r; testimony of Lucas Gallego.

59. Oliver, *Caciques and Cemí Idols*, 168–169; Méndez, *Encomiendas y esclavitud*, 36.

60. Badillo, "Island Caribs," 81.

61. Keegan, *People Who Discovered Columbus*, 222.

62. "Informaciones: Juan González Ponce de Leon," fol. 20r–v.

63. Badillo, "Guadalupe," 47. Juan Garrido, a famous black conquistador, participated in the pacification of Puerto Rico and in the attacks on the Carib islands. One can see a complete description of Garrido's conquests in his *Probanza*, published in Ricardo E. Alegría, *Juan Garrido: El conquistador negro en las Antillas, Florida, Mexico, y California c. 1503–1540* (Puerto Rico: Centro de Estudios Avanzados de Puerto Rico y el Caribe, 1990).

64. "Carta de Don Fernando," February 22, 1512, in Marte, *Santo Domingo en los manuscritos*, 102.

65. Deive, *Española y la esclavitud del indio*, 97.

66. "Auto dado por Diego Colón, jueces y oficiales," July 30, 1513, AGI Justicia 43, no. 2; Méndez, *Encomiendas y esclavitud*, 43.

67. "Carta de Rey Fernando II a Obispo de la Concepción," 1514, transcribed and printed in *La iglesia y el negro esclavo en Santo Domingo: Una historia de tres siglos* by Jose Luis Sáez (Santo

Domingo: Patronato de la Ciudad Colonial de Santo Domingo Colección Quinto Centenario, 1994), 206. This volume contains a brief introduction to Spanish slave policies and the church's involvement in these matters, but it is mainly a compilation of transcribed documents from archives in Sevilla and Madrid, dealing with slavery and the church in Española.

68. Anderson-Córdova, *Surviving Spanish Conquest*, 143.

69. "Carta al Rey," no date, AGI Patronato 14, N.4, R.28, fol. 3r.

70. "Cartas que escribieron los padres de la orden de Santo Domingo que residen en la Española a Mosior de Xevres," 1516, in Marte, *Santo Domingo en los manuscritos*, 175–176. In 1513 the Crown also extended the definition of the "useless" islands to include the "islas gigantes" of Curaçao, Aruba, and Bonaire. In August 1514 the first armada sailed against these islands, capturing up to two thousand Indian slaves. By 1520 Nicolás Peréz declared Curaçao and the other islas gigantes to be depopulated. Jiménez, *Esclavitud indígena en Venezuela*, 128.

71. "De jueces y oficiales de Española," September 6, 1515, Biblioteca de la Real Academia de la Historia, Colección de Juan Bautista Muñoz, vol. 57, fol. 353v.

72. Badillo, "Island Caribs," 82.

73. Seijas, *Asian Slaves*, 38.

74. Zavala, *Instituciones jurídicas*, 77–78.

75. After finding only death and ruin at Navidad, Columbus sailed eastward along the northern coast of the island. Nearly a month later the group decided upon a site, dropping anchor and performing the first mass on January 2, 1494. They named the new colony La Isabela in honor of the queen. Deagan and Cruxent, *Archeology at La Isabela*, 4–5.

76. Deagan and Cruxent, *Archeology at La Isabela*, 7–8; William F. Keegan, *Taíno Indian Myth and Practice: The Arrival of the Stranger King* (Gainesville: University of Florida Press, 2007), 26–27. This community became Concepción de la Vega, the first boomtown of the Americas.

77. S. Lyman Tyler, *Two Worlds: The Indian Encounter with the European, 1492–1509* (Salt Lake City: University of Utah Press, 1988), 138.

78. Deagan and Cruxent, *Archeology at La Isabela*, 57.

79. "Instrucción de Colón a mosén Pedro Margarite," April 9, 1494, AGI Patronato 8, ramo 10, fol. 75v. According to Sauer, in this quotation, Columbus's use of "rescate" is the first time that the term appears in any colonial document. As discussed in the Introduction, this term signifies trade under some pressure, force, or violence and it could mean the commandeering of goods. Sauer, *Early Spanish Main*, 85. "Rescate" was commonly used to describe the capture and forceful trade of Indian slaves in later years.

80. "Instrucción de Colón a mosén Pedro Margarite," fols. 75v–76r.

81. Tyler, *Two Worlds*, 138.

82. Tyler, *Two Worlds*, 139.

83. "Instrucción de Colón a mosén Pedro Margarite," fol. 76r.

84. "Instrucción de Colón a mosén Pedro Margarite," fol. 76v. Following Caonabó's detention, the Spanish soldiers were ordered to dress him since his nudity was indecent.

85. Tyler, *Two Worlds*, 155.

86. Sauer, *Early Spanish Main*, 85.

87. Oviedo claimed that the Taínos refused to plant their crops in the spring of 1494 in hopes of starving the Spaniards and forcing them to abandon the island. Oviedo, *Historia general y natural de las Indias*, 48.

88. Las Casas, *Historia de las Indias*, 1:399.

89. The town, Corral de los Indios, has a central plaza that is more than 125,000 square meters, the largest Taíno plaza in the Caribbean. This suggests that Caonabó was one of the most powerful caciques in the entire region. Keegan, *Taíno Indian Myth and Practice*, 74–75.

90. Keegan, *Taíno Myth and Practice*, 30; Tyler, *Two Worlds*, 162.

91. Keegan, *Taíno Myth and Practice*, 31; Tyler, *Two Worlds*, 153–164.

92. Sauer, *Early Spanish Main*, 87–88; Deagan and Cruxent, *Archeology at La Isabela*, 60; Keegan, *Taíno Myth and Practice*, 32; Las Casas, *Historia de las Indias*, 1:400.

93. Phillips and Phillips, *Worlds of Christopher Columbus*, 207.

94. One official report said that the ship on which Caonabó was held prisoner sank in the harbor of La Isabela before he ever left for Spain. However, this detail or any mention of his arrival in Spain is not included in any of the chronicles, leaving Caonabó's fate a mystery. Keegan, *Taíno Myth and Practice*, 31; Soule, "From Africa to the Ocean Sea," 15.

95. "Carta de Cuneo," in Jane, *Four Voyages of Columbus*, 161; Soule, "From Africa to the Ocean Sea," 16.

96. "De la libertad de los indios y quan deseada y encargada ha sido siempre por nuestros reyes," no date, transcribed and printed in *Biblioteca de autores españoles desde la formación del lenguaje hasta nuestros días: Politica indiana, libro segundo de la política indiana en que se trata de la libertad, estado, y condiciones de los indios*, ed. Juan de Solorzano y Pereyra (Madrid: Lope de Vega, 1972), 135.

97. Las Casas, *Historia de las Indias*, 1:400.

98. Sauer, *Early Spanish Main*, 89.

99. Pauline M. Kulstad, "Concepción de La Vega 1495-1564: A Preliminary Look at Lifeways in the Americas' First Boom Town" (PhD diss., University of Florida, 2008), 39.

100. Tyler, *Two Worlds*, 189.

101. For more on this controversy, see Kulstad, "Concepción de la Vega," 39–41; and Lynne Guitar, "What Really Happened at Santo Cerro? Origin of the Legend of the Virgin of Las Mercedes," *Issues in Indigenous Caribbean Studies* 3, no. 1 (February 2001).

102. For more on the issue of double misunderstanding and double mistaken identity, see James Lockhart, "Sightings: Initial Nahua Reactions to Spanish Culture," in Schwartz, *Implicit Understandings*, 218–248; and Wyatt Macgaffey, "Dialogues of the Deaf: Europeans on the Atlantic Coast of Africa," in Schwartz, *Implicit Understandings*, 249–267.

103. Pedro Mártir de Anglería, *Décadas del nuevo mundo* (Madrid: Ediciones Polifemo, 1989), 44; Fernando Colombo, *The Life of the Admiral Christopher Columbus by His Son Ferdinand* (New Brunswick, NJ: Rutgers University Press, 1959), 149–150; Sauer, *Early Spanish Main*, 90.

104. Colombo, *Life of the Admiral*, 195–196; Sauer, *Early Spanish Main*, 92–95.

105. Sauer, *Early Spanish Main*, 93.

106. Jiménez, *Esclavitud indígena en Venezuela*, 87.

107. "Carta a los reyes de Colón," document 33, in Varela, *Cristóbal Colón*, 407–408.

108. Mira Caballos, "Isabel la Católica," 44–45; Jiménez, *Esclavitud indígena en Venezuela*, 87.

109. Colombo, *Life of the Admiral*, 220–221.

110. "De la guerra, que se levantó en la provincia de Higuey, y porque causa," in Antonio de Herrera y Tordesillas, *Historia general de los hechos de los castellanos, en las islas y Tierra Firme del mar océano*, 4 vols. (Buenos Aires: Editorial Guarania, 1949), 2:13–14.

111. Deive, *Española y la esclavitud del indio*, 73.

112. Troy S. Floyd, *The Columbus Dynasty in the Caribbean, 1492–1526* (Albuquerque: University of New Mexico Press, 1973), 58–59; Las Casas, *Historia de las Indias*, 2:264. According to Las Casas, they hanged thirteen men in honor of Christ and the twelve apostles.

113. Las Casas, *Historia de las Indias*, 2:264. One such slave, baptized as Juan, can be found years later in Sevilla. In 1525, his master, Francisco Velazquez, sought the return of Juan, who had recently fled his household. He described Juan as a slave taken in "just war" in the "war of Higuey." Van Deusen, *Global Indios*, 67–68; Silva, *Esclavitud en Andalucía*, 40.

114. Juan Gil, "Las cuentas de Cristóbal Colón," *Anuario de estudios americanos* 41 (1984): 53.

115. Las Casas, *Historia de las Indias*, 2:265.

116. Shortly after Guarionex's capture, Roldán moved his community to the Jaragua cacicazgo. Farther away from the central Spanish government in Santo Domingo, Roldán created an alliance with cacique Behechio and his sister cacica, Anacaona. Roldán cemented deep ties in Jaragua, including taking a Taíno "wife" and having mestizo children whom he petitioned to bring back with him to Spain as part of his peace settlement in 1498. Jane Landers, "World Colliding: Early Transatlantic Contacts," in *The Atlantic World: A History, 1400–1888*, ed. Douglas R. Egerton, Alison Games, Jane Landers, Kris Lane, and Donald R. Wright (Wheeling, IL: Harlan Davidson, 2007), 12.

117. Herrera y Tordesillas, *Historia general de los hechos de los castellanos*, 2:52.

118. Keegan, *Taíno Myth and Practice*, 33.

119. Herrera y Tordesillas, *Historia general de los hechos de los castellanos*, 2:53; Abulafia, *Discovery of Mankind*, 300. Years later, caciques of Española still sought refuge in Cuba. Notably the cacique Hatuey escaped to Cuba in 1511. Governor Diego Colón then justified the conquest of Cuba through the pursuit of Hatuey. Later that year Hatuey was captured by the Spanish and sentenced to death. According to Las Casas, Hatuey said that he would rather go to Hell than live with Christians in Heaven.

120. "Cédula de la reina," December 20, 1503, in Marte, *Santo Domingo en los manuscritos*, 52–53; Jiménez, *Esclavitud indígena en Venezuela*, 90.

121. However, after 1501 it remained illegal to transport Indian slaves to the Iberian Peninsula to be sold. Repeated violations of the laws led to multiple reiterations of the legislation. For example, in 1511 the Crown again issued a royal order to Diego Colón, governor of the Indies, that no official, governor, or resident of Española could bring or send any Indian slaves to Castile unless they possessed a special license. If they disobeyed the law, they would lose all the Indians they had transported and a third of any other Indians they possessed. If they did not have any other Indians, they would have to pay twenty thousand maravedíes to the royal court. "Prohibición para llevar indios a Castilla," June 21, 1511, AGI Indiferente 418, legajo 3, fol. 91v.

122. Deive, *Española y la esclavitud del indio*, 74–75.

123. "Cartas que escribieron los padres," 171.

124. As many have discussed, the Indians of the Americas lacked immunities to most European diseases, especially those carried by livestock. These included influenzas, smallpox, measles, typhus, the plague, cholera, malaria, and yellow fever. While the first smallpox outbreak did not occur until 1518, there is evidence that several waves of influenza and possibly typhus or measles assailed the island in 1493, 1498, 1502, and 1507. All these outbreaks wreaked havoc on both the rising population of European colonists and the already-declining native Taínos of the Caribbean. Noble David Cook, "Disease and the Depopulation of Hispaniola, 1492–1518," *Colonial Latin American Review* 2, no. 1–2 (1993).

125. The collection of gold to fulfill Spanish tribute took time and laborers away from cultivating crops, hunting, and fishing. And if one did not live near the gold mines or riverbeds where one could find gold, the Taínos replaced their manioc, cassava, and yucca fields with cotton. This led to the first large-scale famine on the island from the fall of 1495 throughout the winter and spring of 1496. Within six months to a year, some historians estimate that up to 40 percent of the Taíno population of Española perished from starvation. The suffering from malnutrition would have made diseases more virulent as well. Wilson, *Hispaniola*, 91–96.

126. While Indian naborías were only supposed to work in the mines or be absent from their homes for eight months out of the year, this regulation was seldom followed. In 1516 Pedro Romero testified that encomenderos often forced their naborías to work year-round, never allowing them to rest or paying them the small salaries they were owed. Esteban Mira Caballos, "El sistema laboral indígena," *Cuadernos de historia latinoamericana* 3 (1996): 21; "Residencia tomado a los jueces de apelación de la isla Española," 1516, AGI Justicia 42, legajo 1.

127. Many chroniclers, including Las Casas, pointed to high rates of suicide and abortions to help explain the catastrophic decline in population. While there no doubt were cases of suicide, there are no accounts of mass suicides, and as late as 1502 the Taínos were still actively resisting the Spanish presence. The rebellion in Higuey serves as one example showing that they had yet to lose hope. Wilson, *Hispaniola*, 96–97.

128. While everyone agrees that Española and the larger Caribbean experienced a sharp decline in indigenous populations following the arrival of the Spanish, many argue over the actual numbers. Much controversy surrounds the pre-contact population estimates of the Caribbean, so it follows that the rate of loss is also disputed. Modern scholars have estimated the 1492 population of Española to have been anywhere from sixty thousand (the very lowest approximation) to nearly eight million (the highest guess). These numbers come from chroniclers (like Las Casas, who claimed that three million Indians perished or were enslaved between 1494 and 1508), censuses conducted in the early sixteenth century, the annual loss of lives, and efforts to establish the island's carrying capacity. Sauer, *Early Spanish Main*, 155. While each estimate has its merits, some of the most reasonable approximations for the pre-contact population of Española are between 500,000 and 750,000, with an upward limit of 1,000,000. Cook, "Disease," 214–220; Massimo Livi Bacci, "Return to Hispaniola: Reassessing a Demographic Catastrophe," *Hispanic American Historical Review* 83, no. 1 (February 2003): 5.

129. "Real cédula," 1510, AGI Indiferente General 418, legajo 2, fol. 7r.

130. Deive, *Española y la esclavitud del indio*, 90.

131. Deive, *Española y la esclavitud del indio*, 92; Jiménez, *Esclavitud indígena en Venezuela*, 124–125; "El rey al almirante," August 14, 1509, in Marte, *Santo Domingo en los manuscritos*, 72.

132. "El rey al Ovando," September 15, 1509, in Marte, *Santo Domingo en los manuscritos*, 73–74.

133. "Licencia para llevar indios," July 21, 1511, AGI Indiferente General 418, legajo 3, fol. 91r.

134. Keegan, *People Who Discovered Columbus*, 220. The northern ports of the island were the preferred locations for the slaving operations into the "useless" islands. Sauer, *Early Spanish Main*, 159.

135. "Carta del licenciado Zuazo a Monsieur de Chievres," January 22, 1518, transcribed and printed in *Cartas y memorias (1511–1539): Alonso de Zuazo*, ed. Rodrigo Martínez Baracs (Mexico City, Mexico: Consejo Nacional Para la Cultura, 2000), 87–88.

136. "Cartas que escribieron los padres," 175–176.

137. Keegan, *People Who Discovered Columbus*, 221. On one expedition, the slaver and encomendero Lucás Vazquéz de Ayllón captured at least nine hundred Indians, half of whom died in pens in the Lucayos while awaiting an additional ship for their voyage to Española. Paul Hoffman, *A New Andalucía and a Way to the Orient: The American Southeast During the Sixteenth Century* (Baton Rouge: Louisiana State University Press, 1990), 5, 44.

138. "Carta de Rodrigo de Figueroa," 1513, AGI Patronato 174, ramo 19.

139. Mira Caballos, "Sistema laboral," 29. Dominican friars gave a lower number of twenty thousand, while Judge Alonso Zuazo estimated fifteen thousand.

140. Otte, *Perlas del Caribe*, 116. For more on pearl ranches, see Molly Warsh, "Enslaved Pearl Divers in the Sixteenth Century Caribbean," *Slavery and Abolition* 31, no. 3 (September 2010); and Michael Perri, "Ruined and Lost: Spanish Destruction of the Pearl Coast in the Early Sixteenth Century," *Environment and History* 15, no. 1 (2009).

141. Juan López Palacios Rubios, a theologian and scholar, developed the requerimiento as part of the response to calls for reform by both Franciscan and Dominican friars. Patricia Seed, *Ceremonies of Possession in Europe's Conquest of the New World, 1492–1640* (Cambridge: Cambridge University Press, 1995), 72. According to Seed, the requerimiento was based on the Muslim ritual of submission characteristic of military *jihad*, or struggle.

142. The requerimiento cites the papal donation of 1493, dividing the globe between the Crowns of Spain and Portugal, as the source of Spanish sovereignty in the Americas. "El requerimiento, que los reyes mandaron hacer a los indios," in Herrera y Tordesillas, *Historia general de los hechos de los castellanos*, 2:127.

143. "Requerimiento, que los reyes mandaron hacer a los Indios," 2:127–128; Seed, *Ceremonies*, 70–72.

144. Seed, *Ceremonies*, 71. Las Casas claimed that he did not know whether to laugh or cry when he read the requerimiento.

145. Zavala, *Instituciones jurídicas*, 79.

146. Jimenéz, *Esclavitud indígena en Venezuela*, 137.

147. "Andres de Haro tesorero a su alteza," August 8, 1515, San Juan, and "Andres de Haro a su alteza," October 6, 1515, Biblioteca de la Real Academia de la Historia, Colección de Juan Bautista Muñoz, vol. 57, fols. 345r–346v. On at least one of these expeditions, the Caribs succeeded in killing four Spaniards.

148. "Jueces y oficiales de la Española," September 15, 1515, Biblioteca de la Real Academia de la Historia, Colección de Juan Bautista Muñoz, vol. 57, fol. 353r; Otte, *Perlas del Caribe*, 134.

149. Otte, *Perlas del Caribe*, 130. Of the forty Indians, there were at least four small children.

150. "Relación de la jornada de Gaspar de Espinosa," 1515, AGI Patronato 26, ramo 7, fols. 1v–2r.

151. "Informaciones del obispo Juan de Quevedo del Darien," 1515, AGI Patronato 26, ramo 5, fols. 36r–43v.

152. Sauer, *Early Spanish Main*, 200–201. Sauer gives the figure of 22,726 Indians of service and naborías while Demorizi estimates 22,336. Emilio Rodríguez Demorizi, *Los dominicos y las encomiendas de indios de la isla Española* (Santo Domingo: Editora del Caribe, 1971), 34.

153. "Instrucción que los reyes dieron a Rodrigo de Alburquerque y al licenciado Ibarra para hacer el Repartimiento general de los indios de la isla Española," 1513, printed in Luis Arranz Márquez, *Repartimientos y encomiendas en la isla Española: El Repartimiento de Alburquerque de 1514* (Madrid: Ediciones Fundación García Arévalo, 1991), 264–273. For the actual text of the Repartimiento and a discussion of the larger Spanish politics surrounding the

creation of the document, see Arranz Márquez, *Repartimientos y encomiendas*, and Demorizi, *Dominicos y las encomiendas*.

154. Arranz Márquez, *Repartimientos y encomiendas*, 204–212; Kulstad, "Concepción de La Vega," 60–62; Demorizi, *Dominicos y las encomiendas*, 34.

155. This led to the rapid depopulation of the island's Spanish residents and the consequent abandonment of some of the island's original towns, like Verapaz. "Memorial de Hernando de Gorjón, acerca de la despoblación de la isla Española," 1520, in *CDI*, 1:428–429.

156. Sauer, *Early Spanish Main*, 201.

157. "Repartimiento de la isla Española" 1514, transcribed and printed in *Colección de documentos inéditos relativos al descubrimiento, conquista, y colonización de las posesiones Españolas en América y Oceanía, sacados en su mayor parte del Real Archivo de Indias*, vol. 1 (Madrid: Imprenta de M. B. de Quirós, 1864), 60–61.

158. Miguel D. Mena, *Iglesia, espacio, y poder: Santo Domingo (1498–1521), experiencia fundacional del nuevo mundo* (Santo Domingo: Archivo General de la Nación, 2007), 285.

159. Arranz Márquez, *Repartimientos y encomiendas*, 242.

160. "Se le encomendó cuarenta y cinco naborías de casas, las que fueron registradas en nombre del almirante Don Diego Colon," "Repartimiento de la isla Española," CDI, 1:109.

161. Charles R. Ewen, *From Spaniard to Creole: The Archaeology of Cultural Formation at Puerto Real, Haiti* (Tuscaloosa: University of Alabama Press, 1991), 27.

Chapter 3

1. "The Advent Sermons of Fray Antonio Montesinos," 1511, translated and printed in *New Iberian World: A Documentary History of the Discovery and Settlement of Latin America to the Early 17th Century: Volume 1: The Conquerors and the Conquered*, ed. John H. Parry (New York: Times Books, 1984), 308.

2. Robert Ricard developed the idea of the "spiritual conquest" in his pivotal work *The Spiritual Conquest of Mexico: An Essay on the Apostolate and the Evangelizing Methods of the Mendicant Orders in New Spain, 1523–1572*, trans. Lesley Byrd Simpson (Berkeley: University of California Press, 1966). For Ricard the "spiritual conquest" was the successful conversion of the natives of New Spain to Catholicism, a process that occurred in concert with the military conquest of Mexico. Since the publication of Ricard's work, the idea of the "spiritual conquest," especially its completion and success, has come under fire from many historians. Now historians like Louise Burkhart and Nancy Farriss portray the "spiritual conquest" as much more of a multilayered negotiation between the Indians and clergy. Others, like William Taylor, have questioned the success of the friars, arguing for the creation of a syncretic Catholicism infused with surviving elements of native culture, ritual, and beliefs constantly evolving over time. For more on this topic, see Louise Burkhart, *The Slippery Earth: Nahua-Christian Dialogue in Sixteenth-Century Mexico* (Tucson: University of Arizona Press, 1989); Nancy Farriss, *Maya Society Under Colonial Rule: The Collective Enterprise of Survival* (Princeton, NJ: Princeton University Press, 1984); William B. Taylor, *Magistrates of the Sacred: Priests and Parishioners in Eighteenth-Century Mexico* (Stanford, CA: Stanford University Press, 1996); Sarah Cline, "Conquest and the Aftermath: Center and Periphery in Colonial Mexico," *Latin American Research Review* 27, no. 3 (1992); and John F. Schwaller, "Franciscans in Colonial Latin America," *Americas* 61, no. 4 (2005).

3. John F. Schwaller, *The Church in Colonial Latin America* (Wilmington, DE: Scholarly Resources, 2000), xiii–xiv; Seijas, *Asian Slaves*, 20; Solorzano y Pereyra, *Biblioteca*, 119–121.

4. Luis N. Rivera, "The Theological Juridical Debate," in Schwaller, *Church in Colonial Latin America*, 10.

5. The Franciscans' early presence in the colonial project can be traced to their support of Columbus's venture. Specifically, Fray Antonio de Marchena and Fray Juan Pérez, two friars from the monastery at La Rábida, were instrumental in gaining Crown support and organizing the first journey. See Lino Gómez Canedo, *Evangelización y conquista: Experiencia franciscana en Hispanoamérica* (Mexico City, Mexico: Editorial Porrua, S.A., 1977), 2.

6. Mariano Errasti, *Los primeros franciscanos en América: Isla Española, 1493–1520* (Santo Domingo: Fundación García Arévalo, 1998), 38. The Jeronymite order was a monastic order; therefore, they were not typical missionaries and played a much smaller role in the colonization of the Americas. For a comprehensive history of the Jeronymite order, see Friar José de Siguienza, *Historia de la orden de San Jerónimo* (Madrid: Bailly Baílliére e Hijos, 1907).

7. Álvarez, *Mitología Taína o Eyeri*, 7; Constance G. Janiga-Perkins, *Reading, Writing, and Translation in the "Relación acerca de las antiguedades de los indios" (c. 1498) by Fray Ramón Pané* (Lewiston, NY: Edwin Mellen Press, 2007).

8. José Juan Arrom, "Estudio preliminar," in *Relacion acerca de las antigüedades de los indios* by Fray Ramón Pané (Mexico City, Mexico: Siglo Veintiuno Editores, S.A., 1974), xiii–xviii.

9. Errasti, *Primeros franciscanos*, 39.

10. Prior to his conversion, Juan Mateo was known as Guaticabanú and was one of sixteen servants or naborías to a small cacique of the Macorix, Guanáoboconel. It was with these servants that Pané made his first inroads into Taíno society. Anthony M. Stevens-Arroyo, "Juan Mateo Guaticabanú, September 21, 1496: Evangelization and Martyrdom in the Time of Columbus," *The Catholic Historical Review* 82:4 (Oct. 1996): 624–625; Jorge Antonio Flores Santana, *La isla Española: Cuna de la evangelización de América* (Santo Domingo: Dirección General de la Feria del Libro, 2011), 41; Canedo, *Evangelización y conquista*, 3.

11. Juan Mateo and his brothers were killed while traveling from Mabiatué's village to the home of their mother near Magdalena. Stevens-Arroyo, "Juan Mateo," 626–628; Pané, *Relación acerca de las antigüedades*, 46–47.

12. Following their baptism by Chaplain Lorenzo Fernández, they received the names Cristóbal and Pedro. Serving as Cristóbal's godfathers were Antonio de Torres and Andrés Balsques. Pedro's godfathers were the brothers Varela. "Partida de bautismo de dos indios criados de Colón," July 29, 1496, Archivo del Real Monasterio de Santa María de Guadalupe, Libro I de Bautismos, fol. 1v. Printed in *Los franciscanos y el nuevo mundo*, ed. José Sánchez Dubé (Sevilla: Guadalquivir Ediciones, 1992), 39.

13. Though it is possible that this many Indians were baptized, what exactly that meant for the Taínos is up for interpretation. Whether or not they truly understood what baptism meant, due to both miscommunication and the difficulties inherent in fully explaining complex religious doctrine, is the first of many questions. While we might never know the answers to these queries, it is important to read the friars' accounts of mass conversions and baptisms with skepticism. Canedo, *Evangelización y conquista*, 4.

14. Originally, thirteen Franciscans were slated to travel to the New World, but only twelve made the journey. The thirteen were Alonso de Espinar, Bartolomé de Turuégano, Antonio de Carrión, Francisco de Portugal, Antonio de los Mártires, Maseo de Zafra, Pedro de Hornachuelos, Bartolomé de Sevilla, Juan de Hinojosa, Alonso de Hornachuelos, Juan de Escalante, Juan Francés, and Pedro Francés. Making up the sixteen clergymen were four lay brothers who remained unnamed in the documentation. Canedo, *Evangelización y conquista*, 6–7.

15. Daniel Castro, *Another Face of Empire: Bartolomé de las Casas, Indigenous Rights, and Ecclesiastical Imperialism* (Durham, NC: Duke University Press, 2007), 45. The soon-to-be-famous Bartolomé de las Casas and Francisco Pizarro, the future conquistador of Peru, were both among the 1502 group.

16. Kulstad, *Concepción de la Vega*, 56. Concepción de la Vega was destroyed by an earthquake in 1562, making Santo Domingo the most populous and important settlement on the island. It is now known as La Vega, a very small town.

17. Errasti, *Primeros franciscanos*, 140.

18. Fray Cipriano de Utrera, *Polémica de Enriquillo* (Santo Domingo: Editora del Caribe, 1973), 136. Franciscans were also sent to Mejoradad del Cotuy and Villa de la Buenaventura. Canedo, *Evangelización y conquista*, 8.

19. Fray Juan Manuel Pérez, *Estos ¿no son hombres? Lectura actual del proyecto apostólico de la primera comunidad de dominicos en el nuevo mundo* (Santo Domingo: Fundación García-Arévalo, 1984), 30.

20. Castro, *Another Face of Empire*, 56.

21. "Sermón de Adviento, 20 de diciembre, 1511," cited in Las Casas, *Historia de las Indias*, 2:441. While there is no written transcription of the Montesinos sermon, we do have firsthand accounts of its content, and the most thorough is that of Las Casas.

22. Patricia Seed, "'Are These Not Men?': The Indians' Humanity and Capacity for Spanish Civilization," *Journal of Latin American Studies* 25, no. 3 (October 1993): 635.

23. Las Casas, *Historia de las Indias*, 2:442–447.

24. Errasti, *Primeros franciscanos*, 204.

25. Mena, *Iglesia, espacio, y poder*, 250–251.

26. Sauer, *Early Spanish Main*, 197; Errasti, *Primeros franciscanos*, 205–206.

27. "Laws of Burgos," in Parry, *New Iberian World*, 342.

28. "Laws of Burgos," in Parry, *New Iberian World*, 344.

29. "Cédula a Pedro de Córdova," June 2, 1513, in Otte, *Cedulas reales relativas a Venezuela*, 65.

30. By 1515, the salt mines of Araya were also fueling the movement of settlers to the region. Otte, *Cedulas reales relativas a Venezuela*, xxviii.

31. "Orden de los gerónimo a los frailes dominicos," September 3, 1516, in Otte, *Cedulas reales relativas a Venezuela*, 78; Las Casas, *Historia de las Indias*, 3:131. For more on this episode and the first missions of Venezuela, see Erin Stone, "Slave Raiders vs. Friars in Tierra Firme, 1513–1522," *Americas* 74, no. 2 (April 2017).

32. "Designación de franciscanos para Indias," June 1512, AGI Indiferente General 418, legajo 3, fol. 316r–v.

33. "Orden de pasaje a fray Alonso de Espinar," July 28, 1512, AGI Indiferente General 418, legajo 3, fol. 329r.

34. "Orden al doctor Sancho de Matienzo," July 30, 1512, AGI Indiferente General 418, legajo 3, fol. 338v.

35. Lino Gómez Canedo, *La educación de los marginados durante la época colonial* (Mexico City, Mexico: Porrúa, 1982), 7.

36. "Orden al doctor Sancho de Matienzo," 1513, AGI Indiferente General 419, legajo 4, fol. 124v.

37. "Orden al provincial de la orden de San Francisco," 1513, AGI Indiferente General 419, legajo 4, fol. 127v. The maravedí was the smallest Spanish coin by the sixteenth century, and it was made only from copper, not gold or silver like the other units.

38. The three friars were Remigio de Faulx, Pedro de Arcabandi, and Guillermo de Podio. Errasti, *Primeros franciscanos*, 140–141. Friar Mejía, one of the original Franciscans to journey to Jaragua, was additionally charged with helping Súarez adapt to the island so that he could most efficiently bring them to the Catholic faith. "Orden a Fray Pedro Mejía," April 19, 1513, AGI Indiferente General 419, legajo 4, fol. 110r.

39. Juan J. Amate Blanco, "La filología indigenista en los misioneros del siglo XVI," *Cuadernos Hispanoamericanos* 500, no. 1 (1992): 55. By the 1550s, Nebrija's *Vocabulario* and *Gramática* were both translated to Nahuatl. Byron Ellsworth Hamann, "Histories in Translation: Antonio de Nebrija, Conceptions of the Past, and Early Modern Global Lexicography," *Journal of the Dictionary Society of North America* 39, no. 1 (2018): 197.

40. "Carta al Rey," June 6, 1534, AGI Santo Domingo 77, ramo 4, no. 77, fol. 1r. Enrique's letter to the Crown indicates his final submission to the Spanish authorities in Santo Domingo. His testament, a document that has yet to be found, is described in a letter from the Audiencia of Santo Domingo to the Crown in September 1535. At least one Spaniard, Captain Alferro, saw the will and states that the cacique left power to his wife, Doña Mencia, and his nephew in his testament. While it is possible that both these documents were written by scribes, Enrique's signature does appear on the letter of surrender. There is additional evidence that the cacique could read Spanish, as he was described by two military captains as reading the pardon signed by both the queen and the royal court of Santo Domingo. "Carta del Audiencia de Santo Domingo," September 1, 1533, AGI Santo Domingo 49, ramo 4, no. 28, fol. 2r.

41. "Carta al emperador de oidor Zuazo y Vadillo," September 4, 1533, Biblioteca de la Real Academia de la Historia, Colección de Juan Bautista Muñoz, vol. 61, fol. 299v.

42. Manuel Arturo Pena Battle, *La rebelión de Bahoruco* (Santo Domingo: Librería Hispaniola, 1970), 74; "Carta al emperador de oidor Zuazo y Vadillo," fol. 300r.

43. Errasti, *Primeros franciscanos*, 134.

44. "Casa para enseñanza en la isla Española," December 22, 1517, AGI Patronato 275, ramo 3, no folio.

45. "Salario de Aquiles Holden, maestro de gramática," June 3, 1523, AGI Indiferente General 420, legajo 9, fol. 97v. The Franciscans began their mission in Santo Domingo years earlier, beginning construction on both their permanent stone monastery and the central cathedral from 1511 to 1512. Errasti, *Primeros franciscanos*, 104–107; Mariano Errasti, *El primer convento de América: Historia y forma de vida de los franciscanos en su convento de la ciudad de Santo Domingo, 1516–1820* (Santo Domingo: Editora Corripio, 2006), 59.

46. "Real cédula al gobernador y oficiales," November 9, 1526, in *CDI*, 1:360–361.

47. Christopher Abel, "The Catholic Church," in *The Cambridge History of Latin America, Vol. 11: Bibliographical Essays*, ed. Leslie Bethell (Cambridge: Cambridge University Press, 1995), 523.

48. Jason M. Yaremko, *Indigenous Passages to Cuba, 1515–1900* (Gainesville: University Press of Florida, 2016), 18–21.

49. It was thought that married men present in the Americas would better fulfill their commitments to indoctrinate and convert the indigenous populations in their care. For more on the policies of marriage and family in the developing Caribbean colonies, see Ida Altman, "Marriage, Family, and Ethnicity in the Early Spanish Caribbean," *William and Mary Quarterly* 70, no. 2 (April 2013).

50. Kulstad, "Concepción de La Vega," 60.

51. The three chosen Jeronymite friars were Luis de Figueroa, Bernardino de Manzanedo, and Alfonso de Santo Domingo. Mena, *Iglesia, espacio, y poder*, 294.

52. Manuel Giménez Fernández, *La jurisdicción jeronomita en las Indias* (Mexico: Universitaria, 1951), 142.

53. Luis Fernández de Retana, *Cisneros y su siglo: Estudio histórico de la vida y actuación pública del Cardenal D. Fr. Francisco Ximénez de Cisneros*, vol. 2 (Madrid: Administración de "El Perpetuo Socorro," 1930), 311–313. Beyond their removal from the political realm, the Jeronymites had recently sheltered Cisneros and the young King Charles during the succession struggle so he had personal ties to the order. Fernández, *Jurisdicción jeronomita*, 71–73.

54. "Los jerónimos enviados a la Española por el Cardinal Cisneros," 1516, in Marte, *Santo Domingo en los manuscritos*, 208–210; Kulstad, "Concepción de La Vega," 62–63.

55. Guitar, "Cultural Genesis," 224.

56. Esteban Mira Caballos, "La primera utopía Americana: Las reducciones de indios de los jerónimos en la Española (1517–1519)," in *La Española*, 348; "The Heronymite Survey," 1517, in Parry, *New Iberian World*, 1:329.

57. Herbert S. Klein, *The Atlantic Slave Trade* (Cambridge: Cambridge University Press, 2010), 13; David Wheat, *Atlantic Africa and the Spanish Caribbean, 1570–1640* (Williamsburg, VA / Chapel Hill: Omohundro Institute / University of North Carolina Press, 2016), 19.

58. "Interrogatorio jerónimo," 1517, AGI Indiferente 1624, ramo 3, no. 1, fols. 49v–52v. The Franciscan was Pedro de Mexia, though his reasons for supporting the maintenance of the encomienda are not clear. He was present in the Indies since at least 1513 and served as provincial of the Franciscan order in Española. He was even instrumental in the creation of the schools for hijos de caciques. "Orden al provincial de la orden de San Francisco," fol. 127v. Mexia, like Espinal, may have personally benefited from the encomienda system since the larger monasteries possessed encomienda grants.

59. "Orden de los gerónimo a los frailes dominicos," 77.

60. "Orden de los gerónimo a los frailes dominicos," 79.

61. Saco, *Historia de la esclavitud de los indios*, 4:3–55.

62. Otte, *Cedulas reales relativas a Venezuela*, xxix.

63. Jiménez, *Esclavitud indígena*, 145.

64. "Comisión al licenciado Zuazo sobre los indios cautivados," January 13, 1518, in Otte, *Cedulas reales relativas a Venezuela*, 101.

65. "Memorial del licenciado Zuazo sobre lo que resulta de las probanzas a los jueces de apelación," 1518, in Baracs, *Cartas y memorias*, 105–106. Zuazo also described many other issues, including the branding of many free Indians and the poor treatment of women.

66. Ida Altman, "The Revolt of Enriquillo and the Historiography of Early Spanish America," *Americas* 63, no. 4 (2007): 597, Sauer, *Early Spanish Main*, 205; and Mira Caballos, "Primera utopía," 351.

67. "Cuentas de Juan Ampiés," 1519, in Marte, *Santo Domingo en los manuscritos*, 260.

68. Mira Caballos, "Primera utopía," 353.

69. Mira Caballos, "Primera utopía," 356–361; Mena, *Iglesia, espacio, y poder*, 299.

70. Demorizi, *Dominicos y las encomiendas*, 252–254.

71. Carlos Esteban Deive, *La esclavitud del negro en Santo Domingo (1492-1844)* (Santo Domingo: Editora Taller, 1980), 78.

72. Mira Caballos, "Primera utopía," 366.

73. "Residencia que tomó el licenciado Lebrón al licenciado Rodrigo de Figueroa," 1521, AGI Justicia 45, N.1a.

74. "Carta al rey y reina por el licenciado Figueroa," April 7, 1519, Biblioteca de la Real Academia de la Historia, Colección de Juan Bautista Muñoz, vol. 58, fol. 91r.

75. Mira Caballos, "Primera utopía," 367–368.

76. Mira Caballos, "Primera utopía," 369.

77. Guitar, "Cultural Genesis," 176.

78. Bozal slaves came directly from Africa, usually the interior, and unlike ladino slaves they did not speak a European language and had not converted to Catholicism.

79. Saco, *Historia de la esclavitud de los indios*, 4:178. Specifically, throughout Tierra Firme, Spaniards were free to take or trade any slaves that were already held as slaves by local Indians. "Confirmación de privilegios de Santo Domingo por los jerónimos," 1518, Biblioteca de la Real Academia de la Historia, Colección de Juan Bautista Muñoz, vol. 58, fol. 89r; "Licencia para traer de Tierra Firme para esclavos los que allí lo son de otros indios. Licencia para traer negros bozales," 1518, Biblioteca de la Real Academia de la Historia, Colección de Juan Bautista Muñoz, vol. 58, fol. 89r.

80. "Licencia a Miguel de Pasamonte para rescatar esclavos," June 19, 1519, AGI Indiferente General 420, legajo 8, fol. 69r.

81. Otte, *Perlas del Caribe*, 136.

82. Deive, *Esclavitud del negro en Santo Domingo*, 169–170.

83. "Licencia para comprar indios a los portugueses," January 9, 1520, AGI Indiferente General 420, legajo 8, fol. 177r–v. The Indians on the northern coast of Brazil were easily categorized as Caribs following the accounts of early explorers, most notably the publications of Amerigo Vespucci after his 1501 journey to Brazil. In perhaps his most inflammatory anecdote he describes how two European men ventured ashore to trade with the Indians, but instead they were captured, killed, cooked, and eaten in full view of the waiting Portuguese vessel. Metcalf, *Go-Betweens*, 36. Other important early colonial accounts that detail cannibalism in Brazil include Jean de Léry's "History of a voyage to the land of Brazil, otherwise called America: Containing the navigation and the remarkable things seen on the sea by the author; the behavior of Villegagnon in that country; the customs and strange ways of life" and Hans Staden's captivity narrative, "Hans Staden's true history: An account of cannibal captivity in Brazil."

84. Saco, *Historia de la esclavitud de los indios*, 2:180.

85. Whitehead, *Of Cannibals and Kings*, 9. In the span of two months alone, six hundred Indian slaves were sold publicly in Santo Domingo. Demorizi, *Dominicos y las encomiendas*, 44.

86. Saco, *Historia de la esclavitud de los indios*, 2:195.

87. Demorizi, *Dominicos y las encomiendas*, 44. It is likely that at least some of these slaves came from the two caravels for which Juan de Cardenás received a license in August 1520. Cardenás could capture and trade for Indian slaves in Barbados, Isla Verde, Trinidad, and along the coast of Paria. "Licencia a Juan de Cardenás para armar carabelas," August 27, 1520, AGI Indiferente General 420, legajo 8, fol. 253r.

88. Figueroa was not the first official to be assigned the difficult task of differentiating between the Caribs who could be enslaved and all the other Indians who were free. In 1515 Francisco de Vallejo had been charged with the job, but slavers actively blocked him from completing the work. Later Las Casas was asked to carry out the task, but he refused to be the man to relegate hundreds or thousands of Indians to slavery, regardless of their practices and ethnicities. Whitehead, *Of Cannibals and Kings*, 13–14. "Información hecha por el licenciado Rodrigo de Figueroa acerca de la población india de las islas e costa de Tierra Firme, e sentencia que dió en nombre de su Majestad," 1520, in *CDI*, 1:380. For the first published English translation of the Figueroa report, see "The Deposition of Rodrigo de Figueroa on the Islands of the Barbarous Caribs" 1520, in Whitehead, *Of Cannibals and Kings*, 115–119.

89. "Información hecha por el licenciado Figueroa," in *CDI*, 1:380.

90. "Memorial de Hernando de Gorjon, acerca de la despoblación de la isla Española," 1520, in *CDI*, 1:428–429.

91. "Información hecha por el licenciado Figueroa," in *CDI*, 1:380.

92. "Información hecha por el licenciado Figueroa," in *CDI*, 1:383.

93. Otte, *Perlas del Caribe*, 141–145.

94. Otte, *Perlas del Caribe*, 186.

95. "Licencia a Juan de Cardenás para armar carabelas," fols. 253v–254r.

96. "Interrogatorio de factor Juan Ampies sobre indios," August 29, 1526, AGI Santo Domingo 74, ramo 1, no. 1, fols. 1r–11r.

97. In 1520 Las Casas received a commission and license from the king to establish three more pueblos with the help of fifty men. These towns received the same support as had previous settlements set up by Dominican and Franciscan friars on the coast of Tierra Firme. The asiento is transcribed in the collection *Descubrimiento y conquista de Venezuela: Textos históricos contemporáneos y documentos fundamentales*, vol. 1, ed. Joaquín Gabaldón Márquez (Caracas: Biblioteca de la Academia Nacional de la Historia, 1962), 357–432.

98. Lawerence A. Clayton, *Bartolomé de las Casas: A Biography* (Cambridge: Cambridge University Press, 2012), 188; Castro, *Another Face of Empire*, 82.

99. "A sus Majestades de los oidores e oficiales reales de Santo Domingo," November 14, 1520, in *CDI*, 1:423.

100. "A sus Majestades de los oidores e oficiales reales de Santo Domingo," in *CDI*, 1:423.

101. "A sus Majestades de los oidores e oficiales reales de Santo Domingo," in *CDI*, 1:424–426.

102. "Orden a los oficiales de La Española," March 11, 1522, AGI Indiferente General 420, legajo 8, fol. 362v.

103. "Representación del Contador Real que fue con Casas a Cumaná," 1524, in Márquez, *Descubrimiento y conquista de Venezuela*, 1:378.

104. "Orden a los oficiales de La Española," fols. 362v–363r.

105. "Extracto de una provisión real, emanada del almirante de la Audiencia y oficiales de Santo Domingo de la isla Española dando instrucciones al capitán Gonzalo de Ocampo para la guerra de los indios," January 20, 1521, in CDI, 1:438.

106. "Extracto de una provisión real," in *CDI*, 1:438.

107. Clayton, *Bartolomé de las Casas*, 191–195.

108. "Representación del Contador Real," 1:378–379.

109. Whitehead, *Of Cannibals and Kings*, 11.

110. Otte, *Perlas del Caribe*, 206–207.

111. Jiménez, *Esclavitud indígena*, 211–212.

112. Kulstad, "Concepción de La Vega," 66; Guitar, "Cultural Genesis," 176.

Chapter 4

1. This pattern is very similar to early exploration and slave raiding on the western coast of Africa by the Portuguese, where privateers and raiders slowly became explorers, slave traders, and commercial brokers between Europe and African communities. For more, see Malyn Newitts, *A History of Portuguese Overseas Expansion, 1400-1668* (New York: Routledge, 2005).

2. There were contemporaneous exploration missions that did not focus on the search for new sources of Indian slaves, most notably the expeditions from Darién to locate an entrance to the South Sea and a path to Asia. Sauer, *Early Spanish Main*, 173–177.

3. It is well documented that certain indigenous groups willingly became Spanish allies and participated in the conquest of other territories. For example, up to twelve thousand Xochimilco troops fought in the siege of Tenochtitlan alongside Cortés's soldiers. Also, many years after the conquest of Mexico, Maya warriors accompanied Pedro de Alvarado to the Andes in 1534. For more on indigenous allies throughout Mesoamerica from the initial conquest forward, see Matthew and Oudijk, *Indian Conquistadors*. Indian leaders also made pragmatic alliances throughout the Americas in many lesser-known episodes: for example, when the Timucua of Northeast Florida allied with the Spanish against the French. These alliances allowed Indian groups access to European goods and an opportunity to attack their enemies using European weapons and soldiers. Indian allies also worked with the Spanish beyond conquest, sometimes facilitating construction of colonial societies and helping the Spanish fulfill labor requirements for nascent economies. For more on these influential characters, or go-betweens, see Metcalf, *Go-Betweens*; and Yannakakis, *Art of Being In-Between*. Nevertheless, the Spanish did not always treat their Indian allies fairly. In many cases they were treated little better than slaves. For more on this, see Matthew Restall and Florine Asselbergs, eds., *Invading Guatemala: Spanish, Nahua, and Maya Accounts of the Conquest Wars* (University Park: Pennsylvania State University Press, 2007), 10–20; and Ida Altman, *The War for Mexico's West: Indians and Spaniards in New Galicia, 1524–1550* (Albuquerque: University of New Mexico Press, 2010), 24–56.

4. For more on this, see chapter 5, "People: The Trade in Indigenous Bodies and Bilingual Minds," in Scott Cave, "Communication and the Social History of Contact in the Spanish Atlantic, 1341–1602" (PhD diss., Pennsylvania State University, 2018).

5. José Ignacio Avellaneda, *The Conquerors of the New Kingdom of Granada* (Albuquerque: University of New Mexico Press, 1995), 11–20. By 1535 the explorers had begun to search for El Dorado, a mythic land full of gold governed by a golden-skinned Indian. According to the story the Indian chief, who lived somewhere in present-day Colombia, covered his body in gold dust once a year prior to rowing to the middle of an enormous lake where he bathed, bestowing the gold as an offering. This legend was first articulated in 1535 and soon after spread throughout Spanish America. For a full discussion of the myth, see the introduction to Sir Walter Raleigh, *The Discoverie of the Large and Bewtiful Empire of Guinana*, ed. V. T. Harlow (London: Argonaut Press, 1928), xlv–xcvi. Though this Indian chief was the source of the specific El Dorado myth, the idea that massive amounts of gold would be located at the equator had been promoted for decades, if not centuries.

6. Deive, *Española y la esclavitud del indio*, 244.

7. Following the failure of Ponce de León were a string of would-be-conquerors (Lucas Vázquez de Ayllón, Pánfilo de Narváez, Hernando de Soto, and Don Tristán de Luna y Arellano), ending with the successful voyage of Pedro Menéndez de Avilés in 1565. For more on Menéndez and the successful conquest of Florida, see Eugene Lyon's seminal works *The Enterprise of Florida: Pedro Menéndez de Aviles and the Spanish Conquest of 1565–1568* (Gainesville: University Presses of Florida, 1974), the document collection *Pedro Menéndez de Avilés* (New York: Garland, 1995), and *Richer Than We Thought: The Material Culture of Sixteenth-Century St. Augustine* (St. Augustine, FL: St. Augustine Historical Society, 1992).

8. Ponce de León was propelled to find new territories after he lost the governorship of Puerto Rico to Diego Colón (Christopher Columbus's son) in 1511. "Asiento con Juan Ponce de León," February 23, 1512, AGI Indiferente General 415, legajo 1, fol. 9r; John E. Worth, *Discovering Florida: First-Contact Narratives from Spanish Expeditions Along the Lower Gulf Coast* (Gainesville: University Press of Florida, 2014), 8–13.

9. "Asiento con Juan Ponce de León," fols. 10r, 11v.

10. Jerald T. Milanich and Susan Milbrath, "Another World," in *First Encounters: Spanish Explorations in the Caribbean and the United States, 1492-1570*, ed. Jerald T. Milanich and Susan Milbrath (Gainesville: University of Florida Press, 1991), 13; and Antonio de Herrera y Tordesillas, "De la navegación de Juan Ponce de Leon, al norte de la isla de San Juan: y descubrimiento de la Florida; y porque la llamó así," in Herrera y Tordesillas, *Historia general de los hechos de los castellanos*, 2:207. Herrera's chronicle was first published in 1601. He was the official royal historian and chronicler at this point for the king of Spain. It is in his transcriptions that we find the only record of Ponce de León's voyage in 1513, so presumably Herrera had the contract in his possession when he penned his chronicle.

11. Herrera y Tordesillas, *Historia general de los hechos de los castellanos*, 2:208.

12. The Ais, whose settlement was located near present-day Cape Canaveral, allied with Menéndez during his search for surviving Frenchmen, and they even invited him and his men to stay in their territory to establish a fort following the defeat of the French. Menéndez gladly accepted their invitation, leaving many of his soldiers with about one hundred French captives in the newly formed Fort Santa Lucia, when he sailed for Havana seeking more men and supplies for the coming winter in Florida. However, those left behind soon found themselves threatened and then abandoned by the Ais, forcing them to travel northward to another river where they encountered another Indian group that continuously attacked them. The Spanish spent the next two months suffering from starvation and attack from various Indians (both those with whom they had previously been friends, and their new enemy, the cacique named Jega), ultimately resorting to cannibalism of the French captives in order to survive. "Méritos y servicios: Diego López," 1569, AGI Patronato 51, no. 3, ramo 3, fols. 1r–22r.

13. Following the arrival of Pedro Menéndez de Avilés, the Spanish maintained a tenuous though friendly alliance with the Calusa for several decades with the sons of cacique Carlos, even traveling to Havana to be schooled in the Catholic faith. For more on the Calusa and their relationship with the early Spanish colonizers, see Ruben Vargas Ugarte, "The First Jesuit Mission in Florida," *Historical Records and Studies*, vol. 25; and Stephen Edward Reilly, "A Marriage of Experience: Calusa Indians and Their Relations with Pedro Menéndez de Avilés," *Florida Historical Quarterly* 59, no. 4 (April 1981): 395–421.

14. Herrera y Tordesillas, *Historia general de los hechos de los castellanos*, 2:209.

15. Worth, *Discovering Florida*, 8.

16. While Herrera refers to the cacique in question as Carlos, it is possible that he is applying the name of a much later cacique of the Calusa to this earlier chief. When Pedro Menéndez de Avilés undertook the conquest of Florida, he encountered a cacique by the name of Carlos with whom he had a complex relationship. However, it is also possible that the Calusa possessed a word describing their chiefs or their ethnic group that sounded like "Carlos" and thus the Spanish mistakenly believed that term to be a proper name. For more on the controversy, see Hann, *Indians of Central and South Florida*, 13–16.

17. Herrera y Tordesillas, "Que Juan Ponce de Leon, acabada su navegación por la costa de la Florida, volvió a la isla de San Juan," in Herrera y Tordesillas, *Historia general de los hechos de los castellanos*, 2:209–210.

18. According to Herrera's chronicle, the ship returned to the Lucayos to locate the true Bimini Island and with it the fabled "fountain of youth." Herrera y Tordesillas, *Historia general de los hechos de los castellanos*, 2:210–211; Douglas T. Peck, "Reconstruction and Analysis of the 1513 Discovery Voyage of Juan Ponce de León," *Florida Historical Quarterly* 71, no. 2 (October

1992): 136. For more on how the legend of the fountain of youth became associated with Florida, see Worth, *Discovering Florida*, 8–13.

19. Vicente Murga Sanz, *Juan Ponce de Leon: Fundador y primer gobernador del pueblo puertorriqueno descubridor de la Florida y del estrecho de las Bahamas* (San Juan: Ediciones de la Universidad de Puerto Rico, 1959), 114.

20. In the end, it did not matter, because Ponce de León died during his second attempt at conquering Florida in 1521, perishing from a wound inflicted during a skirmish with Indians along the southwestern Florida coast. Worth, *Discovering Florida*, 19.

21. Antonio de Herrera y Tordesillas, "Del viaje del piloto Esteban Gómez, y del que hicieron a Chicora los navios del Licenciado Ayllón," in Herrera y Tordesillas, *Historia general de los hechos de los castellanos*, 3:25–26.

22. Herrera y Tordesillas, "Del viaje del piloto Esteban Gómez," 3:25–26.

23. The license was issued by Diego Colón, the governor at the time.

24. The mission also received sponsorship from the secretary of the Audiencia Diego Caballero.

25. Hoffman, *New Andalucía*, 3–6. This slaver was Captain Pedro de Salazar.

26. Paul Quattlebaum, *The Land Called Chicora: The Carolinas Under Spanish Rule with French Intrusions, 1520–1670* (Gainesville: University of Florida Press, 1956), 7; Otte, *Perlas del Caribe*, 113–115. Ayllón owned several boats so that he could more efficiently engage in the Indian slave trade.

27. Hoffman, *New Andalucía*, 10.

28. "El licenciado Juan Ortiz de Matienzo contra el licenciado Lucas Vázquez de Ayllón sobre licencia para descubrir, pacificar, y poblar una tierra nueva en 35 y 37 grados," March 1526, AGI Justicia 3, ramo 3, fol. 27v.

"El licenciado Juan Ortiz de Matienzo," fol. 27v. According to Quejo and Gordillo, the Indians or "naturales" of the land were "nefandos y comían carne humana" (savages who ate human flesh). This testimony appears as part of the much larger case that Matienzo presented against Vázquez de Ayllón in March 1526 in an effort to prevent him from using the license from the Crown to "discover, pacify, and settle" the new lands located between the latitudes of 35 and 37 degrees.

29. Hoffman, *New Andalucía*, 6–11.

30. Hoffman, *New Andalucía*, 21. The name "Chicora" likely comes from the actual name of the region's native inhabitants, the Shakori, whom the Spanish mistakenly called the Chicora. The Shakori practiced the elongation of the skulls of infants, for both cosmetic and practical reasons (to improve eyesight for hunting), which produced bulging eyes in many offspring. This trait could explain why the Spanish referred to the Indian captive as "frog boy."

31. Peter Martyr D'Anghera, *De Orbo Novo: The Eight Decades of Peter Martyr D'Anghera*, 2 vols., trans. Francis Augustus MacNutt (New York: Burt Franklin, 1970), 1:259–263.

32. Hoffman, *New Andalucía*, 15, 40. While Hoffman claims that the Indians were sent to work in a gold mine, this industry was waning by the 1520s in and near Concepción de la Vega. While the Spanish did attempt to replace mining with sugar, sugar plantations did not survive in the Cibao. Instead cattle ranching became the most profitable trade after 1514, so it is possible that Ayllón's lands were used for this purpose instead. Kulstad, *Concepción de la Vega*, 232.

33. "El licenciado Juan Ortiz de Matienzo contra el licenciado Lucas Vázquez de Ayllón," fol. 31r; Hoffman, *New Andalucía*, 17.

34. "Capitulación con el licenciado Ayllón para lo de la Florida," 1523, AGI Indiferente General 415, legajo 1, fol. 23r.

35. "Capitulación con el licenciado Ayllón," fol. 33r.

36. "Capitulación con el licenciado Ayllón," fol. 36r.

37. David B. Quinn, *Explorers and Colonies: America, 1500–1625* (London: Hambledon Press, 1990), 134–135.

38. Herrera y Tordesillas, "Del viaje del piloto Esteban Gomez," 3:27.

39. David J. Weber, *The Spanish Frontier in North America* (New Haven, CT: Yale University Press, 1992), 36–37; Hoffman, *New Andalucía*, 77.

40. It is worth noting that there was a great deal of controversy surrounding Doncel's assumption of power over Captain Francisco Gomez, leading to the arrest of multiple colonists and several assassination plots. For more on this subject, see Hoffman, *New Andalucía*, 76–79.

41. Weber, *Spanish Frontier*, 37; Quattlebaum, *Land Called Chicora*, 24–25. Among the survivors was Antonio de Montesinos, one of the three Dominican friars who accompanied the group with the intention of converting the native peoples of La Chicora.

42. The indigenous groups of Mexico and Cuba might have been ethnically connected, making their relationship closer than with those who lived on other Caribbean islands. Using craniometrics and modern geometric morphometric methods, archaeologists are evaluating possible dispersal theories of Caribbean populations. See Ann H. Ross and Douglas H. Ubelaker, "A Morphometric Approach to Taíno Biological Distance in the Caribbean," in Fitzpatrick and Ross, *Island Shores, Distant Pasts*, 124–125. Mayan pottery found in Cuba presents additional evidence of pre-Hispanic trade routes between the Maya and the Taíno of Cuba. Sauer, *Early Spanish Main*, 212–213.

43. Sauer, *Early Spanish Main*, 213.

44. Hernán M. Venegas Delgado and Carlos M. Valdés Dávila, *La ruta del horror: Prisioneros indios del noreste novohispano llevados como esclavos a la Habana Cuba* (Coahuila: Universidad Autónoma de Coahuila, 2013), 52; Deive, *Española y la esclavitud del indio*, 131.

45. Deive, *Española y la esclavitud del indio*, 131; Sauer, *Early Spanish Main*, 213. The discovery and conquest of the Yucatán and greater Mexico did not stop slaving in the Guanaxas Islands. This continued until 1526 when Pedro Moreno, a slaver living in Trujillo, Honduras, reported that the Guanaxas Islands were depopulated. Anderson-Córdova, *Surviving Spanish Conquest*, 180.

46. Inga Clendinnen, *Ambivalent Conquests: Maya and Spaniard in Yucatan, 1517–1570* (Cambridge: Cambridge University Press, 1987), 4–5; Sauer, *Early Spanish Main*, 214.

47. Saco, *Historia de la esclavitud de los indios*, 2:77–78; Bernal Díaz del Castillo, *The History of the Conquest of New Spain*, ed. Davíd Carrasco (Albuquerque: University of New Mexico Press, 2008), 2.

48. Robert S. Chamberlain, *The Conquest and Colonization of Yucatan, 1517–1550* (Washington, DC: Carnegie Institution of Washington, 1948), 11.

49. Díaz del Castillo, *History of the Conquest of New Spain*, 2.

50. Díaz del Castillo, *History of the Conquest of New Spain*, 3.

51. Díaz del Castillo, *History of the Conquest of New Spain*, 4–5.

52. Silvio Zavala, *Los esclavos indios en Nueva España* (Mexico City, Mexico: Colegio Nacional Luis Gonzalez Obregon, 1967), 1.

53. Matthew Restall, *When Moctezuma Met Cortés: The True Story of the Meeting That Changed History* (New York: HarperCollins, 2018), 300.

54. Zavala, *Esclavos indios*, 2. There is much debate on why the Spanish conquistadors attacked and massacred the leaders of Cholula. While Cortés claimed that they had warning,

from Doña Marina, of an impending attack on their forces, others point to the Tlaxcalans, enemies of the Cholulans. Many believe that the Spanish attack on Cholula was a litmus test proving the alliance to the Tlaxcalans. Stuart B. Schwartz, ed., *Victors and Vanquished: Spanish and Nahua Views of the Conquest of Mexico* (Boston: Bedford St. Martin's, 2000), 100–102; Camilla Townsend, *Malintzin's Choices: An Indian Woman in the Conquest of Mexico* (Albuquerque: University of New Mexico Press, 2006), 79–82.

55. Hernán Cortés, "Segunda carta de relación," 1520, transcribed and printed in Zavala, *Instituciones jurídicas*, 184–185.

56. Restall, *When Moctezuma Met Cortés*, 296–298.

57. Restall, *When Moctezuma Met Cortés*, 302.

58. "Carta escrita al rey por los oidores de la Real Audiencia de la Española," August 20, 1520, Archivo del Museo Naval (hereafter, AMN) 0031, Ms.0039ter/000.

59. Reséndez, *Other Slavery*, 62

60. Van Deusen, *Global Indios*, 67.

61. Restall, *When Moctezuma Met Cortés*, 304.

62. Following the passage of the New Laws in 1542, Gregorio López, a member of the Council of the Indies, conducted an inspection of all indigenous slaves and free Indians in Spain. During the procedure, over one hundred indigenous slaves in Sevilla alone were freed. Van Deusen, *Global Indios*, 16.

63. Van Deusen, *Global Indios*, 72.

64. William L. Sherman, *Forced Native Labor in Sixteenth-Century Central America* (Lincoln: University of Nebraska Press, 1979), 21–32.

65. Restall and Asselbergs, *Invading Guatemala*, 10–12; Sherman, *Forced Native Labor*, 22–27.

66. Linda Newson, *The Cost of Conquest: Indian Decline in Honduras Under Spanish Rule* (Boulder, CO: Westview Press, 1986), 97.

67. Zavala, *Esclavos indios en Nueva España*, 6; Sherman, *Forced Native Labor*, 38.

68. "Memorial de Rodrigo del Castillo a su magestad y autorizado de Samano," 1528, AGI Patronato 26, ramo 5, fol. 138r–v.

69. "Cartas del cabildos seculares," March 20, 1530, AGI Guatemala 44a, no. 17, fol. 2r. Salcedo claimed that some of these Indians were given to him as part of diplomatic meetings, because caciques or principales always brought slaves and other goods to political rendezvous. "Conquista de Trujillo: Diego López de Salcedo," November 11, 1529, AGI Patronato 54, no. 6, ramo 3, no folio.

70. The one hundred slaves were sold in Leon and then transported to Trujillo. For a list of how many slaves each resident purchased and took to Trujillo, see "Esclavos y naborías de ciudad de León a villa Trujillo," February 28, 1529, AGI Patronato 20, no. 4, ramo 4, no folio.

71. "Cartas del cabildos seculares," fol. 2r; Newson, *Cost of Conquest*, 110.

72. Newson, *Cost of Conquest*, 110.

73. David R. Radell, "The Indian Slave Trade and Population of Nicaragua During the Sixteenth Century," in *The Native Population of the Americas in 1492*, ed. William M. Denevan (Madison: University of Wisconsin Press, 1976), 72. Some royal officials held partial ownership of slave ships, including the royal treasurer of Nicaragua, Alonso Cáceres; and conquistadors Francisco Pizarro and Diego de Almagro. Others were directly involved, like governor Francisco de Castañeda, who took seven hundred Indian slaves when he left Nicaragua in 1533. Radell, "Indian Slave Trade," 69–72.

74. Reséndez, *Other Slavery*, 43.

75. Radell, "Indian Slave Trade," 68–75.

76. After the discovery of Peru, many Nicaraguan slaves also found themselves sent to the Andes. In 1535 the number of ships dedicated to Indian slave traffic rose to fifteen or twenty because the captives were in high demand in Peru and Chile. Sherman, *Forced Native Labor*, 41.

77. Sherman, *Forced Native Labor*, 40.

78. Sherman, *Forced Native Labor*, 68–70.

79. For more on the Germans in South America, including the Fuggers and the Welsers, see Spencer Tyce, "The Hispano-German Caribbean: South German Merchants and the Realities of European Consolidation, 1500–1540," in Altman and Wheat, *Spanish Caribbean*, 235–256.

80. Juan Friede, *Vida y viajes de Nicolás Féderman: Conquistador, poblador, y confundador de Bogotá, 1506–1542* (Bogotá: Ediciones Librería Buchholz, 1960), 13–18; Tyce, "Hispano-German Caribbean," 235–242.

81. "Capitulación con los alemanes," March 27, 1528, transcribed and printed in Otte, *Cedulas reales relativas a Venezuela*, 250; Tyce, "Hispano-German Caribbean," 241. The elaboration on the policy of enslaving the Indians of Venezuela, keeping them within the province, appears in the "Real provision del consejo de indios," May 10, 1531, transcribed and printed in Enrique Otte, comp., *Cedularios de la monarquia Española relativas a la provincia de Venezuela, 1520–1561*, vol. 1 (Caracas: Edición de la Fundación John Boulton y La Fundación Eugenio Mendoza, 1965), 97. Accompanying this provision is a license allowing the Germans to transport up to four thousand African slaves to Venezuela.

82. "Historia indiana o primer viaje de Nicolás Féderman," in *Descubrimiento y conquista de Venezuela (textos históricos contemporáneos y documentos fundamentales)*, vol. 2, trans. and ed. Juan Friede (Caracas: Biblioteca de la Academia Nacional de la Historia, 1962), 171–172. This is a firsthand account of the 1530 Féderman expedition written by Féderman himself, first published in German but translated to French in 1916 and then to Spanish by Friede.

83. "Carta de los oficiales de Venezuela de Coro," October 6, 1533, AGI Santo Domingo 206, ramo 1, no. 4, fol. 14v.

84. During some of his more violent encounters with the Indians of Venezuela, Féderman enslaved up to six hundred Indians. Friede, *Vida y viajes de Nicolás Féderman*, 58–67.

85. According to the historian Carl Ortwin Sauer, as early as 1513 the term "ranchear" began to generally mean the sacking of indigenous settlements and taking of captives. An example occurs in the account of exploration of Panama by Balboa and Espinosa. Sauer, *Early Spanish Main*, 283.

86. "Carta de los oficiales de Venezuela de Coro," fol. 20r.

87. The reaction of Spanish officials to the German conquistador's actions could have had larger, geopolitical origins. It is also possible that the Germans themselves did not fully respect the commands of the Spanish Crown, only fueling the tension between the two groups.

88. "Orden al gobernador de Venezuela sobre el cacique Marcos," 1535, AGI Caracas I, fol. 13r–v.

89. Jimenéz, *Esclavitud indígena*, 223–224.

90. "Información y cargos contra Alfinger por juicio de residencia del Dr. Navarro," 1538, AGI Justicia 56, no. 2, fols. 57v–59.

91. "Declaración y relación del entrada del gobernador Alfinger por maestre del campo Esteban Martín," August 18, 1534, AGI Santo Domingo 206, no. 4, fol. 33r–v. He even burned entire settlements, leaving Indians with nowhere to hide. After capturing one group of fleeing

Indians, Alfinger claimed that they fled the Spanish brigade because they feared they had come from Santa Marta. The Indians explained that Spaniards who came from Santa Marta forced them to engage in trade, at first in gold, until none was left. Then they attacked the Indians, taking as many as they could as slaves back to Santa Marta," AGI Santo Domingo 206, no. 4, fol. 27r.

92. Jimenéz, *Esclavitud indígena*, 232. Alfinger sequestered another population, at the town of Yjara, for six months until receiving six thousand pesos of gold for his ransom.

93. "Información y cargos contra Alfinger," fol. 34r–v. The witnesses who made these assertions were Gil Navas and Virgilio García.

94. "Información y cargos contra Alfinger," fol. 55v; Jimenéz, *Esclavitud indígena*, 232.

95. "Carta del Obispo de Santo Domingo," April 16, 1534, AGI Santo Domingo 218, no. 5, fol. 1r.

96. For an overview and description of most of these expeditions, and a few more, from their origins to their outcomes, see Avellaneda, *Conquerors of the New Kingdom of Granada.*

97. Quesada's success came from his discovery and sacking of the Muisca capital of Tunja that provided him and his men with thousands of pesos in gold and hundreds of emeralds. J. Michael Francis, *Invading Colombia: Spanish Accounts of the Gonzalo Jiménez de Quesada Expedition of Conquest* (University Park: Pennsylvania State University Press, 2007), 83–85.

98. "Relación de Santa Marta," 1545, transcribed, translated, and published in Francis, *Invading Colombia*, 65–66. The taking of these Indians occurred in early 1537, prior to Quesada's discovery of great riches.

99. Tyce, "Hispano-German Caribbean," 249.

100. José Ignacio Avellaneda, *Los compañeros de Federman: Cofundadores de Santa Fe de Bogotá* (Bogotá: Academia de Historia de Bogotá, 1990), 31.

101. Jimenéz, *Esclavitud indígena*, 221–222.

102. For a list of at least some of the many caciques (along with their subject Indians) whom Féderman captured (many died soon after) and enslaved, see the bishop of Coro's letter to the king in 1538, located in AGI Santo Domingo 218, N.13, fols. 2r–3r.

103. "Carta de obispo de Venezuela de la ciudad de Coro," April 2, 1538, AGI Santo Domingo 218, no. 12, fol. 2r.

104. Tyce, "Hispano-German Caribbean," 235–242.

105. Spencer Tyce, "Mistaken Identity?—The Welser Company, the Church, and Indigenous Allies in Sixteenth-Century Venezuela," paper presented at the Society of Ethnohistory conference, September 11–15, 2013, p. 14; "Rodrigo de Bastidas: Toma de Cuentas Oficiales de Venezuela," AGI Patronato Real 193, R.25, 1538.

106. For example, in 1528, Pánfilo de Narváez brought an unknown number of Mexican Indian slaves to Florida in the hopes that Indians from New Spain would be able to communicate with the inhabitants of Florida. He might have drawn this conclusion because Mayan Indians could converse with the natives of Cuba.

107. This clause appeared in Narváez's contract with the king, as it did in contracts with many other conquistadors. In an interesting twist Narváez was also ordered to free any indigenous slaves that he encountered being held by the natives of Florida. "Capitulación que se tomo Pánfilo de Narváez para la conquista del Rio de las Palmas," 1526, AGI Indiferente General 415, legajo 1, fol. 96v. Throughout his expedition Narváez captured and enslaved many Indians, through both legal and illegal methods. The best account of this voyage was written by one of its few survivors, the treasurer Alvar Núñez Cabeza de Vaca. Two excellent versions of the

document are *The 1542 Relación (Account) of Alvar Núñez Cabeza de Vaca*, ed. and trans. Rolena Adorno and Patrick Charles Pautz (Lincoln: University of Nebraska Press, 2003); and Alvar Núñez Cabeza de Vaca, *Naufragio* (Barcelona: Diferencias, 2006).

108. Cave, "Communication and the Social History of Contact," 159.

109. Charles Hudson, *Knights of Spain, Warriors of the Sun: Hernando de Soto and the South's Ancient Chiefdoms* (Athens: University of Georgia Press, 1997), 57, 66.

110. Cave, "Communication and the Social History of Contact," 158. Within a few days of the expedition's arrival, these indigenous slaves escaped Soto. During the search for the men, the expedition happened upon Juan Ortiz, a Spaniard who had been shipwrecked ten years prior and had taken several female slaves.

111. Cave, "Communication and the Social History of Contact," 198. In this dissertation, Cave lists the slaves specifically retrieved to serve as expeditionary guides or translators from 1522 to 1550. See pages 199–200.

112. Soto's actual route is still debated by both historians and archaeologists. For more on the possible twists and turns of Soto's travels, see Charles Hudson, Chester B. DePratter, and Marvin T. Smith, "Hernando de Soto's Expedition Through the Southern United States," in Milanich and Milbrath, *First Encounters*, 77–98; Joyce Rockwood Hudson, *Looking for De Soto: A Search Through the South for the Spaniards' Trail* (Athens: University of Georgia Press, 1993); and Gloria A. Young and Michael P. Hoffman, eds., *The Expedition of Hernando de Soto West of the Mississippi, 1541–1543* (Fayetteville: University of Arkansas Press, 1993). On other issues of the expedition, from archaeology and the life of Soto before the expedition to the problems with all the Soto narratives, see Patricia Galloway, ed., *The Hernando de Soto Expedition: History, Historiography, and "Discovery" in the Southeast* (Lincoln: University of Nebraska Press, 1997); and Jerald T. Milanich, *The Hernando de Soto Expedition* (New York: Garland, 1991).

113. Charles R. Ewen and John H. Hann, *Hernando De Soto Among the Apalachee* (Gainesville, FL: University of Florida Press, 1998), 5–8.

114. "Relación de la jornada a Florida con De Soto por Luis Hernández de Biedma," AGI Patronato 19, ramo 3, fols. 3v–4r. Unlike Elvas's account, Biedma's (the journey's treasurer) is the only firsthand relation of the Soto expedition that we possess. For more on the import of the narrative, along with its possible silences and history, see Ida Altman, "An Official's Report: The Hernández de Biedma Account," in Galloway, *Hernando de Soto Expedition*.

115. Charles Hudson, *The Juan Pardo Expeditions: Exploration of the Carolinas and Tennessee, 1566–1568* (Tuscaloosa: University of Alabama Press, 1990), 68–70.

116. While there could be many reasons for the cacica's refusal to supply Soto with Indian porters (as many other native leaders did when encountered by the conquistador), one of the most likely explanations stems from the fact that most of Florida's Indians lived in small societies or chiefdoms. Due to the tight-knit nature of these chiefdoms (often with five hundred or fewer members), the loss of a few individuals had a greater impact on the kinship networks and economic survival of the communities than in a larger state. Hudson, *Juan Pardo Expeditions*, 21–23.

117. "Relacion de la jornada a Florida con De Soto por Luis Hernández de Biedma," fol. 4r. During their campaign to find the cacica, the Spanish also encountered evidence of Spanish tools and trading goods, leading them to believe that they had located one of Ayllón's encampments in the interior.

118. We know the fate of the cacica from two sources. One is the soldier Alaminos, who either briefly deserted Soto or was lost and met with the group of escaped slaves in late May

1540. The other is the explorer Juan Pardo, who journeyed to Cofitachequi and heard the tale of the Soto encounter many years later, following Menéndez's conquest of Florida in 1565. Hudson, *Knights of Spain, Warriors of the Sun*, 192–93; Hudson, *Juan Pardo Expeditions*, 68–82.

119. Hudson, *Knights of Spain, Warriors of the Sun*, 146.

120. "Relación de la jornada a Florida con De Soto por Luis Hernández de Biedma," fol. 3r.

121. The different chronicles disagree on exactly what and how much was lost, but at least ten horses and most of the pearls collected at Cofitachequi were not recovered. Robbie Ethridge, Kathryn E. Holland Braund, Lawrence A. Clayton, George E. Lankford, and Michael D. Murphy, "A Comparative Analysis of the De Soto Accounts on the Route to, and the Events at, Mabila," in *The Search for Mabila: The Decisive Battle Between Hernando de Soto and Chief Tascalusa*, ed. Vernon James Knight Jr. (Tuscaloosa: University of Alabama Press, 2009), 173–174.

122. "Relación de la jornada a Florida con De Soto por Luis Hernández de Biedma," fol. 5r.

123. "Relación de la jornada a Florida con De Soto por Luis Hernández de Biedma," fol. 5v. The Spaniards did not escape unscathed from the massacre, with 250 wounded and twenty dead. For more on the battle of Mabila, from its archaeology and location to a discussion of its portrayal in the various Soto narratives, see Knight, *Search for Mabila*.

124. Some of these indigenous slaves were still alive in 1547, when the Dominican friar Luis Cáncer requested their presence as interpreters on his voyage to southwest Florida in 1549. He planned to establish a mission to peacefully convert the Indians without the influence of secular colonists and soldiers. While he failed in gathering the slaves in Guatemala, he did garner the help of a Tocobaga Indian slave named Madalena. She was likely captured at the start of Soto's expedition and sent back to Cuba. There she served as a household slave for Soto's wife, Isabel de Bobadilla, before returning to Florida with Cáncer in 1549. Scott Cave, "Madalena: The Entangled History of One Indigenous Floridian Woman in the Atlantic World," *Americas* 74, no. 2 (April 2017): 171–173; Worth, *Discovering Florida*, 24.

125. Soto died from an unknown illness along the banks of the Mississippi River in May 1542, effectively ending his dreams and the fruitless search for another Inca Empire in the southern United States. Hudson, *Knights of Spain, Warriors of the Sun*, 349.

126. Clifford M. Lewis and Albert J. Loomie, *The Spanish Jesuit Mission in Virginia, 1570–1572* (Chapel Hill: University of North Carolina Press, 1953), 15.

127. Lewis and Loomie, *Spanish Jesuit Mission*, 26.

128. This was not the first time that religious groups tried to create separate settlements to indoctrinate indigenous populations far from the "corrupting" influences of the larger Spanish populations. For more on the first of these missions in Tierra Firme, see Stone, "Slave Raiders vs. Friars," 150–155.

129. J. Michael Francis and Kathleen M. Kole, *Murder and Martyrdom in Spanish Florida: Don Juan and the Guale Uprising of 1597*, American Museum of Natural History Anthropological Papers 95 (2011): 30.

130. They declined the offer for soldiers, because of both their faith in Luis and their opinion that misbehaving soldiers were the true cause of Indian rebellion and slow conversion to Catholicism.

131. "Carta de Juan Rogel al Francis Borgia," August 28, 1572, in Lewis and Loomie, *Spanish Jesuit Mission*, 104–105. It is difficult to determine Don Luis's ethnic group because the Spanish failed to give any place-name, beyond Jacán or Ajacán, to describe Luis's territory. The only clues can be gathered from the sailors' descriptions of the bays, coastlines, and rivers where they disembarked. By linking these geographic references with the much more detailed records

of Walter Raleigh's expeditions, we can make some guesses of the regions' ethnography during Luis's time, but these are still questionable. Lewis and Loomie, *Spanish Jesuit Mission*, 231–239.

132. Lewis and Loomie, *Spanish Jesuit Mission*, 44–45.

133. "Carta de Juan Rogel," 105. While the historical record shows no impetus for the Indian attack, on the part of the Jesuits, all the documentation of the assault also comes from Jesuit sources, which are naturally biased against the Indians' actions.

134. Vargas Ugarte, *First Jesuit Mission*, 139–142; "Carta de Juan Rogel," 107. Another later relation goes beyond stating that the Indians wore the Jesuits' vestments to claim that they wore them to perform native ritual dances while also drinking sacramental wine from the Jesuits' skulls. However, Rogel does not mention this occurrence, and his is the closest to a firsthand account as he traveled with the boy Alonso. Additionally, Alonso described how Luis seemed repentant following the murder of the friars and asked the boy to help him give the Jesuits a proper Christian burial.

135. The Spanish sent the rescue mission in the summer of 1572 when they received news that Alonso was alive. This information came from a relief expedition sent to Jacán the previous year that located the mission, but instead of finding friars, they found Indians wearing Jesuit robes. This strange sight caused the group to immediately question whether they should go ashore. Their concern was warranted when the Indians sent out several canoes to attack the ship. During the skirmish the Spanish did succeed in capturing two Indians from whom they learned that the boy Alonso was still alive. Lewis and Loomie, *Spanish Jesuit Mission*, 49–51.

136. For more on the eventual English settlement of the Chesapeake Bay, during which they employed many of the same techniques as the Spanish, including Indian intermediaries (both voluntary and coerced), see Karen Ordahl Kupperman, *Indians and English: Facing Off in Early America* (Ithaca, NY: Cornell University Press, 2000).

Chapter 5

1. Otte, *Perlas del Caribe*, 214.

2. This is reminiscent of Columbus's idea for a large Indian slave trade, selling Indians to Andalucía to make the Indies venture both profitable and sustainable.

3. "Los vecinos de la isla de Cuba al rey," July 1540, AGI Santo Domingo 1121, legajo 2, fol. 175v.

4. "Para que el hierro con que se hierran los esclavos se ponga en poder de Villacorta," August 3, 1535, in *Cedulario de la monarquía Española relativo a la isla de Cubagua (1523–1550)*, 2 vols., ed. Enrique Otte (Caracas: Edición de la Fundación John Boulton y la Fundación Eugenio Mendoza, 1961), 15. One gold peso was equal to eight tomines.

5. Wheat, *Atlantic Africa*, 101–102.

6. In one such case a group of captives arrived in the port of Havana in 1628. The majority of the group were young boys and girls, each valued as two-thirds or half a pieza. In the end the cargo was valued as 142 piezas, even though 230 slaves disembarked from the ship. Wheat, *Atlantic Africa*, 102.

7. I use the definition of the commodification of people through slavery postulated by anthropologist Igor Kopytoff in his essay "The Cultural Biography of Things: Commoditization as Process." Here, Kopytoff describes the process of commoditization of a slave: "Slavery begins with capture or sale, when the individual is stripped of his previous social identity and becomes a non-person, indeed an object and an actual or potential commodity. But the process continues. The slave is acquired by a person or group and is reinserted into the host group, within which he is

resocialized and rehumanized by being given a new social identity." Kopytoff, "The Cultural Biography of Things: Commoditization as Process," in *The Social Life of Things: Commodities in Cultural Perspective*, ed. Arjun Appadurai (Cambridge: Cambridge University Press, 1986), 75. While any slave, from the first days of the colonial experiment until abolition, was considered to be a commodity for a period of time, I argue that it is not until the 1530s that the majority of enslaved Indians remained commodities following their initial sale, demonstrating a change in how Spanish colonists perceived Indians and in the overall moral economy of the Circum-Caribbean. Essentially by the fourth decade of colonization, slaves were subject to "terminal commoditization."

8. Scholars from Kenneth Andrews (in *The Spanish Caribbean: Trade and Plunder, 1530–1630* (New Haven, CT: Yale University Press, 1978) and Carl Ortwin Sauer (in *The Early Spanish Main*), to David Abulafia (in *The Discovery of Mankind*) have discussed the lack of authority and control present in the early Spanish colonial world.

9. The legislation also put additional restrictions on conquistadors' actions during the act of conquest to ameliorate some of the excesses committed during the conquest of Central America. Zavala, *Instituciones jurídicas*, 125.

10. Reséndez, *Other Slavery*, 64.

11. Charles Gibson, *Tlaxcala in the Sixteenth Century* (Stanford, CA: Stanford University Press, 1952), 144; Reséndez, *Other Slavery*, 66.

12. Saco, *Historia de la esclavitud de los indios*, 2:101.

13. "Indios o esclavos sacados del Pánuco para las islas," July 5, 1529, AGI Patronato 231, no. 4, ramo 1, fol. 1r.

14. "Indios o esclavos sacados del Pánuco para las islas," fol. 1r. Testimonies against the two officials appear in two documents in the same section, first against Juan Ortiz de Matienzo and later against Nuño de Guzmán. See the testimonies of Cristóbal de Quevedo and Gonzalo Ruiz Solano. Other witnesses include Diego de Padriera, Lope de Sayavedra, Pedro de Barboa, Juan de Cartucha, Juan Pardo, and Gomez Meto.

15. Donald E. Chipman, *Nuño de Guzmán and the Province of Pánuco in New Spain, 1518–1533* (Glendale, CA: Arthur H. Clark Company, 1967), 200.

16. In 1546 the Crown's hopes were fulfilled with the discovery of the silver-rich mines in the nearby province of Zacatecas.

17. Rolena Adorno and Patrick Charles Pautz, "Introduction," in *The Narrative of Cabeza de Vaca*, by Álvar Núñez Cabeza de Vaca, ed. and introd. Rolena Adorno and Patrick Charles Pautz (Lincoln: University of Nebraska Press, 2003), 9; Chipman, *Nuño de Guzmán*, 144–145.

18. Chipman, *Nuño de Guzmán*, 165.

19. Chipman, *Nuño de Guzmán*, 152–153.

20. Chipman, *Nuño de Guzmán*, 10.

21. Chipman, *Nuño de Guzmán*, 145.

22. Chipman, *Nuño de Guzmán*, 165. The removal of Quevedo's Indians was significant to him, even though his encomienda was fairly small. For example, a more famous conquistador like Hernán Cortés controlled close to sixty thousand Indians. Even on the largely depopulated island of Española, an important Crown official, like Judge Zuazo, benefited from two hundred commended Indians. Lesley Byrd Simpson, *The Encomienda in New Spain: The Beginning of Spanish Mexico* (Berkeley: University of California Press, 1982), 165–167; Esteban Mira Caballos, "El sistema laboral indígena en las Antillas (1492–1542)," in *Encomiendas, indios, y españoles*, coord. Julián B. Ruis Rivera and Horst Pietschmann (Munster: Cuadernos de Historia Latinoamericana), 28.

23. "Indios o esclavos sacados del Pánuco para las islas," fol. 3r–v; testimonies of Cristóbal de Quevedo and Gonzalo Ruiz Solano. While Española and Cuba lacked Indians by the 1520s, they did have a surplus of livestock. Within a few years, at least by the 1530s, cattle ranches were one of the more profitable industries on Española. By the 1580s there were over four hundred thousand cattle on the island, enabling ranchers to export up to fifty thousand hides a year. "Carta de Audiencia de Santo Domingo," January 25, 1533, AGI Santo Domingo 49, ramo 4, no. 23, fol. 2r–v; Andrews, *Spanish Caribbean*, 13.

24. Rosa E. Ficek, "Cattle, Capital, Colonization: Tracking Creatures of the Anthropocene in and out of Human Projects," *Current Anthropology* 60, no. 20 (August 2019): 262; Badillo, "Island Caribs," 66. As the Taíno populations decreased across the Greater Antilles so did their agricultural spaces, or *conucos*, where they had once grown squash, yucca, and other crops. Left fallow, they became grazing land for the growing herds of cattle that took over much of the northern portion of Española by the 1520s. Ficek, "Cattle, Capital, Colonization," 261.

25. "Provisión real hecha en Burgos para el factor de Cuba," February 15, 1528, Biblioteca de la Real Academia de la Historia, Colección de Juan Bautista Muñoz, vol. 60, fol. 69v.

26. Sherman, *Forced Native Labor*, 17.

27. For example, slaves in the Yucatán had their heads shaved. Sherman, *Forced Native Labor*, 15.

28. Sherman, *Forced Native Labor*, 15–16. In another exception, some groups in present-day Honduras cut the noses off their slaves.

29. Chipman, *Nuño de Guzmán*, 157.

30. "Indios o esclavos sacados del Pánuco para las islas," fols. 3v, 6v; testimonies of Cristóbal de Quevedo and Diego de Padriera.

31. "Indios o esclavos sacados del Pánuco para las islas," fol. 3v. A pataje or *patache* is a type of boat used during times of war to carry news and to reconnoiter coastlines or guard the entrances of ports.

32. "Indios o esclavos sacados del Pánuco para las islas," fols. 6v, 9v; testimonies of Diego de Padriera and Lope de Sayavedra.

33. "Indios o esclavos sacados del Pánuco para las islas," fol. 3v. Other vessels were owned by Cristóbal Bezos, Alonso Valiente, and Nuño de Guzmán himself. See fol. 9v.

34. "Indios o esclavos sacados del Pánuco para las islas," fol. 12r; testimony of Pedro de Barboa.

35. "Indios o esclavos sacados del Pánuco para las islas," fol. 12r.

36. "Indios o esclavos sacados del Pánuco para las islas," fol. 10v.

37. "Indios o esclavos sacados del Pánuco para las islas," fol. 10v.

38. "Indios o esclavos sacados del Pánuco para las islas," fol. 3v.

39. Donald E. Chipman, "The Traffic in Indian Slaves in the Province of Pánuco, New Spain, 1523–1533," *Americas* 23, no. 2 (1966): 149.

40. Chipman, *Nuño de Guzmán*, 208.

41. "Indios o esclavos sacados del Pánuco para las islas," fol. 13r; testimony of Juan de Cartucha.

42. "Indios o esclavos sacados del Pánuco para las islas," fol. 14r–v.

43. "Indios o esclavos sacados del Pánuco para las islas," fol. 14v.

44. "Indios o esclavos sacados del Pánuco para las islas," fol. 4r. This estimate comes from the testimony of Cristóbal de Quevedo.

45. Chipman, "Traffic in Indian Slaves," 144, 150.

46. "Indios o esclavos sacados del Pánuco para las islas," fols. 4r, 6v–7r, 10v.

47. Chipman, "Traffic in Indian Slaves," 144, 150.

48. Adorno and Pautz, *Narrative of Cabeza de Vaca*, 9; Chipman, *Nuño de Guzmán*, 144–145.

49. Chipman, *Nuño de Guzmán*, 165.

50. Chipman, "Traffic in Indian Slaves," 151.

51. Reséndez, *Other Slavery*, 81.

52. "Carta de Manuel de Rojas," November 10, 1534, AGI Santo Domingo 77, ramo 4, no. 50, fol. 579r.

53. "Indios o esclavos sacados del Pánuco para las islas," fol. 7r.

54. For more on his entrada into Nueva Galicia, which was at least as bloody as his time spent in Pánuco, see Altman, *War for Mexico's West*.

55. Chipman, *Nuño de Guzmán*, 10–11.

56. Chipman, *Nuño de Guzmán*, 28; Altman, *War for Mexico's West*, 42–52.

57. Daniel T. Reff, "Text and Context: Miracles and Fear in the Relación of Alvar Núñez Cabeza de Vaca," *Journal of the Southwest* 38, no. 2 (Summer 1996): 115–138; Rolena Adorno, "The Negotiation of Fear in Cabeza de Vaca's Naufragios," *Representations* 33, Special Issue: The New World (Winter 1991): 163–199. For more on the fascinating story of Cabeza de Vaca's captivity and journey following the failure of Pánfilo de Narváez's entrada in Florida, see Adorno and Pautz, *Narrative of Cabeza de Vaca*; and Fernando Operé, *Indian Captivity in Spanish America: Frontier Narratives* (Charlottesville: University of Virginia Press, 2008).

58. For example, in Española in 1529 Judge Zuazo wrote the Crown, reacting to legislation that required all residents of Santo Domingo to present titles demonstrating the legality of their Indian slaves. Documents or brands would suffice. However, Zuazo reported that almost no one possessed a title of sale and of the branded Indians it was impossible to ascertain whether their brands were legal. "Carta al emperador del electo Ramírez de Fuenleal y de los licenciados Espinosa y Zuazo sobre esclavos indios, la rebelión de Enriquillo y otros asuntos," July 31, 1529, transcribed in Baracs, *Cartas y memorias (1511–1539)*, 355–356.

59. "Real provisión sobre la manera de herrar los esclavos indios," August 24, 1529, in Konetzke, *Colección de documentos*, 1:130–131; Newson, *Cost of Conquest*, 109.

60. Newson, *Cost of Conquest*, 109.

61. "Cartas de oficiales reales de Honduras," June 14, 1533, AGI Guatemala 49, no. 8, fol. 4v; Newson, *Cost of Conquest*, 110.

62. "Carta de los oficiales de Cuba a vuestra magestad," September 15, 1530, AGI Santo Domingo 118, ramo 1, no. 7, fol. 3r.

63. Paid to the Crown, the diezmo was 10 percent of the total value of any merchandise trafficked through, arriving at, or entering a Spanish colonial port.

64. "Carta de los oficiales de Cuba," November 23, 1530, AGI Santo Domingo 118, R.1, N.17, fol. 1r.

65. "Carta de los oficiales de Cuba," August 18, 1534, AGI Santo Domingo 118, ramo 1, no. 30, fol. 1r. One of the most prolific slave traders between the Yucatán and Cuba was Juan de Lerma. Anderson-Córdova, *Surviving Spanish Conquest*, 140.

66. "Carta de Manuel de Rojas de Santiago de la isla Fernandina," November 10, 1534, Biblioteca de la Real Academia de la Historia, Colección de Juan Bautista Muñoz, vol. 62, fol. 17r.

67. Francisco de Montejo tried to conquer and pacify the Yucatán in 1527 without success. He returned in 1531 and by 1537, with the help of thousands of Indian allies, gained at least partial

control of the Yucatán. These years of nearly constant war produced many of the Indian slaves who were captured and sent to be sold in Española and Cuba. John F. Chuchiak IV, "Forgotten Allies: The Origins and Roles of Native Mesoamerican Auxiliaries and Indios Conquistadores in the Conquest of Yucatan, 1526–1550," in Matthew and Oudijk, *Indian Conquistadors*, 178–182.

68. "Documento num X—sobre hacer esclavos," August 1530, transcribed and printed in Zavala, *Instituciones jurídicas*, 243–244.

69. Zavala, *Instituciones jurídicas*, 48. The laws changed again in 1537, placing great restrictions on the Indian slave trade.

70. C. S. Alexander, "Margarita Island, Exporter of People," *Journal of Inter-American Studies* 3, no. 1 (October 1961): 550.

71. Otte, *Perlas del Caribe*, 48.

72. Perri, "Ruined and Lost," 136.

73. Otte, *Perlas del Caribe*, 48.

74. Warsh, "Enslaved Pearl Divers," 346–347.

75. Warsh, "Enslaved Pearl Divers," 346.

76. Otte, *Perlas del Caribe*, 457–460. Most expeditions claimed only around six Indians; however, some ships did contain nearly fifty Indians.

77. Otte, *Perlas del Caribe*, 205–206.

78. Perri, "Ruined and Lost," 137.

79. Alexander, "Margarita Island," 550.

80. Juan de Ampiés organized one such armada to the region in 1524 that gathered eight hundred Indian slaves for Española. Otte, *Perlas del Caribe*, 209.

81. Jiménez, *Esclavitud indígena*, 177.

82. Deive, *Española y la esclavitud del indio*, 263–265; Otte, *Perlas del Caribe*, 210.

83. In 1528 licenses to engage in rescate were issued to Martín Alonso Alemán, Pedro Ortiz de Matienzo, Alvaro Beltrán, Andrés Hernández, Pedro de Alegría, Alonso Díaz de Gibraleón, Diego de la Peña, and Rodrigo de León, among others. Otte, *Perlas del Caribe*, 211.

84. Deive, *Española y la esclavitud del indio*, 268–269.

85. Jiménez, *Esclavitud indígena*, 177–178.

86. Deive, *Española y la esclavitud del indio*, 268–269. Castellón also organized an armada to attack supposed rebellious Indians along the exact same stretch of coast protected in the treaty. During this voyage, he enslaved and branded a number of Indians, though it is not clear how many.

87. Two armadas registered to Gonzalo Hernández and Gonzalo Martel sailed to Cupira where they captured and later sold eight Indian slaves. Another two armadas, licensed to Fernando Riberos and Andrés de Villacorta, journeyed to Piritu and Maracapana. Jiménez, *Esclavitud indígena*, 178.

88. Jiménez, *Esclavitud indígena*, 178.

89. For a discussion about the good of the metropole versus the public good of the colony, specifically in cases of illegal trade and contraband in African slaves, see María Cristina Navarrete Peláez, "De las 'malas entradas' y las estrategias del 'buen pasaje': El contrabando de esclavos en el Caribe neogranadino, 1550–1690," *Historia crítica* 34, no. 1 (July–December 2007): 160–183.

90. Otte, *Perlas del Caribe*, 92.

91. "Carta de Jácome de Castellón para que se haya cierta información," March 13, 1528, in *Descubrimiento y conquista de Venezuela: Textos históricos contemporáneos y documentos*

fundamentales, vol. 2, ed. Joaquín Gabaldón Márquez (Caracas: Biblioteca de la Academia Nacional de la Historia, 1962), 51–52.

92. Otte, *Perlas del Caribe*, 216–217.

93. Otte, *Perlas del Caribe*, 218.

94. Otte, *Perlas del Caribe*, 222.

95. Otte, *Perlas del Caribe*, 217.

96. "Licencia para rescatar en la costa de Tierra Firme," August 17, 1528, in Otte, *Cedulario de la monarquía Española*, 1:72–73; Otte, *Perlas del Caribe*, 230.

97. "Para que el hierro con que se hierran los esclavos se ponga en poder de Villacorta," August 3, 1535, in Otte, *Cedulario de la monarquía Española* , 2:15.

98. "Declaración de Pedro Ortiz de Matienzo," 1528, AGI Justicia 50, fol. 891. This file contains the *residencia*, or report and examination, of judges Cristóbal Lebrón, Lucas Vázquez de Ayllón, Pedro Ortiz de Matienzo, Marcelo de Villalobos, and Pedro León by the judges and treasurer of the royal court of Santo Domingo, led by Judge Gaspar de Espinosa.

99. Perri, "Ruined and Lost," 137.

100. "Declaración de Pedro Ortiz de Matienzo," fol. 867v.

101. For example, in a royal provision executed in 1528, the Crown chastised Caribbean colonists for exceeding slaving allowances, specifically for capturing and enslaving legally free Indians not at war with the Spanish. Because of this behavior, the Crown ordered the officials of the Americas to reread earlier provisions, to make sure they were followed, and to examine the validity of claims of indigenous insurrection. The Crown even required that indigenous populations had to be in a state of rebellion for an extended period to qualify for enslavement. As a rationale, the Crown began by citing both their service to God—"we, looking principally to faithfully serve God"—and the importance of protecting and converting the Indians. However, following this formulaic statement, the royal order continued to cite the negative impacts of Indian rebellion, brought on by unscrupulous slave raiding, on the economic and social stability of the colonies. In this portion of the provision, the Crown's real concerns become clear. They wanted to limit slave raiding not for moral reasons, but to protect the royal purse. "Hostilidad con los indios y su esclavitud: Santo Domingo," November 20, 1528, AGI Patronato 275, R.6, no folio.

102. "Real provisión que no se pueda cautivar, ni hacer esclavo a ningún indio," August 2, 1530, in Konetzke, *Colección de documentos*, 134–136; Jiménez, *Esclavitud indígena*, 180–181.

103. For more on the conquest of New Granada by the German conquistadors, see Avellaneda, *Conquerors of the New Kingdom of Granada*.

104. "Testimonio y requerimiento sobre el quinto de los esclavos," June 19, 1530, AGI Santo Domingo 203, fols. 1r–2v.

105. Deive, *Española y la esclavitud del indio*, 325. Many other slavers looked to the coasts of Brazil and Colombia to engage in the illegal slave trade in the early 1530s. These men also avoided paying royal taxes on their cargo, whether legal or illegal. One such slaving voyage precipitated a case brought against pilots Cristóbal Alvarez and Pedro de Paz, who either purchased or captured an unknown number of indigenous slaves from the province of Santa Marta in the spring of 1531. They then transported these slaves to Española, where they attempted to sell them without paying the requisite diezmo, thereby defrauding the royal treasury. To do this, Paz and Alvarez did not present them to the royal treasurer upon arrival in Santo Domingo to be evaluated and declared as legally captured. When the deceit was discovered, a royal order required the two traders to have the slaves assessed for value and legality and for them to then pay the royal taxes on their cargo. Here, we see that even when the slave trade was illegal, the

Crown chose to enforce taxation of the slaves rather than to return the slaves to their native lands. "Indios esclavos traidos desde S. Marta por Cristobal Alvarez," March 11, 1531, AGI Indiferente General 1120, legajo 1, fol. 73r.

106. Jiménez, *Esclavitud indígena*, 182.

107. Jiménez, *Esclavitud indígena*, 181. Payment for services in Indian slaves, not just in the licenses to capture them, was a common practice. Licenses for other armadas, these only allowing rescate for slaves, were given to Juan de Ribas, Pedro Herrera, Francisco Portillo, and Antón de Jaén in 1531.

108. Jiménez, *Esclavitud indígena*, 182.

109. "Proceso que hacia Antonio Clavijo por Comisión de la Audiencia Real de la Española contra Juan López de Archuleta Veedor de la isla de Cubagua sobre ciertos delitos," August 11, 1530, AGI Justicia 8, N.1, fol. 1r.

110. "Proceso que hacia Antonio Clavijo," fol. 1r. Archuleta, along with many other high-ranking officials in Española and Cubagua, was granted a license to participate in rescate along the coast of Tierra Firme in 1526. However, it is unclear whether the license was still valid in 1529 and 1530 when he was accused of illegally capturing Indians. Deive, *Española y la esclavitud del indio*, 263.

111. "Proceso que hacia Antonio Clavijo," fol. 1r. In addition to the charges regarding Indian slaves, Archuleta was also accused of the more mundane crimes of reselling goods, including wine and flour, purchased from the Crown at excessively high prices. Lastly, he was accused of helping Don Francisco Fajardo escape from prison where he was being held for his treasonous relationship with the French (fol. 1v).

112. Deive, *Española y la esclavitud del indio*, 264.

113. "Proceso que hacia Antonio Clavijo," fol. 30v. See the testimony of the regidor Diego de Leon.

114. "Proceso que hacia Antonio Clavijo," fol. 30v.

115. Otte, *Perlas del Caribe*, 222.

116. "Proceso que hacía Antonio Clavijo," fol. 33v. The history of the friendship between the Spaniards of Nueva Cádiz and cacique Chatima, along with other caciques of the province (for example, the cacique of Macarn and the cacique known as Camayacoa), is described in great detail in a letter to the Crown from several religious officials working in the region in 1533. "Autos hecho por el señor Francisco de Villavarta el beneficiado de la isla," July 1533, AGI Santo Domingo 175, fols. 22r–25v.

117. "Proceso que hacia Antonio Clavijo," fols. 72v–73r.

118. Concurrent with the enslavement of Chatima was the capture of cacique Alonso (a friend of the residents of Margarita) along with several of his men. Otte, *Perlas del Caribe*, 222.

119. "Carta del obispo de Santo Domingo," August 11, 1531, AGI Santo Domingo 93, ramo 1, no. 2, fol. 2r.

120. "Carta del obispo de Santo Domingo," fol. 2r. Cartagena replaced Santa Marta as the most important port in present-day Columbia, perhaps because of the attacks alluded to by the bishop of Venezuela.

121. Van Deusen, *Global Indios*, 75–76.

122. Van Deusen, *Global Indios*, 76. In her work van Deusen tells the story of twelve-year-old Juan and Isabel, both captives from Santa Marta captured during conquest. Juan was eventually freed in Spain.

123. "Carta del obispo de Santo Domingo," fol. 2r.

124. "Carta del obispo de Santo Domingo," fol. 2r.

125. Perri, "Ruined and Lost," 140.

126. Perri, "Ruined and Lost," 142.

127. "Carta de los oficiales de San Juan de Puerto Rico," June 2, 1532, AGI Santo Domingo 166, ramo 2, fol. 110r.

128. "Carta de los oficiales de San Juan," fol. 110r.

129. "Carta de los oficiales de San Juan," fol. 110v.

130. Jiménez, *Esclavitud indígena*, 186.

131. "El asiento de Antonio Sedeño con su magestad sobre la isla de la Trinidad," 1530, AGI Patronato 18, N.9, R.3, fol. 1r. The designation of Trinidad as a Carib island was heavily debated in the early 1500s, with many officials claiming that it was one of the only islands in the Caribbean *not* inhabited by Caribs. Other Spaniards, including Sedeño, reported at least two populations on the island: one being Carib, while the other was Arawak. Newson, *Aboriginal and Spanish Colonial Trinidad*, 17–18.

132. Though it is unclear whether Sedeño enslaved any Indians during his time in Trinidad in 1530, he did not immediately return to Puerto Rico after withdrawing his forces. Instead, he and his surviving companions journeyed to Paria where they engaged in the illegal capture of Indian slaves that they sold upon their return to Puerto Rico. This was the first of many Sedeño slaving voyages to the northern coast of Tierra Firme. "Información sobre tratamiento de indios de Trinidad por Antonio Sedeño," July 24, 1531, AGI Patronato 18, no. 9, ramo 4, fol. 1r–v. Sedeño justified the enslavement of the Paria Indians by claiming that some, including the cacique known as Cariarto, had willingly accompanied him to Puerto Rico as he had rescued them from Trinidadian Caribs. Regardless of the truth behind the matter, Sedeño was ordered to return the Indians to their native lands.

133. "Carta a su magestad del licenciado Francisco de Prado juez de residencia de Cubagua," February 1, 1533, AGI Santo Domingo 183, ramo 4, no. 139, fol. 3r.

134. Angeles Eugenio Martínez, ed., *Congreso de historia del descubrimiento (1492–1556): Actas (ponencias y comunicaciones)*, vol. 3 (Madrid: Real Academia de la Historia, 1992), 628.

135. "Francisco de Lerma, veedor de Cubagua, con Jerónimo de Ortal, de la misma vecindad, sobre haber cautivado ciertos indios pescadores de la isla," 1536, AGI Justicia 974, no. 2, ramo 2, fol. 2r.

136. "Francisco de Lerma," fol. 6r.

137. "Francisco de Lerma," fol. 6r.

138. Perri, "Ruined and Lost," 143.

139. "El proceso contra Gerónimo Ortal," October 11, 1535, AGI Justicia 974, no. 2a, fol. 1r.

140. "Proceso contra Gerónimo Ortal," fol. 1v.

141. "Proceso contra Gerónimo Ortal," fol. 2v.

142. However, he did have the right to engage in rescate while in the provinces conducting his explorations and settling a new colony, which could have produced some of these slaves.

143. "Contra Jerónimo Dortal y otros," April 20, 1536, in Otte, *Cedulario de la monarquia Española relativo a la isla de Cubagua*, 2:86–90.

144. "Proceso contra Gerónimo Ortal," fol. 10v.

145. "Proceso contra Gerónimo Ortal," fol. 16r. See the testimony of mayor Diego Goméz on October 26.

146. "Proceso contra Gerónimo Ortal," fol. 11r.

147. Specifically, the conquistadors encountered one another in the province of Meta, located one hundred leagues in the interior of Venezuela and presumably within greater Paria and close to Rio Huyaporia.

148. "Carta de los oficiales de Cubagua," February 27, 1537, AGI Santo Domingo 183, ramo 4, no. 147, fol. 1r.

149. "Carta de los oficiales de Cubagua," fol. 1r.

150. "Carta de los oficiales de Cubagua," fol. 1r.

151. Saco, *Historia de la esclavitud de los indios*, 1:255; Perri, "Ruined and Lost," 145.

152. "Proceso contra Gerónimo Ortal," fol. 28v.

153. "Proceso contra Gerónimo Ortal," fol. 28v.

154. "Proceso contra Gerónimo Ortal," fol. 10r (testimony of Francisco de Reina) and fol. 16v (testimony of Diego Gomez).

155. "Proceso contra Gerónimo Ortal," fol. 17r.

156. "Carta de obispo de Venezuela de la ciudad de Coro," April 2, 1538, AGI Santo Domingo 218, no. 12, fol. 2r.

157. Tyce, "Mistaken Identity?"; "Rodrigo de Bastidas: Toma de Cuentas Oficiales de Venezuela," AGI Patronato Real 193, R.25, 1538.

158. Martínez, *Congreso de historia*, 3:629–630.

159. Aldemaro Romero, Susanna Chilbert, and M. G. Eisenhart, "Cubagua's Pearl-Oyster Beds: The First Depletion of a Natural Resource Caused by Europeans in the American Continent," *Journal of Political Ecology* 6, no. 1 (1999): 64.

Chapter 6

1. Following Solon's reforms in 594 BCE, it was no longer legal to enslave another Athenian who fell into debt. The subsequent labor shortage, especially as the Athenians began plantation-style cultivation of grapes and olives, resulted in the search for new sources of slaves. Many came from Africa, in addition to the Middle East and other portions of Europe. The trend continued under the Romans. Thomas Wiedemann, *Greek and Roman Slavery* (Baltimore: Johns Hopkins University Press, 1981), 1–3; Klein, *Atlantic Slave Trade*, 2; Sauer, *Early Spanish Main*, 206–207.

2. Green, *Rise of the Trans-Atlantic Slave Trade*, 188; Silva, *Esclavitud en Andalucía*, 72.

3. Ricardo E. Alegria, *Juan Garrido: El conquistador negro en las Antillas, Florida, Mexico, y California* (San Juan: Centro de Estudios Avanzados de Puerto Rico y el Caribe, 1990), 20. While he may or may not have been the first African in the Americas, he was very likely the first *free* African to set foot on Caribbean soil. Garrido, like many of the earliest African Americans, both free and enslaved, was enslaved on the west coast of Africa and then sold in Lisbon. There he became a Christian and, at some point, gained his liberty. It is also possible that he arrived in the New World as a slave and worked as a conquistador to secure his liberty. Matthew Restall, *Seven Myths of the Spanish Conquest* (Oxford: Oxford University Press, 2003), 54–56.

4. Alegria, *Juan Garrido*, 17.

5. Jane G. Landers, "Introduction," in *Slaves, Subjects, and Subversives: Blacks in Colonial Latin America*, ed. Jane G. Landers and Barry M. Robinson (Albuquerque: University of New Mexico Press, 2006), 2.

6. "Primera carta del licenciado Zuazo a su magestad sobre la necesidad del buen gobierno de las Indias, para conservarlas," January 22, 1518, in Baracs, *Cartas y memorias*, 66.

7. Green, *Rise of the Trans-Atlantic Slave Trade*, 188.

8. Restall, *Seven Myths*, 54. For example, Martin Alonso petitioned the Crown for permission to bring two African slaves to serve in his new home in Cubagua in 1528. "Relación de Martin Alonso," March 27, 1528, in Otte, *Cedulario de la monarquia Española*, 1:59.

9. Klein, *Atlantic Slave Trade*, 11.

10. Landers, "Introduction," 2.

11. Silva, *Esclavitud en Andalucía*, 72.

12. Jane Landers, "The Central African Presence in Spanish Maroon Communities," in *Central Africans and Cultural Transformations in the American Diaspora*, ed. Linda M. Heywood (Cambridge: Cambridge University Press, 2002), 234.

13. "Carta de Ovando," 1503, *CDI*, vol. 5, 43–45.

14. African bozal slaves were imported directly from the African continent with little or no prior interaction with Europeans. Guitar, "Cultural Genesis," 173.

15. "Primera carta del licenciado Zuazo," 67.

16. Deive, *Esclavitud del negro en Santo Domingo*, 31.

17. It is unknown how many slaves arrived in the Caribbean as contraband. The problem of an unlicensed trade in slaves in West Africa was well documented from at least 1514. How many of these slaves crossed the Atlantic is unclear, but it is likely that at least some did. A report from 1526 claimed that at least six hundred contraband slaves were delivered and sold in Española in that year alone. Green, *Rise of the Trans-Atlantic Slave Trade*, 191.

18. Jalil Sued Badillo and Angel Lopez Cantos, eds., *Puerto Rico Negro* (Puerto Rico: Editorial Cultural, 1986), 70–71.

19. "Licencias para llevar esclavos," 1519, AGI Indiferente General 420, legajo 8, fols. 37v–38r.

20. Green, *Rise of the Trans-Atlantic Slave Trade*, 187.

21. "Carta de los vecinos de la ciudad de Santo Domingo," April 1518, AGI Santo Domingo 77, ramo 1, no. 3, fol. 79r.

22. Sauer, *Early Spanish Main*, 207.

23. Badillo and Cantos, *Puerto Rico Negro*, 74.

24. It is estimated that more than six hundred slaves arrived without licenses or payment of royal taxes in Puerto Rico alone from 1529 to 1539. Some merchants brought more slaves than their licenses allowed to account for the number of slaves likely to perish during the journey across the Atlantic. Badillo and Cantos, *Puerto Rico Negro*, 93–99.

25. "Licencias para llevar esclavos," fols. 37v–38r; Deive, *Esclavitud del negro en Santo Domingo*, 31.

26. Silva, *Esclavitud en Andalucía*, 76.

27. This was the only Welser participation in the African slave trade. They apparently found the acquisition of Indian slaves easier and ultimately more profitable. Tyce, "Hispano-German Caribbean," 243–244.

28. Hubert H. S. Almes, *A History of Slavery in Cuba, 1511–1868* (New York: Octagon Books, 1967), 8–9.

29. Alejandro de la Fuente, *Havana and the Atlantic in the Sixteenth Century* (Chapel Hill: University of North Carolina Press, 2008), 37.

30. Klein, *Atlantic Slave Trade*, 11.

31. Silva, *Esclavitud en Andalucía*, 77–78.

32. Hernán Maximiliano Venegas Delgado, Carlos Manuel Valdés, and Carlos Manuel Valdés Dávila, eds., *La ruta del horror: Prisioneros indios del noreste novohispano llevados como*

esclavos a la Habana, Cuba (Mexico City, Mexico: Biblioteca Coahuila de Derechos Humanos, 2013), 53–54.

33. Wheat, *Atlantic Africa*, 5–12.

34. Wheat, *Atlantic Africa*, 5. Puerto Rican colonists sought African slaves later than their counterparts in Española or Cuba because they had a more ready supply of indigenous slaves from nearby islands of the Lesser Antilles, many of which were declared as Carib after Agueybana's rebellion. Nevertheless, by the 1530s, they too were beginning to rely more on African slaves. Badillo and Cantos, *Puerto Rico Negro*, 65.

35. Anderson-Córdova, *Surviving Spanish Conquest*, 108.

36. Genaro Rodriguez Morel, "The Sugar Economy of Española in the Sixteenth Century," in *Tropical Babylons: Sugar and the Making of the Atlantic World*, ed. Stuart B. Schwartz (Chapel Hill: University of North Carolina Press, 2004), 104. The price paid depended on a slave's ethnicity, sex, age, health, and skill set. Silva, *Esclavitud en Andalucía*, 79.

37. Badillo and Cantos, *Puerto Rico Negro*, 107.

38. Morel, "Sugar Economy," 107.

39. Lynne Guitar, "Boiling it Down: Slavery on the First Commercial Sugarcane Ingenios in the Americas (Española, 1534–45)," in *Slaves and Subversives: Blacks in Colonial Latin America*, ed. Barry M. Robinson and Jane Landers (Albuquerque: University of New Mexico Press, 2006), 43; Venegas Delgado, Valdés, and Dávila, *Ruta del horror*, 60–61. While the secondary trade benefited some, it led to a dearth of African slaves in Española proper by 1546.

40. Badillo and Cantos, *Puerto Rico Negro*, 67.

41. Alejandro de la Fuente, "Sugar and Slavery in Early Colonial Cuba," in Schwartz, *Tropical Babylons*, 116–117.

42. "El cabildo, justicia, y regimento de la ciudad de Santo Domingo con Melchor de Torres y otros sobre la tasa de los negros," January 1539, AGI Justicia 16, N.1, R.1, fol. 1r–v.

43. "Cabildo, justicia," fol. 22r.

44. In 1532 there were over five thousand Indian slaves and only five hundred African slaves in Cuba. Aimes, *History of Slavery*, 11.

45. Eugenio Fernández Méndez, *Las encomiendas y esclavitud de los indios de Puerto Rico, 1508-1550* (San Juan: Universidad de Puerto Rico, 1976), 70–73.

46. "Relación de Gil Gonzaléz Dávila," 1518, in *CDI*, 1:342–344.

47. Zavala, *Esclavos indios en Nueva España*, 9.

48. Zavala, *Esclavos indios en Nueva España*, 66. See pages 66–75 in Zavala for a table that lists the slave and livestock sale prices from 1525 to 1538 in Mexico City.

49. (One female Indian slave and two slave girls.) Francisco Moscoso, "Un señor de ingenios de Santo Domingo: Francisco Tostado (1520–1528)," *Boletín Museo del Hombre Dominicano* 25 (1992): 126.

50. Moscoso, "Un señor de ingenios," 126.

51. Guitar, "Boiling It Down," 46.

52. For more on the provenance of the African slaves in the census, see Guitar, "Boiling It Down," 58.

53. Guitar, "Boiling It Down," 58–59.

54. Badillo and Cantos, *Puerto Rico Negro*, 88, 144.

55. "Carta de Santo Domingo al majestad," April 10, 1530, printed and transcribed in *Cartas de la Real Audiencia de Santo Domingo (1530-1546)*, ed. Genaro Rodríguez Morel (Santo Domingo: Academia Dominicana de la Historia, 2007), 30–31.

56. Anderson-Córdova, *Surviving Spanish Conquest*, 109.

57. Méndez, *Encomiendas y esclavitud*, 68–69.

58. Guitar, "Boiling It Down," 47.

59. Otte, *Perlas del Caribe*, 116. For more on pearl ranches, see Warsh, "Enslaved Pearl Divers," and Perri, "Ruined and Lost."

60. Warsh, "Enslaved Pearl Divers," 348.

61. Otte, *Perlas del Caribe*, 355.

62. Méndez, *Encomiendas y esclavitud*, 77.

63. The cacique Enrique is a celebrated figure in the history and imagination of the Dominican Republic. For many he is a hero who represents justice and the best of the island's indigenous history. One of the most famous fictional works about the cacique is Manuel de Jesús Galván's novel *Enriquillo*, published in 1882. For an examination of this novel, see Franklin Gutiérrez, *Enriquillo: Radiografía de un héroe galvaniano* (Santo Domingo: Editora Búho, 1999). Enrique, originally named Guarocuya, was the nephew of the famous cacica Anacaona. "De las causas por que Nicolás de Ovando fue a la provincia de Xaragua; que la provincia de Guahabá se puso en armas, y las villas, que Diego Velázquez pobló en la Española," in Herrera y Tordesillas, *Historia general de los hechos de los castellanos*, 2.53. While most historiography on Enrique refers to the cacique as Enriquillo, I prefer to use Enrique to underscore his power and influence as a historical actor. Calling him Enriquillo, a diminutive name given to him by the Spanish, diminishes his importance, agency, and impact on history.

64. For more on the historical significance of this revolt for Latin American history, see Altman, "Revolt of Enriquillo"; and Erin Woodruff Stone, "America's First Slave Revolt: Indians and African Slaves in Española, 1500–1534," *Ethnohistory* 60, no. 2 (Spring 2013): 195–217.

65. Pena Battle, *Rebelión del Bahoruco*, 76–78; Fray Cipriano de Utrera, *Polémica de Enriquillo* (Santo Domingo: Editora del Caribe, 1973), 89; Altman, "Revolt of Enriquillo," 591.

66. The term "cimarrón" is defined by the Real Academia Española as an "esclavo o animal doméstico que huye al campo y se hace montaraz" (a slave or domestic animal that escapes to the countryside and becomes wild). The label was first used to refer to fugitive African and Indian slaves led by cacique Enrique in 1532 by Medina del Campo in a letter to the Crown. For a complete description of the evolution of the term "cimarrón" in the Caribbean, see José Arrom, "Cimarrón: Apuntes sobre sus primeras documentaciones y su probable origen," *Revista Española de antropología americana* 13 (1983).

67. Most scholars explain the cacique's desertion and resistance as personal, assuming the veracity of Las Casas's initial description of the case. According to Las Casas, Enrique revolted following the death of his encomendero, Francisco Valenzuela, in 1517 when Valenzuela's son inherited his father's encomienda. While Valenzuela the elder was described as a good encomendero, the younger Andrés had little respect for his Indians or the Crown's laws. Las Casas, *Historia de las Indias*, 3:260; Altman, "Revolt of Enriquillo," 594–595. Historians who accepted this account include Fray Cipriano de Utrera, Pena Battle, Altman, and Guitar. See Guitar, "Cultural Genesis," 224. It is important to note that Guitar complicates Las Casas's narrative by linking Valenzuela's disrespect to a larger pattern on the island.

68. In his youth he was baptized Enrique and he spent much of his childhood, from as early as 1502, living with Franciscan friars in the monastery located at Verapaz. There he learned to read and write, attended the first school for native leaders (or hijos de caciques), and gained the diminutive "Enriquillo" from his religious professors.

69. According to Las Casas, the younger Valenzuela both stole Enrique's mare (an especially important status symbol for a ladino Indian) and violated Enrique's wife. While it is possible that Enrique experienced some abuse at the hands of Andrés, it is difficult to know for sure whether the encomendero committed these two specific actions. The only source that describes Valenzuela both stealing the mare and raping Mencia is that of Las Casas, a generally problematic chronicler. There is no record either of Enrique's local complaint, which he made to the lieutenant governor of San Juan de la Maguana Pedro de Vadillo, or of his trip to Santo Domingo where he presented his case against Valenzuela. While many colonial documents have been lost over the centuries, it is curious that absolutely no legal or political record of either occurrence exists. The lack of documentation for Enrique's legal suit is contrasted by the plethora of documentation regarding his maroonage and "war" against the Spanish government. Even if these exact allegations against Valenzuela are true, the injustices did not cause Enrique to forsake his allegiance to the Spanish legal and political system. Instead, he first turned to the local official, Vadillo, and then to the larger Spanish court in Santo Domingo. He might even have journeyed thirty leagues, approximately 105 miles, to present his case to the royal court. The court found in Enrique's favor and provided him with documents demanding that Vadillo return his mare and provide refuge for his wife from Valenzuela's advances. These actions demonstrate that Enrique was literate, educated, and at one point believed in the accountability of the Spanish justice system. Las Casas, *Historia de las Indias*, 3:260.

70. In 1514 Enrique's cacicazgo included ten elderly Indians, seventeen children, and eighty-two Indians of working age and ability. Utrera, *Polémica de Enriquillo*, 136; "Repartimiento de la isla Española," 1514, in *CDI*, 1:218.

71. "Repartimiento de la isla Española," in *CDI*, 1:198. Valenzuela was granted eight naborías from García Soler's dissolved encomienda in Verapaz. Hernandez received another four naborías or house servants from an unknown source.

72. For example, even after two rebellions against the Spaniards, Guarionex remained at least nominally in power of his cacicazgo because the Spanish firmly believed they needed him in order to control his subjects and keep the island at peace.

73. "Repartimiento de la isla Española," in *CDI*, 1:197–198.

74. The Spaniards might have been trying to dilute Enrique's influence by combining his broken cacicazgo with that of other caciques and foreign Indian slaves. Maybe they hoped that his loss of status and separation from his wife would make him docile or easier to manipulate.

75. Las Casas addressed the larger social impact of the displacement in his letter to the king where he attempted to explain, and in some ways excuse, Enrique's rebellion and maroonage by stating that the cacique had simply returned to the "mountains where he was born and the location of his patrimony." Carta de Las Casas," April 30, 1534, AGI Santo Domingo 95, ramo 1, no. 11, fol. 1v.

76. "Residencia que Lebrón tomó a Rodrigo de Figueroa," AGI Justicia 47, transcribed and printed in Utrera, *Polémica de Enriquillo*, 108.

77. "Carta de Pasamonte el tesorero: Población y gastos guerra del Bahoruco," 1529, AGI Patronato 174, ramo 53, fol. 304r; Las Casas, *Historia de las Indias*, 3:261.

78. Pena Battle, *Rebelión del Bahoruco*, 79.

79. Utrera, *Polémica de Enriquillo*, 108.

80. Utrera, *Polémica de Enriquillo*, 165.

81. Guitar, "Boiling It Down," 49.

82. Guitar, "Cultural Genesis," 363.

83. Carlos Deive, *Los guerrilleros negros: Esclavos fugitivos y cimarrones en Santo Domingo* (Santo Domingo: Fundacion Cultural Dominicana, 1989), 33.

84. "Cartas de Audiencia," 1530, AGI Santo Domingo 49, ramo 1, no. 2, fol. 1r.

85. Guitar, "Cultural Genesis," 393. For more on maroon societies formed throughout the Atlantic World and how they helped shape African American culture in slave societies, see Timothy James Lockley, *Maroon Communities in South Carolina: A Documentary Record* (Columbia: University of South Carolina Press, 2009); Jane Landers, *Atlantic Creoles in the Age of Revolution* (Cambridge, MA: Harvard University Press, 2010); Kenneth Bilby, *True-Born Maroons* (Gainesville: University Press of Florida, 2008); and Richard Price, *Maroon Societies: Rebel Slave Communities in the Americas* (Baltimore: Johns Hopkins University Press, 1979).

86. Sylviane A. Diouf, *Servants of Allah: African Muslims Enslaved in the Americas* (New York: New York University Press, 1998), 19–20.

87. Guitar, "Boiling It Down," 45–50; Restall, *Seven Myths*, 61.

88. B. Vega, "Arqueologia de los cimarrones del Maniel del Bahoruco," *Boletin del Museo del Hombre Dominicano Saint-Domingue 8*, no. 12 (1979): 134–151.

89. Deive, *Guerrilleros negros*, 37. The Spanish declared war because of "los grandes daños y muertes y robos y escándolos que los indios y negros que andan alzados hacen" (the great injuries and deaths and thefts that the rebel Indians and blacks have commited).

90. "Consulta del Consejo de Indias," 1532, AGI Indiferente 737, no. 25, fol. 1r.

91. "Consulta del Consejo de Indias," fol. 1r.

92. "Carta al emperador por el licenciado Espinosa y Zuazo de Santo Domingo," July 19, 1528, Biblioteca de la Real Academia de la Historia, Colección de Juan Bautista Muñoz, vol. 60, N.701, fol. 127r; "Guerra contra los indios levantados en la Española," 1529, AGI Patronato 172, ramo 33, fol. 382r.

93. "Carta de la Audiencia de Santo Domingo: Asuntos de gobierno," February 28, 1529, AGI Patronato 174, ramo 52, fol. 295v.

94. "Carta al emperador del electo Ramirez de Fuenleal y de los licenciados Espinosa y Zuazo sobre esclavos indios, la rebelión de Enriquillo y otros asuntos," July 31, 1529, in Baracs, *Cartas y memorias*, 356.

95. "Guerra contra los indios levantados en la Española," fol. 382r.

96. "Carta de la Audiencia de Santo Domingo," fol. 294r. This sum was in addition to more than eight thousand pesos spent by Santo Domingo in combat against the maroons in 1525. "Carta al emperador de licenciado Zuazo y Espinosa de Santo Domingo," March 30, 1528, transcribed and printed in Marte, *Santo Domingo en los manuscritos*, 332.

97. "Carta al emperador de los oficiales de Santo Domingo," July 9, 1532, Biblioteca de la Real Academia de la Historia, Colección de Juan Bautista Muñoz, vol. 61, no. 36, fol. 105r.

98. Otte, *Perlas del Caribe*, 239–240.

99. "Carta al emperador por el licenciado Espinosa Zuazo de Santo Domingo," fol. 127r.

100. Las Casas, *Historia de las Indias*, 3:266.

101. "Carta al emperador por el licenciado Espinosa Zuazo de Santo Domingo," fol. 127r.

102. Utrera, *Polémica de Enriquillo*, 230.

103. Pena Battle, *Rebelión del Bahoruco*, 115–116.

104. "Repartimiento de la isla Española," in *CDI*, 1:60.

105. "Repartimiento de la isla Española," in *CDI*, 1:110–111.

106. Ewen, *From Spaniard to Creole*, 29.

107. Las Casas, *Historia de las Indias*, 3:268.

108. Tamayo's concentration on this one region could suggest that his ancestral territory lay nearby.

109. "Carta del Audiencia de Santo Domingo," February 20, 1532, AGI Santo Domingo 49, ramo 2, no. 14, fol. 1r.

110. "Carta del Audiencia de Santo Domingo," February 20, 1532, fol. 1r.

111. Ewen, *From Spaniard to Creole*, 29.

112. "Carta a su magestad del Doctor Infante," February 20, 1532, in Morel, *Cartas de la Real Audiencia de Santo Domingo*, 70. In the letter, Infante describes escaped African slaves as "negros bellacos y los cimarrones" (violent blacks and maroons).

113. Prior to his return to Spain in late 1516, Remigio penned a letter to the newly elected regent Cisneros, imploring him to send more clergy to help with the evangelization of the Indians. He also described the deplorable situation on the island, recently made worse by the Repartimiento in 1514. "Carta de los franciscanos al Cardinal Cisneros," February 15, 1516, AGI Patronato 174, R.3, no folio. Remigio was chosen by his fellow Franciscans to lead a delegation to Europe to meet with Cisneros. While in Europe, Remigio also journeyed to Rouen, France. There he convinced fourteen Franciscans of the French Order to accompany him to the New World. These missionaries began their work in Cuba a few years later. Errasti, *Primeros franciscanos*, 143.

114. Errasti, *Primeros franciscanos*, 140.

115. "Carta al emperador por el licenciado Espinosa Zuazo de Santo Domingo," July 29, 1528, Biblioteca de la Real Academia de la Historia, Colección de Juan Bautista Muñoz, vol. 60, no. 701, fol. 126v. By drowning Rodrigo, it is possible that Enrique's supporters were trying to facilitate his voyage to the underworld, as water often symbolized portals connecting this world with the next in Taíno mythology. Within their cosmology, the Taíno underworld and resting place for the dead, known as Coaybay, was a watery underground. Charles D. Beeker, Geoffrey W. Conrad, and John W. Foster, "Taíno Use of Flooded Caverns in the East National Park Region, Dominican Republic," *Journal of Caribbean Archaeology* 3 (2002): 3; Pané, *Mitología Taína o Eyeri*, 28.

116. Altman, "Revolt of Enriquillo," 603–604; Errasti, *Primeros franciscanos*, 142.

117. "Guerra contra los indios levantados en la Española," fol. 381v.

118. Altman, "Revolt of Enriquillo," 605–608.

119. "Guerra contra los indios levantados en la Española," fol. 381v.

120. "Guerra contra los indios levantados en la Española," fol. 381v.

121. Pena Battle, *Rebelión del Bahoruco*, 105.

122. "Carta a su magestad de los oficiales de Santo Domingo," September 1, 1533, in Morel, *Cartas de la Real Audiencia de Santo Domingo*, 139. Since the 1520s the government of Española had organized cuadrillas, which were basically groups of colonists, soldiers, Indians, and Africans sent into the countryside to combat Enrique's maroon community, among other threats. These quasi-militias operated from Puerto Plata, La Vega, Yaguana, and other locales.

123. "Asiento: Audiencia Santo Domingo y Francisco de Barrionuevo," 1533, AGI Patronato 18, no. 1, ramo 7, fols. 1r–10r.

124. Pena Battle, *Rebelión del Bahoruco*, 190.

125. Altman, "Revolt of Enriquillo," 597.

126. "Carta al emperador de oidor Zuazo y Vadillo," September 4, 1533, Biblioteca de la Real Academia de la Historia, Colección de Juan Bautista Muñoz, vol. 61, no. 68, fol. 299r.

127. Pena Battle, *La Rebelión Rebelión del Bahoruco*, 91.

128. Pena Battle, *Rebelión del Bahoruco*, 128. Romero brought up to 120 pesos' worth of goods to Enrique's community. "Carta al emperador de oidor Zuazo y Vadillo," fol. 299v.

129. "Carta al emperador de oidores Zuazo y Vadillo," September 1533, in Marte, *Santo Domingo en los manuscritos*, 365; "Heronymite Survey," in Parry, *New Iberian World*, 1:329.

130. "Carta al emperador de oidores Zuazo y Vadillo," 365.

131. "Carta de Audiencia de Santo Domingo," October 20, 1533, AGI Santo Domingo 49, ramo 4, no. 30, fol. 1r–v.

132. "Carta a su magestad de los oficiales de Santo Domingo," September 1, 1533, in Morel, *Cartas de la Real Audiencia de Santo Domingo*, 139.

133. For more on this controversial part of the agreement, see Altman, "Revolt of Enriquillo," 605–606.

134. "Carta del Audiencia de Santo Domingo," September 1, 1533, AGI Santo Domingo 49, ramo 4, no. 28, fols. 2v–7v; Altman, "Revolt of Enriquillo," 606.

135. "Carta a su magestad de los oficiales de Santo Domingo," September 1, 1533, in Morel, *Cartas de la Real Audiencia de Santo Domingo*, 143.

136. "Carta de Las Casas," fol. 1v.

137. Beyond describing his encounter with the cacique, Las Casas claimed that he played an essential role in Enrique's surrender. He dismissed actions taken by military leader Francisco de Barrionuevo, arguing that he barely interacted with the cacique. Las Casas also failed to mention the presence of Remigio at the meeting, perhaps both to highlight his importance and to minimize the influence that the other friar had with the cacique. Additionally, he asserted that if he had been involved in earlier attempts of negotiation, the conflict would have been resolved ten years earlier, saving the Spanish Crown untold amounts of money and soldiers lost during futile attacks on Enrique's maroon community. "Carta de Las Casas," fol. 1v. Interestingly, Las Casas named his last attempt at the creation of a religious settlement, this time in Guatemala, Verapaz, perhaps after the birthplace of Enrique whom the friar so admired.

138. "Carta del Audiencia de Santo Domingo," September 1, 1533, fols. 2v–3r. For more on the various encounters and negotiations, see Altman, "Revolt of Enriquillo," 605–608; and various sections of file AGI file Santo Domingo 49.

139. Altman, "Revolt of Enriquillo," 11.

140. "Carta de Enrique," 1534, AGI Santo Domingo 77, ramo 2, no. 77, fol. 1r.

141. "Carta a su magestad de los oficiales de Santo Domingo," August 1, 1534, in Morel, *Cartas de la Real Audiencia de Santo Domingo*, 165; Vega, "Arqueologia de los cimarrones," 158.

142. "Carta de Capitan Alferro," 1535, AGI Santo Domingo 77, ramo 2, no. 90a, fol. 1r.

143. "Carta a su magestad de los oficiales de Santo Domingo," October 12, 1535, in Morel, *Cartas de la Real Audiencia de Santo Domingo*, 183.

144. Deive, *Esclavitud del negro en Santo Domingo*, 445.

145. Altman, "Revolt of Enriquillo," 608.

146. Carlos Esteban Deive, "Las ordenanzas sobre esclavos cimarrones de 1522," *Boletín Museo del Hombre Dominicano* 25 (1992): 135–137.

147. This set of laws was signed by Alonso de Zuazo, Antonio de Espinosa, and Esteban de Pasamonte. Deive, "Ordenanzas sobre esclavos," 133–134.

148. For example, there is evidence of a sizable maroon community, made of escaped African slaves, but possibly also with some indigenous residents, in southeastern Española, the former cacicazgo of Higuey. The site, called Maniel de Jose Leta, dates from the late seventeenth century or early eighteenth century. While most archaeological evidence points to African slaves in residence, a few indigenous or Taíno ceramics have been found. Manuel A. García Arévalo, "El Maniel de Jose Leta: Evidencias arqueológicas de un posible asentamiento cimarrón en la región sudoriental de la isla de Santo Domingo," in *Cimarrón* by José Juan Arrom and Manuel A. García Arévalo (Santo Domingo: Fundación García Arévalo, 1986), 31–55.

149. Arévalo, "Maniel de Jose Leta," 38.

150. Deive, *Esclavitud del negro en Santo Domingo*, 445.

151. Deive, *Esclavitud del negro en Santo Domingo*, 449. The leader of this group was none other than the famous Lemba.

152. Guitar, "Boiling It Down," 62–63.

153. "Carta de Santo Domingo al rey," July 25, 1547, AGI Santo Domingo 95, fol. 1v. Enrique said that he would search all the mountains of the island to locate and return runaway and rebellious Indians and Blacks. "Carta de Audiencia de Santo Domingo," October 20, 1533, fol. 1r–v.

154. "Carta de Santo Domingo al rey," fol. 1v.

155. (Blacks and Indians who have rebelled.) Badillo and Cantos, *Puerto Rico Negro*, 183.

156. Badillo and Cantos, *Puerto Rico Negro*, 184–187.

157. Green, *Rise of the Trans-Atlantic Slave Trade*, 192.

158. "Real cédula a Gonzalo de Guzmán," November 9, 1526, in *CDI*, 1:351–354. Another group of thirty to fifty Indians rebelled in 1528, murdering at least seven Spaniards. "Carta al emperador por los oficiales de la isla de Fernandina," March 17, 1528, Colección de Juan Bautista Muñoz, vol. 60, N.684, fol. 69r.

159. "Carta de gobernadores," 1532, AGI Santo Domingo 99, ramo 4, no. 17, no folio.

160. "Relacion de Manuel de Rojas," February 13, 1533, AGI Santo Domingo 1121, legajo 1, fol. 156v.

161. José L. Franco, "Maroons and Slave Rebellions in the Spanish Territories," in Price, *Maroon Societies*, 41. It is important to note that others advocated less harsh treatment of maroons, and in fact they blamed abusive encomenderos for motivating the Indians and Africans to run away. "Licenciado Padre Fray Miguel Ramírez obispo de la isla de Fernandina sobe los indios alzados," September 28, 1532, AGI Santo Domingo 1121, legajo 1, fol. 111r.

162. "Visita de los indios de cuba," March 27, 1537, AGI Santo Domingo 77, no. 61, fols. 625r–630v.

163. "Visita de los indios de cuba," fol. 626r. For example, Juan de Castillo was fined three gold pesos for not adequately instructing his slaves in the Catholic faith, and in particular for not giving them Sundays off.

164. "Visita de los indios de cuba," fol. 625r–v.

165. "Visita de los indios de cuba," fols. 625r–630r.

166. "Respuesta de los oficiales de la isla Fernandina al rey," February 21, 1539, AGI Santo Domingo 1121, legajo 2, fols. 126r–130v; "Carta de Santiago de Cuba al rey," August 4, 1540, AGI Santo Domingo 74, R.1, N.52, fol. 52v.

167. "Carta de la Audiencia de Panama," April 1536, AGI Panama 235, legajo 6, fol. 24v.

168. Warsh, "Enslaved Pearl Divers," 350.

169. These laws followed years of debate, pressure from religious leaders like Las Casas and Pope Paul III, and a visible decline in the indigenous population of the Americas. In 1537 Pope Paul III

issued a papal decree against the enslavement of America's indigenous peoples or the seizure of their property. In the decree the pope sided with Dominican friars like Montesinos and Las Casas, concluding that Amerindians possessed the capacity to be converted to Christianity through teaching and did not need to be conquered by force. Elena Isabel Estrada de Gerlero, Donna Pierce, and Clare Farago, "Mass of Saint Gregory," in *Painting a New World: Mexican Art and Life, 1521–1821*, ed. D. Pierce, R. Ruiz Gomar, and C. Bargellini, 94–102 (Denver, CO: Frederick and Jan Mayer Center for Pre-Columbian and Spanish Colonial Art at the Denver Art Museum, 2004), 98.

170. The New Laws made the inheritance of encomiendas illegal. Following the death of an encomendero, his encomienda and all its future profits would default to the Crown. The laws also prohibited the issuance of any new encomiendas. Mark A. Burkholder and Lyman L. Johnson, *Colonial Latin America* (Oxford: Oxford University Press, 2001), 119–120.

171. David Eltis, *The Rise of African Slavery in the Americas* (Cambridge: Cambridge University Press, 2000), 9.

Conclusion

1. "Real provisión que los caciques ni principales no puedan hacer a los indios esclavos," December 6, 1538, and "Real cédula que ninguna persona compre ni rescate de los caciques ni otra persona indio alguno por esclavo," December 6, 1538, transcribed in Konetzke, *Colección de documentos*, 188–191.

2. In 1537 Pope Paul III issued a papal decree against both the enslavement of the Americas' indigenous peoples or the seizure of their property. In the decree the pope sided with Dominican friars, concluding that Amerindians possessed the capacity to be converted to Christianity through teaching and did not need to be conquered by force. Elena Isabel Estrada de Gerlero, Donna Pierce, and Clare Farago, "Mass of Saint Gregory," in Pierce, Ruiz Gomar, and Bargellini, *Painting a New World*, 98.

3. Zavala, *Instituciones jurídicas*, 94; Martínez, "Esclavitud indígena," 625.

4. John Manuel Monteiro, *Negros da terra: índios e bandeirantes nas origens de São Paulo* (São Paulo: Companhia das Letras, 1994), 51–52.

5. Colonists also fought for the continuation of the encomienda system, another institution attacked by the New Laws. One of the most famous proponents of the system was Juan Ginés de Sepulveda, Las Casas's ardent opponent. Sepulveda argued that there was a natural hierarchy that included natural servants or slaves, in this case Indians. The Indians were "natural slaves" due to their lack of reason, a "fact" proven by their idolatry and cannibalism. "Sepulveda on the Justice of the Conquest," 1547, in Parry, *New Iberian World*, 1:323; Vanita Seth, *Europe's Indians: Producing Racial Difference, 1500–1900* (Durham, NC: Duke University Press, 2010), 44.

6. Whitehead, *Of Cannibals and Kings*, 9–10.

7. In 1547 the Crown exempted male Caribs from the New Laws, making their enslavement legal. William Arens, *The Man-Eating Myth: Anthropology and Anthropophagy* (Oxford: Oxford University Press, 1979), 49.

8. "Carta al Rey," AGI Santo Domingo 94, no. 14, fol. 1r.

9. "Carta de Caracas," April 21, 1551, AGI Santo Domingo 207, no. 17, fol. 1v.

10. "Carta de los oficios de la isla Española," September 12, 1536, AGI Santo Domingo 74, ramo 1, no. 35, fol. 2r–v.

11. Alexander Marchant, *From Barter to Slavery: The Economic Relations of Portuguese and Indians in the Settlement of Brazil, 1500–1580* (Baltimore: Johns Hopkins University Press, 1966), 72–73.

12. Marchant, *From Barter to Slavery*, 78; Monteiro, *Negros da terra*, 33–34.

13. Monteiro, *Negros da terra*, 34.

14. It was only after the campaigns that the Jesuits succeeded in building their mission villages. Metcalf, *Go-Betweens*, 111–112.

15. Monteiro, *Negros da terra*, 51–52.

16. Despite the passage of the New Laws, male Caribs could still be enslaved if they attacked Christian colonies. Expeditions continued to enslave Caribs throughout the Caribbean islands and into Tierra Firme well into the seventeenth century, though not to the extent as the armadas of the 1530s. For more on these later slave raids, see Deive, *Española y la esclavitud del indio*, 354–368.

17. "Carta del Doctor Mexia de la Española," October 10, 1568, AGI Santo Domingo 71, legajo 1, fol. 491v.

18. "Carta de los oficiales de Santo Domingo, incluyendo Mexia, Caceres, licenciado Peralta, y licenciado Santiago de Vera," August 26, 1569, AGI Santo Domingo 71, legajo 1, fol. 535r–v.

19. "Carta de arzobispo Fray Andrés de Carvajal de Santo Domingo," August 25, 1569, AGI Santo Domingo 71, legajo 2, fol. 452r.

20. "Carta de Fray Diego de Santa Maria de Santo Domingo," April 30, 1573, AGI Santo Domingo 71, legajo 2, fol. 196r. He too focused on the fact that the Brazilian Indians were cannibals to legitimize their enslavement.

21. Daniel S. Murphree, *Constructing Floridians: Natives and Europeans in the Colonial Floridas, 1513–1783* (Gainesville, FL: University of Florida Press, 2006), 39.

22. "Daños of the Indians of Florida," petition by Menéndez to the royal court, in *Spanish Borderlands Sourcebooks: Pedro Menéndez de Avilés*, trans. Eugene Lyon (Gainesville, FL: University of Florida Press, 1983), 427–429.

23. "De Juez Montanez al rey," July 21, 1547, AGI Santo Domingo 95, ramo 1, fols. 1r–3v. In his letter Montanez describes the trials that he and others faced in discerning which Indians were legally enslaved and which were free. Then they had to figure out what to do with the newly freed Indians, though they were few in number, especially those from distant provinces like Nueva España and the coast of Tierra Firme. Of interest here is that Montanez noted most indigenous peoples on Española at this point were from the mainland, not native to the island or its neighbors. "De Fray Bartolomé de las Casas obispo de Chiapa," April 20, 1544, in Marte, *Santo Domingo en los manuscritos*, vol. 65, fol. 206r.

24. "Al emperador de licenciado cerrato y grajedo de Santo Domingo," April 23, 1545, in Marte, *Santo Domingo en los manuscritos*, 66.

25. When you peruse the court cases dealing with freeing Indian slaves in Spain, a clear pattern emerges. The cases often hinge on the slave's origins being in Nueva España and on the age that they were enslaved. Most successful claimants seem to have been taken captive and sold as children with their master's only defense resting on their brand, not on written documentation. For some examples, see AGI Justicia 741, N.3; AGI Justicia 757, N.3; AGI Justicia 1022, N.1, R.1–4; and AGI Justicia 1023, N.2, R.2.

26. Nancy E. van Deusen, "Seeing *Indios* in Sixteenth-Century Castile," *William and Mary Quarterly* 69, no. 2 (April 2012): 211–213.

27. Van Deusen, "Seeing *Indios*," 227–228.

28. A perfect example of this can be seen in Mexico, when in 1552 Prince Philip created a plan to both fulfill and circumvent the New Laws. While he abolished all indigenous slavery and set all Indians working in the mines free, he also made the now-free Indians even more

dependent on the Spanish. He passed laws that required all Indians to work for their sustenance/nominal wage. Only elderly Indians would not be compelled to work. Reséndez, *Other Slavery*, 70–71; Zavala, *Esclavos indios*, 185–190.

29. Reséndez, *Other Slavery*, 87–93.

30. Jimenéz, *Esclavitud indígena en Venezuela*, 247–249.

31. Jimenéz, *Esclavitud indígena en Venezuela*, 262–264. As late as 1561 religious officials in Margarita wrote to the Crown about Indian slaves, many of them women and children, from Guyana, Paria, and Trinidad. "Carta al rey de Margarita," September 1561, AGI Santo Domingo 172, no. 32, fols. 161v–162r.

32. Seijas, *Asian Slaves*, 16.

33. Seijas, *Asian Slaves*, 36. This was partially because the indigenous elite of Manila refused to give up their slaves or the slave trade, as slave ownership reaffirmed their elite status (46).

34. As late as the 1590s there are records of Spanish leaders, such as a Captain Berrio, torturing and enslaving indigenous peoples, even caciques, in Guyana. Supposedly this treatment is what allowed the English to make further progress into the interior of the province in 1595. Sir W. Raleigh, *The Discoverie of the Large, Rich, and Bewtiful Empyre of Guiana*, trans. and annot. Neil L. Whitehead (Norman: University of Oklahoma Press, 1997), 133.

35. Raleigh, *Discoverie of the Large, Rich, and Bewtiful Empyre of Guiana*, 179.

36. Navarette Peláez, "'Malas entradas.'"

37. Carolyn Arena, "The Carib/Anglo-Dutch/Arawak War: Strategic Knowledge and Alliance Formation in the 17th Century Caribbean," paper presented at "Transmitting Knowledge in the Early Modern Dutch World," December 6–7, 2013, 10–12.

38. Gallay, *Indian Slave Trade*, 1–9.

39. Rushforth, *Bonds of Alliance*, 10–12.

40. Carl J. Ekberg, *Stealing Indian Women: Native Slavery in the Illinois Country* (Urbana: University of Illinois Press, 2006).

41. Lennox Honychurch, "The Leap at Sauteurs: The Lost Cosmology of Indigenous Grenada," paper presented at Grenada Country Conference, University of the West Indies, January 2002, 6.

42. Francisco Moscoso, *Caciques, aldeas, y población Taína de Boriquén (Puerto Rico), 1492–1582* (San Juan: Academia Puertoriqueña de la Historia, 2008), 22–23; Stevens-Arroyo, *Cave of the Jagua*, 4–5.

43. Marriage and baptismal records show the extent of intermarriage between Maya slaves and native Taínos. They also show marriage between indigenous slaves and African slaves by the seventeenth century. Jason M. Yaremko, *Indigenous Passages to Cuba, 1515–1900* (Gainesville: University Press of Florida, 2016), 98–99.

44. Yaremko, *Indigenous Passages*, 169–170.

45. Irving Rouse and José M. Cruxent, *Venezuelan Archaeology* (New Haven, CT: Yale University Press, 1963), 134–135.

46. Stephan Lenik, "Carib as a Colonial Category: Comparing Ethnohistoric and Archaeological Evidence from Dominica, West Indies," *Ethnohistory* 59, no. 1 (Winter 2012): 80–81.

47. The Dominican government even passed legislation replacing "Carib" with "Kalinago" in the Dominican constitution in 2010. Lenik, "Carib as Colonial Category," 82.

48. Lenik, "Carib as Colonial Category," 87–88; Corrine Hofman, Angus Mol, Menno Hoogland, and Roberto Valcárcel Rojas, "Stage of Encounters: Migration, Mobility, and

Interaction in the Pre-Colonial and Early Colonial Caribbean," *World Archaeology* 46, no. 4 (2014): 599–600.

49. Santos-Granero, *Vital Enemies*, 19.

50. Lenik, "Carib as Colonial Category," 84.

51. Elsa M. Redmond, "Meeting with Resistance: Early Spanish Encounters in the Americas, 1492–1524," *Ethnohistory* 63, no. 4 (October 2016): 673.

52. Whitehead, *Wolves from the Sea*, 12.

BIBLIOGRAPHY

Archives Consulted

Archivo del Museo Naval. Madrid, Spain.

Archivo General de Indias. Sevilla, Spain.

Archivo General de la Nación. Bogotá, Colombia.

Archivo General de la Nación. Santo Domingo, Dominican Republic.

Archivo General de Simancas. Simancas, Spain.

Archivo Histórico Nacional. Madrid, Spain.

Archivo Histórico Provincial de Santa Cruz de Tenerife. La Laguna, Spain.

Archivo Histórico Regional de Boyacá. Tunja, Colombia.

Biblioteca de la Real Academia de la Historia. Madrid, Spain.

Sociedad de Bibliografós. Santo Domingo, Dominican Republic.

Archaeological Collections Consulted

Museo Arqueológico Regional de Altos de Chavón. La Romana, Dominican Republic.

Museo de la Naturaleza y Arqueología. Santa Cruz de Tenerife, Spain.

Museo del Hombre Dominicano. Santo Domingo, Dominican Republic.

Museo del Oro. Bogotá, Colombia.

Museo del Oro Tairona. Santa Marta, Colombia.

Museo Histórico de Cartagena. Cartagena, Colombia.

El Museo y Parque Arqueológico Cueva Pintada. Gáldar, Gran Canaria, Spain.

Sala de Arte Pre-Hispanico de García Arévalo. Santo Domingo, Dominican Republic.

Published Primary Sources

Various comps. *Colección de documentos inéditos para la historia de Ibero-America/Hispano-América*. 15 vols. Madrid: Compañía Iberoamericana de Publicaciones, 1925–1937.

Various comps. *Colección de documentos inéditos de ultramar (CDI)*. 2 vols. Madrid: Real Academia de la Historia, 1885.

Various comps. *Colección de documentos inéditos relativos al descubrimiento, conquista, y colonización de las posesiones Españolas en América y Oceanía, sacados en su mayor parte del Real Archivo de Indias*. Vol. 1. Madrid: Imprenta de M. B. de Quirós, 1864.

Abad y Lasierra, Don Iñigo. *Relación de el descubrimiento, conquista y población de las provincias y costas de la Florida*. Madrid: Librería General de Victoriano Suárez, 1912.

Arranz Marquez, Luis. *Repartimientos y encomiendas en la isla Española (el repartimiento de Albuquerque de 1514)*. Santo Domingo: Ediciones Fundación Garcia Arévalo, 1991.

Ayala, Juan de. *A Letter to Ferdinand and Isabella, 1503*. Translated by Charles E. Nowell. Minneapolis: University of Minnesota Press, 1994.

Baracs, Rodrigo Martínez, ed. *Cartas y memorias (1511–1539): Alonso de Zuazo*. Mexico City, Mexico: Consejo Nacional Para la Cultura y las Artes, 2000.

Castillo, Bernal Díaz del. *The History of the Conquest of New Spain*. Edited by Davíd Carrasco. Albuquerque: University of New Mexico Press, 2008.

Colombo, Fernando. *The Life of the Admiral Christopher Columbus by His Son Ferdinand*. New Brunswick, NJ: Rutgers University Press, 1959.

D'Anghera, Peter Martyr. *De Orbo Novo: The Eight Decades of Peter Martyr D'Anghera*. Translated by Francis Augustus MacNutt. New York: Burt Franklin, 1970.

Friede, Juan. *Descubrimiento y conquista de Venezuela (textos históricos contemporáneos y documentos fundamentales)*. Vol. 2. Caracas: Biblioteca de la Academia Nacional de la Historia, 1962.

Gil, Juan. *Cristóbal Colon: Textos y documentos completos*. Madrid: Alianza Editorial, 1992.

Herrera y Tordesillas, Antonio de. *Historia general de los hechos de los castellanos, en las islas y Tierra Firme del mar océano*. 4 vols. Buenos Aires: Editorial Guarania, 1949.

Jane, Cecil, ed. and trans. *The Four Voyages of Columbus: A History in Eight Documents Including Five by Christopher Columbus, in the Original Spanish with English Translations*. New York: Dover Publications, 1988.

Konetzke, Richard, ed. *Colección de documentos para la historia de la formación social de Hispanoamérica, 1493–1810*. Vol. 1. Madrid: Consejo Superior de Investigaciones Científicas, 1953.

Las Casas, Fray Bartolomé de. *Historia de las Indias*. 3 vols. Edited by Lewis Hanke and Agustín Millares Carlo. Mexico City, Mexico: Fondo de Cultura Economica, 1951.

———. *In Defense of the Indians: The Defense of the Most Reverend Lord, Don Fray Bartolomé de las Casas, Against the Persecutors and Slanderers of the peoples of the New World Discovered Across the seas*. Translated and edited by Stafford Poole. Dekalb: Northern Illinois University Press, 1974.

Léry, Jean de. *History of a Voyage to the Land of Brazil*. Translated by Janet Whatley. Berkeley: University of California Press, 1990.

Márquez, Joaquín Gabaldón, ed. *Descubrimiento y conquista de Venezuela: Textos históricos contemporáneos y documentos fundamentales* 2 vols. Caracas: Biblioteca de la Academia Nacional de la Historia, 1962.

Márquez, Luis Arranz. *Repartimientos y encomiendas en la isla Española: El repartimiento de Albuquerque de 1514*. Madrid: Ediciones Fundación García Arévalo, 1991.

Marte, Roberto, ed. *Santo Domingo en los manuscritos de Juan Bautista Muñoz*. Vol. 1. Santo Domingo: Ediciones Fundación García Arévalo, 1981.

Mártir, Pedro de Anglería. *Décadas del nuevo mundo*. Ediciones Polifemo: Madrid: 1989.

Medina, Miguel Angel, O.P. *Doctrina cristiana para instrucción de los indios redactada por Fr. Pedro de Córdoba, O.P. y otros religiosos doctos de la misma orden*. Salamanca: Editorial San Esteban, 1987.

Morel, Genaro Rodríguez. *Cartas de los cabildos eclesiásticos: Santo Domingo y Concepción de la Vega en el siglo XVI*. Santo Domingo: Amigo del Hogar, 2000.

———. *Cartas de la real audiencia de Santo Domingo (1530–1546)*. Santo Domingo: Archivo General de la Nacion, 2007.

Otte, Enrique. *Cedulario de la monarquía Española relativo a la isla de Cubagua (1523–1550)*. 2 vols. Caracas: Edición de la Fundación John Boulton y la Fundación Eugenio Mendoza, 1961.

———. *Cedularios de la monarquía Española relativas a la provincia de Venezuela, 1520–1561*. Vol. 1. Caracas: Edición de la Fundación John Boulton y la Fundación Eugenio Mendoza, 1965.

———. *Cedulas reales relativas a Venezuela (1500–1550)*. Caracas: Edición de la Fundación John Boulton y la Fundación Eugenio Mendoza, 1963.

Oviedo y Valdés, Gonzalo Fernández de. *Historia general y natural de las Indias*. 5 vols. Madrid: Graficas Orbe, 1959.

Pádron, Francisco Morales. *Primeras cartas sobre América (1493–1503)*. Sevilla: Universidad de Sevilla, 1990.

Pané, Ramón. *Mitología Taína o Eyeri Ramón Pané y la relación sobre las antiguedades de los indios: El primer tratado Etnográfico hecho en América*. Edited by Angel Rodríguez Alvarez. San Juan: Editorial Nuevo Mundo, 2009.

Parry, John H., ed. *New Iberian World: A Documentary History of the Discovery and Settlement of Latin America to the Early 17th Century*. 5 vols. New York: Times Books, 1984.

Quinn, David B. *New American World: A Documentary History of North America to 1612*. Vol. 2. New York: Arno Press, 1979.

Raleigh, Sir W. *The Discoverie of the Large, Rich, and Bewtiful Empyre of Guiana*. Transcribed and annotated by Neil L. Whitehead. Norman: University of Oklahoma Press, 1997.

Saéz, José Luis. *La iglesia y el negro esclavo en Santo Domingo: Una historia de tres siglos*. Santo Domingo: Patronato de la ciudad colonial de Santo Domingo Colección Quinto Centenario, 1994.

Sanz, Vicente Murga. *Juan Ponce de Leon: Fundador y primer governador del pueblo puertorriqueno descubridor de la Florida y del estrecho de las Bahamas*. San Juan: Ediciones de la Universidad de Puerto Rico, 1959.

Sousa, Gabriel Soares de. *Tratado descriptivo do Brasil em 1587*. São Paulo: Companhia Editora Nacional, 1938.

Staden, Hans. *The True History of His Captivity*. Translated by Malcolm Letts. London: George Routledge and Sons, 1928.

Utrera, Fray Cipriano de. *Polémica de Enriquillo*. Santo Domingo: Editora del Caribe, 1973.

Vaca, Alvar Núñez Cabeza, de. *Naufragios de Alvar Núñez Cabeza de Vaca*. Barcelona: Diferencias, 2006.

Varela, Consulo, ed. *Cristóbal Colón: Textos y documentos completos*. Madrid: Alianza Editorial, 1992.

Vespucci, Amerigo. *Letters of the Four Voyages to the New World*. Translated by Bernard Quaritch. Hamburg: Wayasbah, 1992.

Williams, Eric, ed. *Documents of West Indian History: From Spanish Discovery to the British Conquest of Jamaica*. New York: A&B Publishers, 1994.

Zavala, Silvio A, ed. *Las instituciones jurídicas en la conquista de América*. Mexico City, Mexico: Editorial Porrúa, 1971.

Select Secondary Sources

Abulafia, David. *The Discovery of Mankind: Atlantic Encounters in the Age of Columbus*. New Haven, CT: Yale University Press, 2008.

Altman, Ida. "The Revolt of Enriquillo and the Historiography of Early Spanish America." *Americas* 63, no. 4 (2007): 587–613.

Altman, Ida, and David Wheat, eds. *The Spanish Caribbean and the Atlantic World in the Long Sixteenth Century*. Lincoln: University of Nebraska Press, 2019.

Anderson-Córdova, Karen F. *Surviving Spanish Conquest: Indian Fight, Flight, and Cultural Transformation in Hispaniola and Puerto Rico*. Tuscaloosa: University of Alabama Press, 2017.

Armas, Antonio Rumeu, de. *La conquista de Tenerife, 1494–1496*. Madrid: Aula de Cultural de Tenerife, 1975.

Arrom, José Juan. *Cimarron*. Santo Domingo: Fundación Garcia-Arévalo, Inc., 1986.

Avellaneda, José Ignacio. *Los compañeros de Federman: Cofundadores de Santa Fe de Bogotá*. Bogotá: Academia de Historia de Bogotá, 1990.

Bacci, Massimo Livi. "Return to Hispaniola: Reassessing a Demographic Catastrophe." *Hispanic American Historical Review* 83, no. 1 (February 2003): 3–51.

Badillo, Jalil Sued. *Agueybana el bravo*. San Juan: Ediciones Puerto, 2008.

———. "Facing Up to Caribbean History." *American Antiquity* 57, no. 4 (October 1992): 599–607.

———. "Guadalupe: ¿Caribe o Taina? La isla de Guadalupe y su cuestionable identidad caribe en la época pre-Colombina: Una revisión etnohistorica y arqueológica preliminar." *Caribbean Studies* 35, no. 1 (2007): 37–85.

Cassá, Roberto. *Los Taínos de la Española*. Santo Domingo: Editora Búho, 1990.

Castro, Daniel. *Another Face of Empire: Bartolomé de las Casas, Indigenous Rights, and Ecclesiastical Imperialism*. Durham, NC: Duke University Press, 2007.

Chipman, Donald E. *Nuño de Guzmán and the Province of Panuco in New Spain, 1518–1533*. Glendale, CA: Arthur H. Clark Company, 1967.

Clayton, Lawerence A. *Bartolomé de las Casas: A Biography*. Cambridge: Cambridge University Press, 2012.

Cook, Noble David. *Born to Die: Disease and New World Conquest, 1492–1650*. Cambridge: Cambridge University Press, 1998.

Deive, Carlos Esteban. *La esclavitud del negro en Santo Domingo (1492–1844)*. Santo Domingo: Editora Taller, 1980.

———. *La Española y la esclavitud del indio*. Santo Domingo: Fundación García Arévalo, 1995.

Demorizi, Emilio Rodríguez. *Los Dominicos y las encomiendas de indios de la isla Española*. Santo Domingo: Editora del Caribe, 1971.

Errasti, Mariano. *Los primeros franciscanos en América: Isla Española, 1493–1520*. Santo Domingo: Fundación García Arévalo, 1998.

Fitzpatrick, Scott M., and Ann H. Ross, eds. *Island Shores, Distant Pasts: Archaeological and Biological Approaches to the Pre-Columbian Settlement of the Caribbean*. Gainesville: University Press of Florida, 2010.

Goetz, Rebecca. "Indian Slavery: An Atlantic and Hemispheric Problem." *History Compass* 14, no. 2 (2016): 59–70.

Guitar, Lynne. "A Cultural Genesis: Relationships Among Indians, Africans and Spaniards in Hispaniola, First Half of the Sixteenth Century." PhD diss., Vanderbilt University, 1998.

Hoffman, Paul. *A New Andalucía and a Way to the Orient: The American Southeast During the Sixteenth Century*. Baton Rouge: Louisiana State University Press, 1990.

Hofman, Corinne L. M., L. P. Hoogland, and A. L. van Gijn, eds. *Crossing the Borders: New Methods and Techniques in the Study of Archaeological Materials in the Caribbean*. Tuscaloosa: University of Alabama Press, 2008.

Hofman, Corinne L., and Anne van Duijvenbode, eds. *Communities in Contact: Essays in Archaeology, Ethnohistory, and Ethnography of the Amerindian Circum-Caribbean*. Leiden: Sidestone Press, 2011.

Hulme, Peter. *Colonial Encounters: Europe and the Native Caribbean, 1492-1797*. New York: Metheun and Co., 1986.

Jiménez, Morella A. *La esclavitud indígena en Venezuela (siglo XVI)*. Caracas: Fuentes para la Historia Colonial de Venezuela, 1986.

Keegan, William F. *Taíno Indian Myth and Practice: The Arrival of the Stranger King*. Gainesville: University Press of Florida, 2007.

Kulstad, Pauline M. "Concepción de La Vega 1495-1564: A Preliminary Look at Lifeways in the Americas' First Boom Town." PhD diss., University of Florida, 2008.

La Fuente, Alejando de. *Havana and the Atlantic in the Sixteenth Century*. Chapel Hill: University of North Carolina Press, 2008.

Lamarche, Sebastián Robiou. *Taínos y Caribes: Las culturas de aborígenes antillanas*. San Juan: Editorial Punto y Coma, 2003.

Lenik, Stephan. "Carib as a Colonial Category: Comparing Ethnohistoric and Archaeological Evidence from Dominica, West Indies." *Ethnohistory* 59, no. 1 (Winter 2012): 79–107.

Lyon, Eugene. *The Enterprise of Florida: Pedro Menéndez de Aviles and the Spanish Conquest of 1565-1568*. Gainesville: University Press of Florida, 1974.

Mena, Miguel D. *Iglesia, espacio, y poder: Santo Domingo (1498-1521), experiencia fundacional del nuevo mundo*. Santo Domingo: Archivo General de la Nación, 2007.

Méndez, Eugenio Fernández. *Las encomiendas y esclavitud de los indios de Puerto Rico, 1508-1550*. San Juan: Universidad de Puerto Rico, 1976.

Mol, Angus A. A. *Costly Giving, Giving Guaízas: Towards an Organic Model of the Exchange of Social Valuables in the Late Ceramic Age Caribbean*. Leiden: Sidestone Press, 2007.

Moya Pons, Frank. *La Española en el siglo XVI, 1493-1529: Trabajo, sociedad, y politica del oro*. Santiago: Universidad Catolica Madre y Maestra, 1978.

Oliver, José R. *Caciques and Cemí Idols: The Web Spun by Taíno Rulers Between Hispaniola and Puerto Rico*. Tuscaloosa: University of Alabama Press, 2009.

Otte, Enrique. *Las perlas del Caribe: Nueva Cádiz de Cubagua*. Caracas: Fundación John Boulton, 1977.

Pena Battle, Manuel Arturo. *La rebelión de Bahoruco*. Santo Domingo: Librería Hispaniola, 1970.

Perri, Michael. "Ruined and Lost: Spanish Destruction of the Pearl Coast in the Early Sixteenth Century." *Environment and History* 15 (2009): 129–161

Phillips, William D., Jr., and Carla Rahn Phillips. *The Worlds of Christopher Columbus*. Cambridge: Cambridge University Press, 1992.

Reséndez, Andrés. *The Other Slavery: The Uncovered Story of Indian Enslavement in America*. Boston: Houghton Mifflin Harcourt, 2016.

Saco, J. A. *Historia de la esclavitud de los indios en el nuevo mundo*. 2 vols. Havana: Librería Cervantes, 1932.

Sahlins, Marshall. *Islands of History*. Chicago: University of Chicago Press, 1985.

Sauer, Carl Ortwin. *The Early Spanish Main*. Berkeley: University of California Press, 1966.

Schwartz, Stuart B. *Implicit Understandings: Observing, Reporting, and Reflecting on the Encounters Between Europeans and Other Peoples in the Early Modern Era*. Cambridge: Cambridge University Press, 1994.

Sewell, William H., Jr. *Logics of History: Social Theory and Social Transformation*. Chicago: University of Chicago Press, 2005.

Sherman, William L. *Forced Native Labor in Sixteenth-Century Central America*. Lincoln: University of Nebraska Press, 1979.

Soule, Emily Berquist. "From Africa to the Ocean Sea: Atlantic Slavery in the Origins of the Spanish Empire." *Atlantic Studies* (2017): 16–39.

Stevens-Arroyo, Antonio M. *Cave of the Jagua: The Mythological World of the Taínos.* Albuquerque: University of New Mexico Press, 1988.

Stone, Erin Woodruff. "America's First Slave Revolt: Indians and African Slaves in Española, 1500–1534." *Ethnohistory* 60, no. 2 (Spring 2013): 195–217.

———. "Chasing 'Caribs': Defining Zones of Legal Indigenous Enslavement in the Circum-Caribbean, 1493–1542." In *Slaving Zones: Cultural Identities, Ideologies, and Institutions in the Evolution of Global Slavery,* edited by Jeff Fynn-Paul and Damian Alan Pargas, 118–150. Leiden: Brill Publishers, 2017.

———. "Slave Raiders vs. Friars in Tierra Firme, 1513–1522." *Americas* 74, no. 2 (April 2017): 139–170.

Utrera, Fray Cipriano de. *Polémica de Enriquillo.* Santo Domingo: Editora del Caribe, 1973.

van Deusen, Nancy E. *Global Indios: The Indigenous Struggle for Justice in Sixteenth-Century Spain.* Durham, NC: Duke University Press, 2015.

Vega, B. "Arqueología de los cimarrones del Maniel del Bahoruco." *Boletin del Museo del Hombre Dominicano Saint-Domingue* 8, no. 12 (1979): 134–151.

Warsh, Molly A. "Enslaved Pearl Divers in the Sixteenth Century Caribbean." *Slavery and Abolition* 31, no. 3 (September 2010): 345–362.

Wheat, David. *Atlantic Africa and the Spanish Caribbean, 1570–1640.* Williamsburg, VA / Chapel Hill: Omohundro Institute / University of North Carolina Press, 2016.

Whitehead, Neil, L. *Of Cannibals and Kings: Primal Anthropology in the Americas.* University Park: Pennsylvania State University Press, 2011.

Zavala, Silvio A. *Los esclavos indios en Nueva España.* Mexico City, Mexico: Colegio Nacional Luis González Obregon, 1967.

INDEX

ACKNOWLEDGMENTS

It is difficult to thank everyone who helped during the formation of this project. First and foremost I have to thank Jane Landers, the best PhD adviser I could imagine. She not only helped me with content, approach, and revisions, but also supported me emotionally throughout my time at Vanderbilt. I also must thank my Vandy family who inspired, entertained, and pushed me in uncountable ways. I look fondly at my time in the classroom (often with wine!) with Eddie Wright-Rios, Steve Wernke, Dan Usner, Marshall Eakin, William Caferro, and Jim Epstein. I will never forget the trivia nights, happy hours, and games of flip cup with my friends and colleagues: Miriam Martin Erikson, Courtney Campbell, Nick Villanueva, Steve Harrison, Bill Hardin, Pablo Gomez, Will Bishop, Angela Sutton, Frances Kolb, Ansley Quiros, Matt Owen, Jeremy DeWaal, Clay Poupart, Nicolette Kostiw, David LaFevor, David Wheat, Ty West, Caree Banton, Erica Hayden, Lance Ingwerson, Rachel Donaldson, Kara Shultz, Tizoc Chavez, and Daniel Genkins. I love you all and thank you for keeping me sane!

In addition to the faculty and colleagues at Vanderbilt, I must extend my gratitude to many professors who helped guide this project over the years. I want to thank Kris Lane, Matthew Restall, Matt Childs, Lin Fisher, and Alan Gallay for feedback, advice, and companionship at many conferences over the years. You all inspired me and my work. To Marcy Norton and Carla Pestana, I will be forever grateful for the seminars you led on the Atlantic and Caribbean worlds. Both provided me with the scholarship to ground my work. Finally, I need to extend my gratitude to Ida Altman, Nancy van Deusen, and Tatiana Seijas for reading my work at various stages and for pushing me to make it better.

I sincerely thank all those who helped me research and enjoy life in both the Dominican Republic (DR) and Spain. I would not have survived my time in the DR without my wonderful friend and mentor Lynne Guitar. Lynne, words cannot express how much I loved and needed your company in Santo

Domingo, Santiago, and during our trips across the island. From our nights of rum at La Piedra to the beach days on the north coast, I cannot thank you enough for showing me the hidden DR. I also want to thank all the archivists in the AGI, especially Fran and Luis, who made my Fulbright year in Sevilla fantastic and so very productive. Likewise, I can never forget my fellow Fulbrighters Josh Brown, Ryan Rockmore, Kate Margolis, Patrick Funicello, and Max Deardorff. Our many dinner parties and flamenco nights brought my Fulbright experience to new heights. I am forever grateful to my larger Archivo General de Indias family, especially to Michael Francis who taught me sixteenth-century Spanish paleography and introduced me to the archival world. Onces would not be the same without my fellow researchers: Katy Kole de Peralta, Spencer Tyce, James Hill, Kaja Cook, and Jesse Cromwell. You all made Sevilla brighter.

I will forever be grateful to the University of West Florida (UWF), my home while I finished the book. The university provided funds for me to finish my research (the New Faculty Research Grant) and introduced me to lifelong friends. Amy Mitchell-Cook, Bill Lees, Monica Beck, Matt Pursell, Greg Cook, Steve Belko, Gabi Grosse, MT Champagne, John Jensen, Karen Belmore, and Jamin Wells have enriched my life personally and academically. In addition to funding from UWF, I am grateful for many other organizations that supported my research, including the Tinker Field Research Grant, Harvard University's Atlantic History Research Grant, the Vanderbilt Graduate School, Herbert and Blanche Henry Weaver Fellowships, the William Campbell Binkley Graduate Education Fund, the Vanderbilt College of Arts and Sciences, the University of Minnesota's Program for Cultural Cooperation between Spain's Ministry of Culture and United States Universities, the IIE Graduate Fellowship for International Study, the University of Florida Center for Latin American Studies, and the Albert J. Beveridge Research Grant of the American Historical Association. I could not have completed the book without assistance from all these amazing institutions.

Finally, I must thank my family who supported me over the past ten years of work and travel. Madre, thank you for always being there for me, whether as a shoulder to cry on, a sympathetic listener, or a dog sitter. I love you more than I can say. To Padre, thank you for financially supporting many of my travels and for driving me around the DR in 2010 and for journeying into the Colombian jungles in 2014. We have made great memories. Lastly, I thank my amazing husband, Rick Stone. Thank you for pushing me to complete my dissertation in five years. Thank you for being my chauffeur and bodyguard in the DR, Spain, Colombia, and Puerto Rico. Thank you for making all my maps and my website for the job market. Thank you for listening to me talk about the colonial Caribbean for hours on end. Thank you for taking care of the house and dogs while I conducted research. I literally could not have done this without you.

CPSIA information can be obtained
at www.ICGtesting.com
Printed in the USA
LVHW090530250321
682389LV00001B/5